Women and Conflict in the Nigerian Civil War

sm

WOMEN AND CONFLICT

IN THE NIGERIAN CIVIL WAR

Egodi Uchendu

Africa World Press, Inc.

P.O. Box 1892
Trenton, NJ 08607

P.O. Box 48
Asmara, ERITREA

Africa World Press, Inc.

P.O. Box 1892
Trenton, NJ 08607

P.O. Box 48
Asmara, ERITREA

First Printing 2007

Book and Cover design: Saverance Publishing Services

Library of Congress Cataloging-in-Publication Data

Uchendu, Egodi.
Women and conflict in the Nigerian civil war / Egodi Uchendu.
p. cm.
Includes bibliographical references and index.
ISBN 1-59221-472-X (hardcover) -- ISBN 1-59221-473-8 (pbk.)
1. Nigeria--History--Civil War, 1967-1970--Women. 2. Women, Igbo--Social conditions--20th century. I. Title.

DT515.836.U24 2006
966.905'2--dc22

2006004359

To Chuka

And to Chisom, Oluoma, and Izuchukwu

Table of Contents

Maps and Illustrations

Acknowledgements

Many individuals contributed toward making this book possible, but just a few can be mentioned here. I am greatly indebted to my interviewees for their cooperation. They were most kind and hospitable. Some accommodated me in their homes for upwards of three or more days, during which time they took care of my needs and acted as my guides as I moved from quarter to quarter and from town to town. A notable feature that characterized them was their willingness to share their civil war experiences or part of them, not minding how unpalatable or embarrassing some of the revelations were. I cannot translate into words how honored I feel to have their confidence and to be the recipient of such intimate revelations. Among them were those who allowed me access to, and free use of, their recollections on the war but who insisted on being treated anonymously. They are as important as their colleagues who accepted to have their identities disclosed.

I have so much to thank Christina Hein, Margie and Rod Hinkle for. The same goes to Professor Onwuka Njoku and my other colleagues in the Department of History, University of Nigeria. It has been an interesting experience working with them. Much assistance, suggestions, and encouragement came from Professor Emeritus Simon Ottenberg, who read the manuscript in all its stages of preparation, and from Professor Emeritus Murray Last with whom I had very interesting discussions. I also appreciate most warmly the help from Chuka, my best friend and husband, who did his job and mine during my long absences from home and while I was writing up my findings. Chisom, Oluoma, and Izuchukwu managed wonderfully without me, and Izuchukwu, only eight months old, endured unsolicited and uncomfortable trips to Anioma. The Fulbright Commission (USA) and the Leventis Research Cooperation Program of the Center of African Studies, School of Asian and African Studies (SOAS) of the University of London financially supported this study with their fellowship awards while Patricia Allen and Damola Ifaturoti saw to the production of this book.

It is not possible incorporating in one book all that occurred in Anioma, the Igbo homeland west of the River Niger, during the Nigerian civil war. With the detailed interviews conducted in towns in the three sections of Anioma, I least will assert that I exhausted all that could be said about women in Anioma during the hostilities. What has been recorded is just a part of the story and I take full responsibility for what I have put down. The views expressed are mine and represent my understanding and interpretation of the data collected for this work.

Berlin, 2006

Abbreviations

ALL	Asaba Ladies League
BOFF	Biafran Freedom Fighters
BCGA	British Cotton Growing Association
CMS	Church Missionary Society
EPLF	Eritrean People's Liberation Front
GOC	General Officer Commanding
IIA	Ika Igbo Association
NIFOR	Nigerian Institute for Oil Palm Research
RCM	Roman Catholic Church
RNC	Royal Niger Company
ROB	Republic of Benin
UNHCR	United Nations High Commissioner for Refugees
UNDP	United Nations Development Program
UNICEF	United Nations International Children Education Fund

Foreword by Simon Ottenberg

The subject of women in the wars and conflicts in Africa has not been well examined. Women were involved in many ways in the precolonial African wars. They were also involved in these events during the period of the colonial conquest of Africa, helping their men to resist and spying for them. They were involved in the anticolonial wars of the 1950s – 1980s, as certain countries attempted to gain their independence through military efforts, particularly Angola, Mozambique, Guinea-Bissau, and Zimbabwe, and later in the multiple small-scale conflicts leading up to the end of apartheid in South Africa. During the colonial period in Africa women sometimes vigorously demonstrated against their colonial rulers, as in the 1929 Aba riots or Women's War in Nigeria. They have been involved in all of Africa's post-independence civil wars, whether in the Ivory Coast, Liberia, Sierra Leone, Guinea-Bissau, Nigeria, Somalia, Burundi, Rwanda, Sudan, or the Congo. They have played multiple roles, engaging the enemy as fighters, supplying food and goods to the military forces, carrying out espionage, and providing entertainment for their fighters. Some moved with the troops, and others have migrated here and there to protect themselves and their families as they sought food and shelter, sometimes with tragic consequences for them. Rarely have they been passive in Africa's wars.

While some journalistic accounts and novels have been written on this topic, there have been few serious studies of women in Africa's wars. Professor Egodi Uchendu's study stands out as a detailed analysis of women's wartime roles in Anioma, a region of south-central Nigeria; Anioma, where the most westerly Igbo-speaking people reside. Her writing focuses on women during the major Nigerian civil war of 1967–1970, also called the Biafran War. While maintaining a scholarly objectivity, her writing is sympathetic to the women involved, yet without romanticizing their wartime activities. She draws on interviews with women who survived the war; some of them were adults then, and others were children at the time of the conflict. She has carefully screened her interviews for memory distortion and loss some thirty or more years later, supplementing these often very personal and tragic accounts taken over a number of years of field research, with published and archival materials from the federal, Anioma, and Biafra sides, both civilian and military. She blends all of this information together into a finely crafted study. She has also grounded herself well in the earlier studies of Igbo women, carried out in the years before and after the war, a treasure of thoughtful scholarship.

Dr. Uchendu begins with a description of the changing prewar social and cultural conditions in Anioma in a modernizing Nigeria. The activities of Anioma women, their roles, and their relationships and statuses in terms of men are carefully delineated. This information provides a necessary background to an understanding of women's activities during the war. This is followed by a description of the disruptions and confusion that occurred during the short period of actual military conflict in Anioma, and the migration of women here and there to live, to protect themselves, and to find security. Many hardships occurred, but the women are not passive but active in their responses to the war. The fighting was soon over in Anioma, although it continued for several years more in the major battle areas of Igbo country east of the Niger. While the conflict continued elsewhere Anioma was under federal military occupation. Dr. Uchendu relates the various activities and maneuvers that Anioma women carried out to survive in their search of nourishment, lodging when their homes were destroyed or taken over by federal troops, and where women were subject to aggressive actions on the part of the military, and even sometimes individual federal civil servants and groups. Their hardships are sympathetically described without sentimentality. Often without their male counterparts, who were at war or had gone elsewhere, women became the heads of their families, which included not only their young but often the very old. As with other Igbo and southern Nigerians of their gender, in prewar times they were used to a good deal of independence in their daily lives and in trade, which they attempted to continue and even to extend during the period of the federal government military control. The accounts of women's activities that Dr. Uchendu explored during the occupation are finely detailed, providing vivid images of women under occupation. During this period some Anioma women also surreptitiously traded with the Biafrans at war on the east side of the Niger River, though they were in danger of being caught by the military; and some Anioma women were able to maintain contacts with kin, trading partners, and friends in Biafra.

The author then turns to the period of postwar reconstruction in Anioma. Again, this was a difficult time; when promised federal assistance often did not materialize. There were the problems of locating relatives and friends, restarting full family life, earning a sound living, and for many women, getting back into trade or farming or both. Dr. Uchendu carefully surveys the damage to Igbo culture and tradition that the fighting and occupation in Anioma created, with particular reference to women. She also explored the painful slowness of the region's revival following the end of the war in Anioma.

One theme that runs as a thread through Dr. Uchendu's work is the question of the ethnic identity of Igbo women in Anioma. They have always considered themselves and their men (and have been considered by the few scholars who have been interested in studying them until now) as being somewhat different from the vast majority of Igbo to the east, on the other side of the Niger River; thus the term *Anioma*, which they employ for themselves.

Yet they have strong links to these other Igbo to the east. On the other hand, they have had, for a number of centuries, contacts with the Edo peoples to their west, including from its important capital of Benin City, even though the Edo speak a different tongue; they have been subject to cultural infusions from the Edo and even at times to domination under them. The people of Anioma have looked both east and west in culture, trade, and in ethnic identity. Dr. Uchendu skillfully explores how these identity issues played out for Anioma women before, during, and after the conflict. They still exist today.

Dr. Uchendu, herself of Igbo heritage, was, unlike many foreign scholars of Igbo, able to interview Anioma women in the Igbo language. Trained at one of the best history departments in Nigeria, at the University of Nigeria, Nsukka, she is in the growing tradition of Africans studying their own societies in intelligent ways, full of wisdom and ideas, and yet capable of being objective about their own societies. The book is a major contribution to studies of women in wartime conditions in Africa. Further, most of the accounts of the Biafran War, whether from the Biafran or the federal side, pay only brief attention to the events in Anioma, concentrating on those that occurred in the main Biafran region, so that beyond its emphasis on women, this work is a valuable contribution to the history of the tragic civil war in Nigeria. This war turned out to be a forewarning of political, social, and economic troubles, which have plagued Nigeria since its end in early 1970. It has also been a forerunner of the numerous postcolonial civil wars that have occurred in Africa since that time. This war was a harbinger of postcolonial troubles ahead in Africa, which largely went unheeded.

Simon Ottenberg
Professor Emeritus
University of Washington
Seattle WA 98105

INTRODUCTION

The twentieth century was replete with wars. It was a century of turbulence, crisis, and bloodshed, all of which bequeathed many legacies to nations and peoples in the contemporary world. With as many as a hundred and fifty wars fought since 1945, the world recorded roughly twenty-six days of peace[1] by the close of the century. Modern warfare has become a sophisticated affair involving the use of terribly destructive weapons and unspeakable violence unlike the small-scale skirmishes common in Africa in precolonial times, where warriors depended on charms, clubs, machetes, and crude guns that utilized split stones as bullets.[2] War is generally regarded as the business of men because of the popular definition of war as "being in combat."[3] But warfare involves many activities as well as locations besides the exact contact between armed men; and, women share many stakes in wartime just as in peacetime.[4]

Women may rarely have taken part in the decision of any group to resort to violence, but when conflicts arise they take a heavy toll on the female gender. In the 1990s alone it was estimated that about 90 percent of the casualties in wars around the globe were civilians.[5] It has also been observed that the advent of high-altitude bombing, more powerful bombs, and a strategy of total warfare have practically ended the distinction between combatants and civilians as targets of war, making women and children the majority of the mounting numbers of casualties.[6]

Women are not spared during internal and external disturbances. They are directly and indirectly affected by the fighting. Many join in the fighting, either out of choice or necessity. Others are forcefully displaced, threatened, and intimidated; and both combatants and noncombatants suffer various abuses during such crises. They are challenged by starvation and epidemics when they occur and are confronted with increased workloads. Many inherit the responsibility for the survival of their families, the protection and maintenance of their elderly relatives, and, sometimes, their husbands. Countries facing war situations automatically inherit a state of emergency. War and a state of emergency heighten privations and make it all the more difficult for women to cope with their enlarged responsibilities. Searching for food with which to feed their dependants becomes strenuous and demanding. If women are forced to flee their homes, their burdens exacerbate. In crisis situations pregnant women and nursing mothers are the most vulnerable to food shortages and lack of medical attention. These privations occasion an alarming increase in their mortality rate.

Confessions of women from countries that have known civil disturbances help to illustrate the ordeal of the female gender and the challenges they grapple with during episodes of violence and civil strife. Sabaah, a Somali woman who took refuge in Ethiopia following the civil war in Somalia, recalled her trauma with these words: "We are always worried about how to feed our children and look after them for we have become both mothers and fathers."[7] Similarly, a displaced Ethiopian woman shared this testimony:

> With my husband, my parents and my home all gone, there were times when I just wanted to give up, just lie down and die. But I couldn't. What would happen to my children? ... Later I found out that when I had to speak up, I could. When I had to learn new ways, I did. I'm stronger now than I ever dreamed I could be.[8]

As tragic as wars or other crisis situations are, there could be a positive aspect to them. From the Ethiopian we see the development of inner strength and the acquisition of abilities to do what she previously could not do. That, however, in no way supports the existence of conflict situations. No matter the argument proffered, the odds far outweigh anything positive about war, and this includes the suggestion of Uta Klein that they liberate and expand women's roles in the labor market.[9] War situations generate conditions for rape and mental suffering in women in addition to obvious physical trauma and can also lead to personality developments. All these features typically impacted women in Anioma during the Nigerian civil war of 1967–1970.

Anioma is the Igbo area west of the Niger. It was one of the minority groups of the old Western Region that were reconstituted within the Midwest Region by the 1963 referendum and was renamed Midwest State in 1967 when Nigeria was split into twelve states. In 1976 the Midwest became Bendel State and in 1991 Bendel State was divided into two: Edo and Delta states, with Anioma in the latter. Anioma is the second largest ethnic group in Delta State, next to the Urhobo/Isoko. The other groups in the state are the Itshekiri and the Ijaw. The Anioma have categorized themselves into three subsections on the basis of dialectical variations that are mutually intelligible. The three subsections are Aniocha in the northeast, Ika in the northwest, and Ndokwa or Ukwuani, mispronounced Kwale by British colonial officials, in the south.[10] Ndosimili,[11] the riverine area of Ukwuani, is liable to flooding in the rainy season, making it necessary for residents to rely on canoes in moving from house to house. The division of Anioma into Aniocha, Ika, and Ukwuani also corresponds with Anioma's administrative division by the government of the Midwest (1967–1976) into Asaba, Ika, and Aboh divisions and does not in anyway imply the existence of any profound cultural diversity in Anioma.

Map of Nigeria, 1960, showing the division into three regions

The story of Nigeria from independence in 1960 until the *coup d'état* of 15 January 1966 that precipitated the civil war is relatively well known. The major incidents that culminated into war will be outlined here for better understanding of the events that led up to it. At independence in 1960, Nigerians looked forward to a bright and excellent future, but that expectation was short-lived. The euphoria of independence soon dissipated as the country became tossed by one crisis after another, each of which severely tested the parliamentary democracy inherited from Britain.

The first major incident took place in 1962 in the Western Region, when a rift occurred in the leadership of the Action Group, the dominant political party of the region. The rift, which led to the revocation of the region's premier, degenerated into disorder and violence and affected the peace of the entire nation. This incident was followed by the controversy over the 1962 – 63 population census – Nigeria's first postindependence census. The census was important because seats in the Federal

House of Representatives were allocated to the three regions according to their population strengths. The 1962–63 census figures were grossly inflated. Alleged rigging, miscounting, and inflation of figures discredited the 1963 recount and destabilized the country as contending regional premiers resorted to threats and lawsuits and disorganized existing political partnerships in the regions and at the federal level.

The 1964 federal elections, again Nigeria's first postindependence elections, occasioned more serious upheavals. The campaigns and the conduct of the elections revealed the bitter struggle for power among politicians of the major political and regionally based parties.[12] Mutual accusations of evil intentions, sabotage, and fraud, with incidents of violence and political assassinations, characterized the exercise, threatening to tear the nation apart. The impact on the nation of the 1964 federal elections seemed mild when compared with the Western regional election of 1965. This latter incident reduced previous events to mere child's play. As one writer noted, Western Nigeria became the country's problem area.[13] Politically disaffected individuals and groups within the region employed force and threats in redressing grievances. Those in possession of power blatantly resorted to violence in order to suppress opponents. The Nigerian police admitted their difficulty in maintaining law and order in many districts in the region.[14] The confusion and total breakdown of law and order from the disastrous 1965 Western regional elections and the inability of the central government to arrest the situation provided the stimulus for the January 1966 coup led by Major Chukwuma Nzeogwu from Anioma, which ended Nigeria's experiment at postindependence civil rule.

Among many classes and ethnic groups in the country, the immediate reaction to the putsch and the consequent change of government was one of relief.[15] The welcome accorded the incident by Nigerians and their unrestrained jubilation at the restoration of peace waned especially in the north with the British press announcement that the putsch was an Igbo coup, a judgment based on the preponderance of Igbo officers among the plotters.[16] No matter the virtues of the coup, the Northern Region, the most affected in the killings, would not be pacified. The coup, unintentionally, split the country into two.

Northern Nigerians were soured by the reorganized political structure that resulted from the coup, which they considered unfavorably. Their feelings of political and economic incapacitation were made acute by their lack of educated manpower when compared to either the Eastern or Western regions. The atmosphere in the north became gloomier when Major General J. T. U. Aguiyi-Ironsi, the new head of state and an Igbo, announced the promulgation of Decree 34 on 24 May 1966, prescribing a unitary government for the country. In the north it was interpreted as a device for the more educationally advanced south, particularly easterners, to overshadow and lord it over them.[17]

Northern military officers and their civilian populace attempted to redress their grievances through the pogroms of May and July 1966 in which they massacred the Igbo on a large scale, particularly those in the north of the country. Among those killed was Major General Aguiyi-Ironsi. More massacres occurred in September and October of that year, mostly affecting military officers of Igbo origin. The killing of the Igbo in 1966, as a direct consequence of the January coup, was indiscriminate. Although most Igbo lived east of the Niger River, it also affected those on the west of the Niger otherwise known as the Anioma. Everywhere, the death toll was higher on the men's side than on the women's. In the disturbances wives, daughters, and sisters were spectators to the decimation of their husbands, fathers, and brothers. The prevailing lawlessness degenerated into an exodus of the hunted Igbo from the Northern and, to a lesser degree, the Western regions.

Horrid tales of the incidents and assaults, with pictorial proof of the maimed and the disfigured, enraged the entire Igbo nation. The evolving tragedy culminated in the secession of the Eastern Region, the core Igbo area, from the Nigerian federation on 30 May 1967.

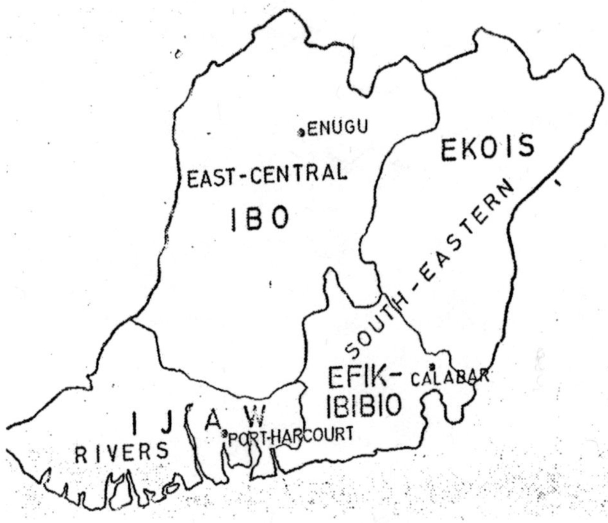

Biafra, 30 May 1967

The secession was unacceptable to Lt. Col. Yakubu Gowon, who took over as head of state from Major General Aguiyi-Ironsi, and he promptly declared war on the Eastern Region, now the Republic of Biafra. The opposing factions perceived the civil war differently. To Biafrans it was a war to protect their lives and property and to assert their independence from Nigeria. To the federal government it was to prevent secession and to keep Nigeria as one; hence the popular federal slogan during the hostilities became "One Nigeria."

Even though in the Midwest,[18] and therefore under a different administrative unit from the Eastern Region, the Anioma were in support of Biafrans with whom they shared the traumatic experiences of 1966. Notwithstanding, Anioma did not become a war theater until 9 August 1967, when Biafran troops invaded the Midwest and attempted to reach Lagos, Nigeria's capital. On 17 August 1967 the Biafran government announced Major (M.D.) Albert Nwazu Okonkwo from Anioma as the administrator of Midwest State, which it renamed the Republic of Benin. For a very short time, Asaba became the capital of the ill-fated new republic. Less than a week after the installation of a pro-Biafran government in Midwest, the Second Infantry Division of the Nigerian Army recaptured Benin, the original capital of Midwest State.

Biafra's entry into the Midwest attracted the federal army into that territory. The arrival of the federal troops provided a cover for an uprising against the Anioma by non-Igbo groups, especially the Bini [Edo] and the Urhobo/Isoko. The rampage resulted in the egregious slaughter of the people of Anioma in different parts of the Midwest. This act of unrestrained violence sent the survivors fleeing back to their towns from the non-Igbo areas. By November 1967, the Nigerian forces had recaptured the entirety of Midwest State.

In the attempt to wrest the state from Biafran control, and during the period of occupation of Anioma until the end of the war, women in Anioma were subjected to untold brutality by federal troops. The subsequent decimation of men in Anioma in the course of the conflict left the women unprotected and vulnerable. They had to devise means of coping with the war and its aftermath. How they survived the military occupation of Anioma is the concern of this work.

Beginning with the colonial period (1890–1960), many studies have been carried out on the Igbo. At present a commendable handful focus on Igbo women. The Aba Women's War of 1929 (called the Women's riot by British colonial officers and early scholars on Igboland) is credited with launching Igbo women into the limelight, resulting in the British colonial office and its administrators commissioning studies on the "Igbo social organization and about the women."[19] Among the pioneer British scholars who studied Igbo women were Sylvia Leith Ross (1939) and Margaret Green (1947), besides G. T. Basden (1938), the Archdeacon of the Anglican Communion at Onitsha; and Dr. Percy Amaury Talbot (1926 and 1932), a colonial Resident officer. They gave descriptions of life as it appeared to be lived in Igbo communities. M. M. Green aptly observed the existence of local variations within the larger Igbo society, which calls for some degree of caution in generalizing issues about the Igbo. The present work confirms the need for this caution for scholars working on the Igbo and particularly on Igbo women. The American anthropologist Phoebe V. (Ottenberg) Miller (1959, 1965, and 1982), with Simon Ottenberg (1962),[20] falls within this early group of scholars of Igbo women's history with her reasonably extensive studies on Afikpo women.

To these early works on Igbo women have been added many others and of a varied nature by postcolonial authors from different parts of the world and different ideological persuasions such as Judith Van Allen (1976), Kamene Okonjo (1976), Ifi Amadiume (1987), Gloria Chuku (1995), 'Zulu Sofala (1998), and Misty Bastian (2002). Unlike Igbo women, east of the Niger, Anioma women, west of the Niger, did not receive similar scholarly attention. There was no major sociopolitical upheaval involving them and that would trigger similar colonial attention as found east of the Niger. Nevertheless, G. T. Basden, in his *Niger Ibos*, discussed aspects of Anioma women's activities during the early colonial period, and Elizabeth Isichei (1970) and Don Ohadike (1994)[21] make reference to Anioma women in their books. On the whole Anioma women have received far less scholarly attention than their sisters east of the Niger, making them one of the least studied groups in southern Nigeria.

Anioma also doubles as an under-studied area with regard to the Nigerian civil war. The neglect of Anioma and its women in the writings on the civil war could be attributed to two factors. The first is Anioma's geographical location, i.e., outside core Igbo territory. The second derives from the assumption that because women were not formally involved in actual combat they faced little or no threat from the war, played no role during the crisis, and had no experience worth investigating. Contrary to these assumptions, the civil war represented a unique ordeal and a horrendous challenge to Anioma women. Of course, their experiences varied from person to person according to localities and they responded differently to the challenges of the war, all of which are worth investigating in order to be appreciated.

Claude Phillips in 1984 described the Nigerian civil war as the most notorious conflict ever witnessed in Africa.[22] (That was before the complete degeneration to utter lawlessness of the states of Liberia, Sierra Leone, and Rwanda.) The notoriety of the Nigerian civil war is undisputed, but unfortunately it has been observed that where war is the worst and suffering is at its greatest the least is known.[23] This was acknowledged in the statement, made a decade ago, that the Nigerian civil war has not received a deserving academic attention by Nigerian scholars.[24] We must agree that many burning questions remain, not least of all the various experiences of women during the conflict. The present study is a contribution in this direction. It explores and analyses women's experiences during that war.

The concentration on women's war experiences in Anioma derives from the certitude that what people undergo and how they react to war vary according to sex, time, and situation. Women do not all respond in the same way to the same situation. It is misleading to assume that the experiences of the men speak for all classes and genders of the society. The accounts of the activities of men during the civil war, which dominate the contents of the majority of works on the subject,[25] are in no way holistic but rather lopsided. A study incorporating the actions of both men and women will give a more balanced historical picture of the civil war in Nigeria. Reconstructing the history of women in Anioma from their narratives permits an integration of other members of the society, instead of just a part of it, in the events that took place during the period under investigation. This study should not only enrich the growing corpus of literature on the Nigerian civil war but will incorporate Anioma into the mainstream of events that occurred in the nation between May 1966 and January 1970, because it deals with neglected issues relating to the crisis: the Igbo homeland west of the Niger and the place of women in that conflict. It shows that Anioma, the Igbo area west of the river Niger, was no neutral territory during the crisis but was drawn into the cauldron within three months of the outbreak of hostilities. The research also provides insight into the life of Anioma women during the occupation of the area. Women felt the brunt of the war in a unique way. With much of the males killed by the federal army in their bid to combat the challenge of Biafra, a substantial number of women had no male family member to protect and maintain them during the crisis, as was the custom. They were left to contend with the soldiers; in order to cope with the situation, they adapted themselves to the challenges it engendered. The results of the investigation of Anioma women contributes to an evaluation of how well the Nigerian army observed Lt. Col. Yakubu Gowon's Code of Conduct, given to guide federal troops in their prosecution of the war and treatment of civilians.

The silence in traditional war narratives about women's role and experiences during armed hostilities both within and outside Africa would appear to be the rule rather than the exception. Accounts of the conflicts in Ethiopia and in Zimbabwe illustrate this with regard to Africa.[26] Jenny Hammond with Nell Druce (1990) and Tanya Lyons (2004), in trying to give a voice to women who have experienced conflict situations, have discussed the experiences of women guerilla fighters in Ethiopia from 1975 and in the Zimbabwean liberation struggle from 1972.[27] These authors, writing on latter incidents that took place in other parts of Africa after the Nigerian civil war, have demonstrated the growing involvement of women in warfare, but most especially the challenges female combatants encounter. The Zimbabwean anticolonial liberation struggle against white minority rule had a different objective from the Tigrayan revolution. The Tigrayans of Ethiopia, like the Biafrans, took up arms against their central government because of post-independence oppression; but unlike the Biafrans who sought political independence from Nigeria, the Tigrayans fought for "self-determination within a united, democratic and socialist Ethiopia."[28] Both works emphasize the exclusion of the accounts of African women participants in warfare. In general the contribution of Tigrayan and Zimbabwean women to warfare was more elaborate than that of Igbo women during the Nigerian civil war.

The present study goes well beyond the civil war itself; to the long-range consequences of the conflict up to 1979. At the expiration of military operations in January 1970, the people of Anioma, devastated by the conflict, undertook the difficult task of rehabilitating themselves and their communities. This immense task took years to accomplish; though the scars of the tragedy remain evident even today.

RESEARCH METHOD

This account of Anioma and its women strongly depends on primary sources that exist in the form of oral information obtained from individuals, mostly women, who experienced the war, and male observers from the sidelines; official reports, gazettes, and private papers found in the archives and in government establishments.

Interviews were conducted in towns in the three sections of Anioma between November 1999 until June 2001 and again between November 2002 and April 2004. There were no preplanned considerations to determine which group of women, or men, to interview. Efforts were made to seek audiences with local leaders and all categories of resource persons. But in order to get a good picture of women's experiences, as many women as possible who could recall the events of the civil war were interviewed excepting those who declined to speak. And, quite a number of women refused to be interviewed, wanting to avoid recollection of events they had made efforts to forget. In all, over a hundred and fifty-five persons were interviewed. Out of this number, three were from the Igbo area east of the Niger. A few interviews were not recorded because the interviewees objected to the recording.

Besides the interviews, archival materials and government papers were collected. These were useful in tracing the history of Anioma and in presenting an account of the events in the area until the eve of the crisis and also during the war. Cultural dictates determined in most cases women's perception of the war and their responses to it, which will be discussed in the next chapter.

The heavy reliance on oral testimonies for this work arises from the dearth of written primary sources on the subject. The Midwest government was silent on federal military activities in Anioma and on most occurrences in the area during the crisis. Whatever records were kept have not been made available to the public. Also, all through the occupation of Anioma, the state's newspaper stories tried to exclude events in the militarized areas, instead concentrating exclusively on other sections of the state. This was presumably a strategy aimed at protecting the interest and image of the Nigerian federal government during the crisis.

Oral tradition, in the process of being made available to the historian, is beset with problems. These include the problem of chronology, feed back, personal influence, or distortion of true experiences. The question of chronology is not a serious matter with regard to this study because of its relatively recent occurrence and the educated status of many interviewees. Extensive interviews and cross-examination of discussants have proved helpful in analyzing and assessing received information to ensure accuracy. This method also makes it easy to identify exaggerated testimonies as well as feedback from places outside the survey area that are passed off as source materials for the area and period under study. The research benefited from necessary contributions from scholars in other fields of study and makes reference to existing secondary materials that throw light on the themes of this discourse.

Beyond this Introduction, the work is organized into six chapters. Chapter 1 is a brief historical discussion of Anioma, its culture, and its women before the outbreak of the war. It considers the social and economic functions of women in their respective towns and mentions their token part in local administration.

The chapter enables the reader to appreciate the extent to which Anioma women were challenged by the civil war.

The remaining five chapters deal with the crux of the study. Chapter 2 discusses the extension of the war to the Midwest, with Biafra's operation there. Chapter 3 considers federal military reprisals on Anioma, whose eastern counterparts were fighting for secession. The chapter incorporates the immediate reaction of Anioma women to the sudden presence of federal soldiers in their midst and how the myth of insulation from the crisis was shattered by the militarization of their localities. Also discussed is women's recourse to rumor as a means of getting their bearings right.

Chapter 4 treats the impacts of the Biafran and federal occupations of Anioma, especially on cultural observances. It includes women's efforts to aid the war. Women were not drafted into any military unit by the two armed forces but interested ones, by their enlistment into the Biafran militia, were given the chance to participate in Biafra's struggle for survival. A detailed discussion of this is handled in this chapter. Chapter 5 covers the responses of women to the emergency situations that attended the war; how they survived the hostilities, and the experiences of those who found themselves in territory under the supreme control of the Nigerian federal government. The challenges of rehabilitation constitute the content of Chapter 6, which is followed by the Conclusion.

Chapter 1

ANIOMA AND ITS PEOPLE

Delta State stretches approximately 18,000 square kilometers with more than 50 percent of the area occupied by riverine communities.[29] The vegetation is lacking in uniformity. Thick mangrove swamp forests dominate the coastal area, while savanna vegetation covers the northern section. The ethnic groups in the state – the Urhobo/Isoko, Igbo (Anioma), Itshekiri, and Ijaw – merge into one another,[30] with communities along ethnic boundaries intermarrying. Sections of Ukwuani in Anioma, whose people intermarry with the Urhobo/Isoko, are bilingual. The same applies to the Urhobo/Isoko and Itshekiri groups, as well as to the Ika section of Anioma and their Edo neighbors. The different peoples of Delta State share some cultural usage arising from their consanguinity and affinity. No ethnic group has developed in isolation, untouched by marriage, trade, migration, or war with neighboring ethnic and linguistic groups. The culture is, therefore, a blended version of many patterns indicating the diversity of origin, environmental influence, and cross-cultural contacts. Asaba, the capital and situated in Anioma, is one of the oldest towns in Nigeria. Before Nigeria's emergence as a nation, it was the civil headquarters of the territory ruled by the Royal Niger Company (RNC) from 1886 until 1899. The British acquired Asaba and its environs when Asaba leaders and those of the hinterland signed the British Treaty of Friendship and Peace in 1884.[31]

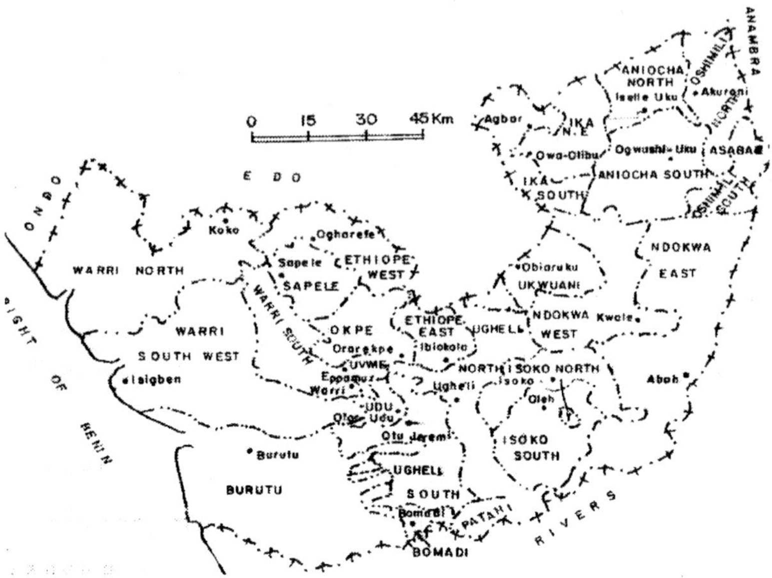

Map of Delta State

Delta State has twenty-five local government areas, nine of which make up Anioma.[32] The Anioma, on the west of the river Niger, has come a long way in evolving a distinct identity. Before the Nigerian civil war the people were known as the Ika Igbo. In the 1970s, Anioma, meaning the "good land," emerged as their nomenclature. The name is preferred by the people to the old appellation the *Western Igbo* – given by the British,[33] or the *Ika Igbo*, as other peoples of the state previously addressed them and by which they were known until the outbreak of the war. In 1991 Anioma's population was 785,777, with women in excess of men by 18,317.[34] Anioma is the smaller part of Igboland. The larger section is found east of the river Niger and comprises five states: Anambra, Enugu, Imo, Abia, and Ebonyi, and part of Rivers State. Don Ohadike has already observed that the Anioma are descendants of those Igbo men and women who, because of land shortages and the population explosion, began to cross the Niger River in the ninth century to occupy some sites on the west bank of the river.[35]

Elizabeth Isichei, in *The Ibo People and the Europeans* (1970), wrote that the history of many peoples begins with a migration and a founding father.[36] A people's origins relate to their rationalizations as to how they evolved as a sociopolitical and cultural entity and why they came to be where they are at present. Their convictions about their roots generally form their perspectives and ideas of life, and condition their minds and hearts to think of themselves and others in specific ways.[37] The history of town origins in Anioma has received scholarly attention from two leading Anioma historians: Elizabeth Isichei in the above-mentioned work and Don Ohadike in *Anioma, A Social History of the Western Igbo People* (1994). It is unnecessary to repeat an account of the origin of the Anioma; rather, what may be necessary is a brief comment on where the people came from.

Anioma lacks a common tradition of origin. Like the state in which it is located, it reflects cultural influences from more than one direction. The fifteenth to early eighteenth centuries constitute a period of intense economic activity around the Niger River and was also the period of the eastward expansion of the Benin kingdom. This period saw movements of people and cultures from different areas into Anioma. The main language groups connected with the influx are the Igbo east of the Niger, the Edo from the northwest, and the Igala from the north. In addition, there were minor influxes from the Yoruba, Ishan, and Urhobo/Isoko into the area.

Communities in Anioma claim to have migrated from one or the other of the above-mentioned places. It cannot be said with any certainty whether the immigrants only went to enlarge existing sparse settlements or to found entirely new ones. Both conclusions are possible. It is common to hear different sections of a town claim origin from different places and to be at pains to state categorically who settled first in that environment. It would be rash to state unequivocally the origin of the earliest inhabitants of Anioma. A careful study of their culture and way of life reveal that the Igbo are likely the earliest and most dominant immigrants. The Igbo influence appears more entrenched and of longer duration than that of either the Edo or any other group.

The indigenous political organizations in Anioma did not completely remain as they were before the late nineteenth century. Changes in the political structure became evident after the complete pacification of Anioma towns in May 1910. The basic political organization found in the Aniocha section of Anioma in the first two decades of the twentieth century closely resembled the segmented pattern or village republics found in Igbo communities east of the Niger, which centered on kinship groupings and title associations. Towns in Aniocha that claimed Edo origin manifested a combination of the village republics and kingship administration. The kinship or lineage system in Aniocha, Ika, and Ukwuani areas was identical.[38] It started with the *ezi n'uno* (the household or family), then the *umunna* (extended family), the *idumu* (minimal lineage); and ended with the *ebo* or *ogbe* (maximal lineage), preferably called a "quarter" by the people.[39] The lineage groupings were all patrilineal. The *ezi n'uno* was made up of a man and his wife or wives and their sons and daughters. The *umunna* was a compound comprising households that traced origin to a common ancestor. The *idumu* comprised a group of *umunna* that claimed a common ancestor. Apart from claims of common descent, there were other bonds of unity in the minimal and maximal units. These were: having a common *ilo* (entrance into the unit), a single shrine for *ani*, the earth goddess, where all who claimed descent offered their sacrifices; one *diokpa* or *okpara* (male leader of the unit), who held the staff of office, and joint ownership of farm and forest lands. Marriages were forbidden between members of the same lineage.[40]

In Aniocha and Ukwuani, each of the units – *uno*, *umunna*, *idumu*, and *ogbe*— was headed by a *diokpa* or *okpara*, the oldest man of the unit in accordance with the patrilineal system of most African communities. In the Ika area headship in these units was by primogeniture and not necessarily by age. No section of Anioma was matrilineal. Before the civil war, it was the responsibility of these male leaders of the kindred units to perform prescribed political and ritual functions as the representatives and embodiments of the authority of the ancestors. They regulated the conduct and affairs of those under them and, when necessary, represented them at the next level of the kinship structure. Members of the kinship units held their leaders in reverence and submitted to their authority. Of all the units, the household and the quarter were the most important economically and politically. This kinship structure has remained the same up till the present.

Social groupings based on age commonly referred to by the Igbo as "age-grades" were a special feature of the grassroots political organization before the 1960s in Aniocha and Ukwuani, excluding the Ndosimili section of Ukwuani. An age-grade was formed by several age sets. Each age grade could have in its membership persons born within a six-year period depending on the number of years approved by each community to compose an age group. If a community accepts six years as its standard limit for an age group, then persons born anytime within a six-year period belonged to one age group. Age-sets were formed at shorter intervals of two or three years. Various units of age-sets of men and women made up age-grades, and these cut across families and quarters. Women's age-grades were considered by men to be of no political importance.[41] For male age-grades, three main groupings could be observed, and each had their functions. *Otu umuaka* was for children between the ages of seven and fifteen, *otu ikolobia* for youths, and *otu ikei* for older adults for age of sixty and upwards. Within the last century, the age-grade system in most towns in Anioma gradually died away. The title system, unlike the age-grades, has remained a feature of these communities to the present time. The two main categories of titles found in Aniocha were those acquired by purchase and those conferred on individuals by local rulers. Titles were a source of personal prestige rather than of power except for holders of the most prominent ones, which were called *alo and obi.* (In some communities the obi title is called *eze.*) Wives could assist their husbands to acquire titles by paying for them. One method most women used to assist their husbands to acquire titles was by contributing their labor to help raise the crops that would translate into capital for purschasing the title. They shared in the honor conferred by each of the titles, yet, being women, they were ineligible for titles. Local rulers and elders, most of whom held the title eze, chaired the local councils.

The indigenous and precolonial political organization in Anioma was reorganized during the colonial era with the introduction of native administration and its instruments of native authority and native treasury. Although Aboh, Agbor, and towns in Aniocha claiming Benin ancestry, had paramount chiefs, none ruled a very vast territory. British colonial administrators approved certain male representatives to assist with governance at the village and town levels and issued them with certificates called "Warrants" as proof of their authority. Initially, the warrant chiefs were rarely chosen from among the ruling class. Most local rulers, suspicious of British intentions, put forward junior members of their community or even slaves for the conferment of warrant. The warrant chiefs became very powerful and also very corrupt. As a result, their emergence in Anioma in the late 1920s and their corruption resulted in wide spread feelings of discontent among the people. The disdain for these new upstarts, as they were seen, prompted a modification in the new system after 1929 and recourse to something similar to what existed before the British advent.[42]

In Ukwuani, for instance, the political restructuring that occurred afterwards, from 1920 until 1959, did not affect local administration at the family and lineage levels. Only the town's administration was altered to accommodate a borrowed culture. Individuals were at first allowed to use the political facility they preferred: either the indigenous system that operated at the lineage levels or the modernized local administration at the town level with its unfamiliar judicial and executive apparatuses. But as the colonial administration became more formalized, the latter,

Map of Anioma showing Aniocha, Ika, and Ukwuani (Ndokwa) sections[43]

preferred by the colonial authorities, superceded the former in importance. In the effort to reorganize the local administration to resemble what existed before the onset of colonialism, some aspects of the local apparatus were negatively affected. The age-grades and title systems lost their historical importance, respect for community elders gradually eroded, and the position of the monarchs became subservient to that of British colonial officers. Moreover, the monarchs lost their sacredness. The basic political structure in Anioma survived the colonial era but not in the form it was by 1910.

Slavery existed in Anioma until the second decade of the twentieth century. Slaves were at the base of the social structure and were regarded as expendables. The Anioma acquired their slaves from outside their geographical area. It was thus easy to isolate them from most of the activities of the people. Slaves served a variety of purposes. Strong and capable male slaves were used in agriculture. Child slaves served as palace servants who carried the rulers' emblems of office. Attractive female slaves were used mostly as concubines.[44] Concubinage was customary in Anioma. Freeborn citizens[45] sometimes kept slave concubines, but children from such unions became *ipso facto* slaves except in Aboh. Female slaves were also acquired for the purpose of serving as wives to male slaves. It was the responsibility of slave owners to provide wives for their male slaves. Where a master had no female slave for his male slave, he married one for him from another slave owner. In such instances, the offspring of the slave couple was shared with the owner of the female slave. Most slave owners did not consider it economically advantageous to acquire a slave from another master. They therefore kept female slaves and from their stock provided a male slave with a female partner. Domestic slaves were also used for human sacrifices and some were buried along with their masters after functioning as pallbearers or diggers at their master's burials. These helped to check their own population to prevent its threatening that of the freeborn citizens.

Prior to the abrogation of slavery in Nigeria in 1916, there were slave settlements called *ilo ugwule*,[46] where wealthy men housed their slaves to create some distance between them and the freeborn. Slaves built their own houses and settled down to as normal a life as possible. Their routine involved moving daily to and from the settlements to their masters' houses or farms. While slaves in Aniocha and Ika areas lived in slave settlements outside the normal residential areas of the freeborn, in Aboh in Ukwuani they intermingled with the freeborn without relinquishing their servile status. Offspring of female slaves and freeborn fathers in

Aboh acquired the status of their father, unlike those in other sections of Anioma, where children born to a slave parent, either male or female, retained the status of servitude.[47] Proximity to non-Igbo groups appears to be responsible for the mild disposition of the people of Aboh to their slaves.

Slaves responded in different ways to the antislavery proclamations of the British colonial government. Many walked away and were never heard of again. Some remained in their communities, exacting equal treatment, access to land, and full membership in their communities.[48] Female slaves suffered a serious social handicap, and the stigma of servitude remained for men and women after their emancipation. In Aniocha and Ika areas freeborn men did not marry former female slaves from their towns but could marry one from another town even though such alliances were not common immediately following emancipation. By the outbreak of the war, the lines of demarcation between former slaves and freeborns in most towns in Anioma had become blurred. Nevertheless, the issue of slaves and former slaves remained particularly strong in Asaba, Ogwashi-ukwu, and Issele-ukwu even after the war.[49] In Asaba in 2002 older members of the society could still point to male descendants of former slaves who are still denied certain social rights such as title taking.[50]

ANIOMA WOMEN BEFORE THE CIVIL WAR

Excluding slaves, no member of Anioma society before the civil war was regarded as a "nobody." Each had duties assigned according to their assumed physical and mental capabilities. In line with the patrilineal nature of Anioma, male elders controlled local politics; while women, taken to be lacking in physical capabilities, were in charge of the domestic sphere. Intelligent male youths were permitted to take part in the deliberations of the elders at the lineage levels but their female counterparts were not.[51] This was in line with the constitutive principle of the Igbo family–the principle of domination, which in practice implies male domination.[52] Women were under the control of men both before and after marriage. Thus, for the greater part of their lives they were regarded as minors, except for older women who enjoyed greater respect for their age in a society that put a premium on age.

The first wife of a man, called *anasi*, was considered an important figure in the family because of her position as the mother of the family. Younger wives looked up to her, and she took precedence over her cowives in the affairs of the household. She was honored along with her husband in the event of his taking a title and observed with him the taboos associated with the title. If the husband took the highest title in Anioma, the title of obi or eze, she enjoyed the following privileges: wearing the hair style associated with her husband's title; tying a wrapper around her chest instead of wearing a blouse[53]; having threads on her ankles, and being greeted with the honorific title of *igwe*. It was unlawful for her to carry loads on her head, and she could neither divorce her husband nor remarry after taking a title with him.[54]

Cowives in a polygynous marriage, common in Anioma and in the Igboland heartland until the outbreak of the war, had an ambiguous relationship among themselves. Malice, rivalry, and intrigue often featured. Sometimes the first wife was not the favorite wife. Such a situation undermined her position and fostered rebellion from her cowives. Wives formed alliances among themselves according to their personal interests. While they could cooperate occasionally against their husbands, they also could pool forces together against one or the other of their colleagues whose attitude might be obnoxious to the others. Usually, they collaborated among themselves during festivals and public functions in order to present a good image of their household to the public. Modalities over sharing a husband's sexual attention and rivalry associated with being the first to have a male child were two basic issues known to cause quarrels among cowives.[55]

It was often said in Anioma that "women did not sit with men to discuss the affairs of the town,"[56] meaning that women did not take part in the political life of Anioma. The only exception was

Installation of the oza-omu, female chief, of Okpanam in 1999

for female chiefs, called *omu*, found in some towns in Aniocha. From childhood women were assigned domestic roles and confined to the domestic side of life. Their age-grades supervised female social functions and, in comparison with the age-grades of the men, were described as lacking in purpose and without focus.[57] But, women maintained a female-focused administration that paralleled what existed in the lineage levels through the omu institution and through *umuada* (daughters of the lineage) and inyemedi (wives of the lineage) associations.[58]

The omu, who were in effect women leaders, were famous for their ritual and secular duties. In reference to their ritual duties, they were called sorcerers and witches.[59] They represented women in the local administration and were in charge of women affairs, which included the control of the markets, local trade, and the supervision of women's conduct in the society. They worked closely with a female group of counselors called *otu-omu*, until male ritual specialists were introduced into the group towards the end of the colonial era.[60] The institution changed with the times. The colonial period saw it losing much of its administrative influence first to warrant chiefs from 1900 to 1929 and afterwards to local government officials. The transformation continued after independence in 1960 when Christianity and modernization made it difficult for the omu to exercise their authority and influence in towns that have become heterogeneous. The institution brought into the limelight very few women in Aniocha. No town had more than one omu. A single female office holder in the midst of a group of many male office holders in any town is not an indication that power was shared equally between men and women. Such privileged women do not have much of an impact on the political life of their communities since they could be intimidated or manipulated by the male majority to yield to their judgment in the affairs of their town.

Ada, a generic name for female daughters in Igboland, was also an honorary title in parts of Anioma. In Ukwuani they were called *ada-obodo*; in Aniocha, *ada isi*. The office of ada was not inherited, acquired with money, or bestowed on the basis of wealth. It was bestowed on the basis of age. In Ukwuani, where the ada was the highest female position in the society, she was regarded as the counterpart of the *okpara-ukwu* (or *odua* as he was called in Aboh), the recognized male local ruler. The ada's honorific title was *erumeru* or *ofase.* In both Ukwuani and Aniocha, occupants of this stool were the oldest women in their minimal lineage where they assisted with the administration of the women and were the venerators of most female deities that operated at that level. Because of their debility as a result of age, they depended on stronger women to discharge their responsibilities, which included the supervision of female rituals and the purification of the lineage in cases of abomination or desecration of a person, an institution, or a shrine.[61] The ada institution in Aniocha existed before the omu institution and operated at the lineage level, but the popularity of the omu at the major lineage level has overshadowed the office of the ada and restricted its influence to the minimal lineage.[62]

Both the ada and the omu acquired male status, the only condition under which they could wield power in traditional Igbo society, and returned to their fathers' lineages on acceding to office. In Ukwuani, the ada attended local council meetings held by men as an observer. She was required to sit outside the normal male meeting circle and had no right to make any input in the discussions of the men.[63] These strictures provide evidence that the ada only enjoyed an incomplete male status. Unlike the Aniocha and Ukwuani areas, there was no elevated female position in the Ika area.

The life of Anioma women revolved around rituals. The omu, ada, and umuada featured prominently in the various rites performed. Some were associated with social and biological changes, regarded as rites of passage, but others were incorporated in the religious ceremonies of the people. Female rites of passage involved numerous ceremonial events that marked the transition of any female from one social status to another. These rites were proof that human existence was marked by changes that were not always allowed to go unnoticed. Many of the important rites performed before the war were connected with the biological stages of life: birth, maturity, reproduction, and death. They provided entertainment for the people and were approved means of participating in pleasurable activities. Presently, modern forms of entertainment compete with them for importance

Children were treasured in colonial Igboland. In Anioma the life of a female child was dotted with interesting moments from birth till death, but to the modern woman they might not be interesting at all. Developmental stages were events to be remembered and were marked with simple or elaborate ceremonies, depending on the stage reached and its culturally accorded importance. A mother rejoiced at the birth of her daughter because she has delivered a live-in assistant to help her with her many household chores and a dependable companion in old age. This, however, did not stop her from anticipating with all eagerness the birth of a son. Male children perpetuated the family line and ensured that their mothers were maintained by their husbands' families at the death of their spouses. Consequently, male children more than the females strengthened their mothers' social and economic status in Igboland. While baby girls were welcomed in every family, it was unthinkable to a woman, before the war, not to have a son.

Birth marked the beginning of the life cycle. In a home birth, a baby's cry announced her arrival to the wider world. In Ubulu-ukwu the women responded with a guttural sound made by beating their hands on their mouths and the comment "nne i gwa gi okwu, i nulu ife; nna i gwa gi okwu, i nulu ife"; i.e., "pay attention to your mother's instructions; pay attention to your father's instructions."[64] Until weaned, the baby remained at the center of her family's affection and the focus of their attention.

Rites performed for a baby girl in the first few weeks of life were to adapt her to life on earth before exposing her to the public. The rites served a variety of purposes: They celebrated the sex of the child and laid the foundation for her life in the future. The important ones were the naming ceremony, burying the umbilical cord, and female circumcision; that is, female genital mutilation. The latter was widely done in the Aniocha and Ika areas in early childhood. Even though today female circumcision is dying out, some families still hold to it as an important female rite.

The naming ceremony transcended simply giving the child a name; it served as the first public and formal presentation of the infant to the gods of the land and to the society as a whole. The ceremony was always well attended by members of the family and their friends. It began with a prayer to the ancestors and the gods of the land by the head of the family unit, requesting that these entities watch over the child and bless her life on earth. The spirit beings received tokens of drinks and pieces of kola nut in the course of prayer. Today, the pervading presence of Christianity has altered this practice significantly from what it was before the war. Many families hold naming ceremonies for their children according to the pattern common in the past but without the ritual prayer to the gods and the ancestors. Some make mention of these spirit beings as well as God, on the notion that all are spirits and work towards similar goals. It is also normal now for parents to name their children without formal ceremony.

Parents named their children after careful consideration. Names might reflect the social status or expectations of the couple for themselves and for the child or the circumstances of its birth. After the naming ceremony the next focus for non-Christian parents was the safety of their child. The fear of malevolent spirits and of human beings attacking the child was so real before the war that parents took certain precautions, which often involved the services of a diviner, in order to safeguard the life of their child. Burying the child's umbilical cord was done after the naming ceremony.

Prepuberty rites for baby girls and boys were identical except for the piercing of the ear, a mark of beauty in girls, and genital mutilation. Female genital circumcision, involving the excision of part of the clitoris was performed on girls in the Aniocha and Ika areas within the first eight days of life, but not in the Ukwuani area. In the prewar period the practice was highly rated by nonliterate women and men who considered it humiliating for a girl to escape it. The virtues of this act, as some are quick to point out, have remained an obstacle to its total extinction in

Anioma. Present supporters of the rite justify it as the antidote to nymphomania and poor personal hygiene,[65] although the latter is doubtful. Its importance actually is hinged on ability to reduce female sexual desire, which promised social advantages to parents by ensuring that their daughters did not compromise their chastity, a development that would taint the image of the girl and her family.[66]

Mother and child concluded the ceremonies involving the birth of the child and processes of adjustment to life on earth with an outing after the period of postnatal confinement observed in the first three months of the baby's life. The concentration of birth rituals within this period made it an important and action-packed one for babies in Anioma.

The most common rites for adolescent girls focused on their future sexual and reproductive roles. In most parts of Anioma the marriage process served as girls' initiation into adult society. It involved many ceremonies and rituals commemorating the transition to adulthood. Marriage, which figured prominently as creating a union of a woman and a man as a basic social unit, was regarded as the prerequisite to parenthood. For this reason, betrothal and the marriage ceremony were very important events in girls' lives, resulting in their being socialized, from an early age, into mothering roles.

The marriage process was a rite of passage in the Aniocha and Ika areas. A standard marraige followed a slightly lengthy process that began with the finding of a marriageable girl and terminated with the young bride joining her husband. The important event in any marriage process was the payment of the bridewealth. Before the 1930s it was common to pay the bridewealth in the form of labor services, but this was eventually replaced with money, so that by 1975 the concept of paying bridewealth through rendering services to the bride's family appeared strange and outmoded. Bridewealth as money comprised whatever was agreed on by the two contracting families in addition to specified or unspecified gallons of palm-wine, tubers of yam, and a host of presents for the bride and her mother.[67] Postwar inflation and community reconsiderations resulted in an increase in the bridewealth paid in Anioma since 1970. The acceptance of the bridewealth by a bride's family sealed the marriage contract and marked the accession of a girl to womanhood.

Other forms of marriage in Aniocha and Ukwuani, such as marriage by abduction and concubinage, existed and were common before the war. In recent times modernization and the entrenchment of Christianity have given girls more options regarding the type of marriage they submit to. Especially in the past three decades, it has become unfashionable to settle for concubinage or to accept the position of a second wife in a polygynous marriage.

Nwunye and *mgba* marriages existed in the Ika area. *Mgba* was a form of concubinage and was preferred because of its flexibility and advantages for women. It enabled people of lower social status to marry without obstacles, in the hope that it discouraged promiscuity. A couple that contracted an *mgba* marriage shared their children equally among themselves and if they had just one child, it belonged to the woman.[68] Parents unwilling to separate with their daughters in the manner *nwunye* marriage allowed married them off through *mgba* marriage. *Nwunye* marriage, on the other hand, was regarded as a form of slavery. It was contracted by a sacrifice to the ancestor cult. Only *nwunye* wives served as priestesses when the need arose and carried out purification rites in their extended families. A daughter given out in *nwunye* marriage was solely her husband's, along with all she owned.[69] At death she was buried in his village unlike the cultural practice of returning women to their natal families when dead. To revert from *nwunye* to *mgba* a woman sacrificed a goat to the ancestor cult to nullify the sacrifice made at the commencement of the *nwunye* marriage. Members of the Agbor royal family married only *nwunye* wives and their submission to their husbands was never to be questioned.[70] Investigations into the social history of the girl's family were unnecessary for *nwunye* marriage, unlike in the normal marriage contract first described, but the suitor must pay everything demanded as bridewealth by the parents of the bride.

Contrary to what obtained in the Aniocha and Ika areas, young women in Ukwuani confirmed their transition to adulthood with adolescent "circumcision" performed in the first trimester of pregnancy. Despite the declining status of this practice it was abnormal in Ukwuani for women to be buried with their clitoris intact. A variant of adolescent circumcision in the Ika area was the incisions made on the lower abdomen of a bride before she moved in with her husband. The incisions served as both her initiation into womanhood and a prayer by her family for her fruitfulness.

From the moment a lady's bridewealth was paid, she starts to observe the taboos associated with marital status. Initiation ceremonies were held for young brides in Aniocha within the extended family unit. It was at such ceremonies that they were taught the taboos in their respective husband's family units and the norms governing marital relationships in their new lineages. From this moment onwards, other women subtly observed the activities of a bride for signs of marital infidelity, a heinous crime in Igboland—when committed by a woman. Adultery committed by women was not always concealed because of the belief that severe repercussions from the deities befall the confidante and the culprit; and unless handled according to the custom the husband of an unfaithful wife might die and the children would become ill. Men rarely exonerated a wife caught in adultery, but they themselves were free to enjoy intimacies with women outside their homes at no expense to anyone. There were no profound changes in the marriage process in Anioma between what it was before the war and what obtains presently except that inflation has resulted in an appreciable increase in the bridewealth, and that ceremonies are now more ostentatious. Also, many couples proceed to hold a church wedding after the traditional marriage. Contemporary families demand more from a suitor who is from another town or from outside the Igbo area than they would from one who is from the same town as the bride.[71] The most important change, however, is the official abrogation of marriage by abduction and the wide range of marital choices open to girls to choose from.

The final passage rite associated with life transitions among women relates to death. The Anioma regarded death as a reversal of birth and therefore a transition from the land of the living to that of spirits. The burial ceremony embraced certain rites performed to speed a dead woman in her journey to the spirit world. These rites had a variety of emphases, meaning different things to different people. Some stressed the incorporation of the deceased into the realm of the departed and, for the mourners, their separation from the dead.[72]

Inquiries were made concerning the circumstances of a person's death to confirm whether it was a good or a bad end. Bad deaths were not celebrated; those that occurred in the course of pregnancy, by execution or suicide (usually by hanging), as a result of an incurable disease (through adultery), or as a consequence of taking a false oath. Before 1930, it included a widow dying before the completion of the burial ceremony of a deceased spouse. This was also taken as an indication that she was responsible for the death of her husband.[73]

The burial ceremony in Anioma was in two parts: the first and the second burials. The former was much simpler and entailed the burial of the body. Through the second burial the soul, the focus of the rituals at this stage, was sent to the ancestral land. Unmarried adolescents and children were not given a second burial. Death was handled carefully among the Igbo. A bereaved husband diplomatically notified his in-laws of the death of their daughter. He would need their consent to return the body for burial, which was the norm in Anioma. Where the relationship between a man and his wife's family was strained the latter might constitute an obstacle to the easy burial of the deceased.

The second burial ceremony involved considerable expense and commenced any time after the burial of the body but when the deceased's family was financially able to handle it. In many towns, it was announced with a gunshot, followed by the ritual sacrifice of a goat, representing the deceased's unrealized expectations and aspirations and as atonement for the deceasesd's sins. Sacrificing a goat replaced human sacrifice, which was the practice before the 1920s.[74] The goat to be sacrificed was killed by hitting its head on the mock coffin, *igbudu*, which represented the deceased's body. After other rituals to appease the deceased to preclude her coming out to disturb her family, her former business associates, if she had any, and the community, the mock coffin was buried. Her husband and children observed an all-night vigil in her honor before the first part of the ceremony was concluded.

In Ukwuani husbands mourned their wives for nine or twelve days but among the Ika the mourning period did not exceed seven days. Three months after the death of the wife a man was free to remarry.[75] Women, unlike men, were subjected to some dehumanizing practices during the burial processes of their deceased spouses. The burial rites in honor of a dead man in Anioma took a form that suggested that the widow was responsible for her husband's death and was being punished for it. This sometimes progressed from mere impression to real assumption. As a result, women in Anioma were visibly worried and anxious at the death of their spouses, and this is still the case even though the burial rites have undergone some modifications over the decades. Blaming women for the death of their husbands was not peculiar to Anioma. Such thinking existed among some of the cultural groups in the Nigerian middle belt, the Hindu of India,[76] and the Dobu Islanders of the Western Pacific.[77] The practice of burying a prominent man with as many as ten to forty male and female slaves ended with the effective implementation of the British colonial administration and, therefore, did not feature in Anioma after 1916.

Two customs that widows in Anioma found extremely distressing were the ritual separation from a husband after his death and the farewell visit by masqueraders—representing the ancestors, the latter believed to have been borrowed from Igala.[78] The ritual separation, known as *iya-isi* in some towns, involved laying a widow beside, but in opposite directions to the body of her dead husband with their heads facing opposite ends of the room. In Aboh, the widow was not only laid beside the corpse but was carried across it four times for the separation to be complete. The purpose of the ritual was to prevent the spirit of the dead man from killing any future husband of the woman, which most often was a relation of the deceased, unless the widow rejected to being inherited by one of her husband's brothers and returned to her family. She was not free until she returned the bridewealth paid on her, thereby severing all links with her late husband's family. At present in Asaba the lid of the casket may take the place of the actual body of the deceased, yet women still report that the ritual is frightening.

The rite involving masqueraders, called *egwugwu* in Asaba, paying their last respects to a dead man was observed for every freeborn male in Asaba, Illah, Obamkpa, Ukala-uno, and Ukala-okwute, all in Aniocha. In Asaba, on the night slated for this, in complete disregard to weather conditions, the widow sits alone in the open for a last "discussion" with the spirit of the husband, which involved being questioned by the masqueraders over her husband's death. And this occurred in Anioma, where women like those in the Igbo heartland were socialized to dread and avoid masqueraders because they represented the ancestors. Women were intimidated into observing these rites with threats of excommunication from their community and separation from their children. As disconcerting as these rituals were to women, they have survived to the present. In summary, burial rites in Anioma engender gender violence, reduce women's self-esteem, deny them the right to free movement, expose them to health hazards during the period of mourning, and provide grounds for the total disinheritance of the widow.[79] Yet some widows who passed through these rituals were unwilling to permit their abrogation.[80]

Anioma women pursued a wide range of economic activities before the civil war, but agriculture was their common engagement. Others were trading, weaving, production of pottery wares and white chalk, processing vegetable oils, and working as ritual specialists. Men cultivated farms while their wives assisted in planting crops. This did not include yams, which were the responsibility of male farmers. Women received portions of land from their husbands or male relatives and on these raised a variety of crops, mostly vegetables. All the crops cultivated in Anioma were not indigenous to the area. Banana, plantains, and some species of cocoyam were introduced into Nigeria from Asia between the sixteenth and eighteenth centuries. Maize and coconut came from the Caribbean, while cassava (manioc) came to West Africa from Brazil, through the Portuguese in the fifteenth century and diffused into Anioma at the end of the nineteenth century.

Most women had their vegetable gardens close to their compounds. The nearness of the gardens saved them the trouble of walking far and exerting themselves unduly in order to obtain what they needed for meal preparation. The gardens were cultivated by the women themselves or with the help of their adolescent children and sometimes of their husbands. They retained and enhanced the soil fertility by sweeping animal droppings into their gardens, pouring the ash from the daily sweepings of the kitchen on the land, and by practicing rough rotational cultivation. Ash was widely used as an insect repellent. Women carefully and habitually tended their farms assisted by their children or their friends whom they helped on their own farms.

The main food staple in Anioma was yam. Yam was so important that it was ritualized in the *Ifejioku*, a yearly festival used to mark the Igbo calendar. But already before 1960 cassava had become an important variable to yam, and women adopted it as a better option to the cocoyam, the famed female crop and the variant to yam. Cassava had some advantages over yam. It was easy to crop and thrived well under soil and climatic condition changes in which other food crops failed. It had a low-labor requirement and the harvested tubers could be processed in a variety of ways. Despite its comparatively recent introduction in Anioma it has emerged as the food crop with the highest potential. The Ika area and Asaba were important cassava-producing zones before the war,[81] and Ika has remained so.

Among the things that affected agriculture in Anioma were communal land tenure, soil types, and climatic conditions. The land-tenure system was deeply rooted in local institutions and constituted one of the most formidable human influences affecting farming. Women had no direct access to land except what was assigned to them by their husbands in farms already planted with yam. Women utilized the spaces between the mounds for their crops. A widow claimed land on behalf of her male children. One of her husband's male relatives leased a portion of her deceased husband's farm to her or gave her an allocation from his.[82] In like manner, mature but unmarried women who needed farmland gained access to temporary land allocations by the grace and favor of their male relatives. Although colonial rule hastened increased household production of agricultural crops for sale, and women were the chief suppliers of labor during the period,[83] rigid compliance with the local land-tenure system did not encourage large-scale farming among women before 1960. In the riverine area, the people faced the problem of insufficient land for farming. With about 80 percent of the land swampy and water logged for most part of the year, farming was difficult and not widely practiced as it was in the Ika and Aniocha subsections, and in the nonriverine communities in Ukwuani.[84]

The role of women in farming did not end with cultivating their own gardens and working the portions given them in their husbands' farms. They participated actively in harvesting the crops in the months of October and November. Though many crops were harvested long before then, for some, the process lasted for a considerably long period. Crops that were reaped and consumed early were vegetables and maize. Other proceeds lasted much longer if properly handled. Women were careful to preserve their harvests and thus were able to retain most of their proceeds long after the planting season.

Animal husbandry was another aspect of the agricultural activities of Anioma women. The animals reared were local fowls, pigeons, *muturu* cattle (the Nigerian short horn), goats (the West African dwarf breed), pigs, and dogs. The animals were not restricted in pens but allowed to graze freely in a few restricted areas. The parent stock was procured through livestock tenancy, gifts, or by purchase. The last two conferred on owners total rights to the animals and to their offspring. The benefit of animal tenancy was the possibility it extended to poor women to own livestock without having to raise the initial capital for their purchase.

Processed animal feeds were unavailable in rural areas before the war, hence animal owners fed their stock mostly on maize in addition to left over meals and yam peelings. At the onset of the farming season, farmers took care to rein in their animals to preclude their eating up farm produce. Animal farming was important to the local population for through it they met the demand for rituals and sacrifices and had access to animal protein. It was also a form of investment against future needs.[85] The setback to animal husbandry, however, was the rate of mortality through endemic diseases. Popular diseases were *pestes des petit ruminant* (PPR), a viral infection peculiar to small ruminants; and *helminthiasis,* which is an increase in worm burden in the gastrointestinal tract of animal species.

Ossissa, Akoku, and Ashaka women in Ukwuani engaged in fishing,[86] a lucrative otherwise masculine activity widely practiced in Ukwuani and in parts of Aniocha. Women fished with baskets and not with hooks and lines. Fishing by women was done towards the end of the rainy season when the water level had subsided and risks minimized. Because of the presence of bodies of water in the Ukwuani area girls acquired appreciable skill in swimming. Only good female swimmers could fish, because of the considerable risk of being drowned or swept away by the current in the process of pursuing a targeted fish. Female fishing was not primarily for commerce but for individual consumption. The fish caught, along with lobster and some crayfish, were preserved in the sun or by smoking them over slow fires. Fishing did not prevent women from buying them from the market to supplement their catch, but those who caught more than they needed at any one time disposed of the rest through trade.

Processing vegetable oils was a common female engagement in Anioma. Oil palm, an indigenous plant in the tropics, was widely available. Women were involved in different aspects of the palm produce industry as a cottage business because of the abundance of palm bushes and the economic importance of the palm tree. The oil palm tree was the source of the following: oil, wine, ropes, brooms, building materials, soap, and ointment. Its diverse economic importance made it a cherished tree. Excluding the extraction of palm wine, handled exclusively by men, the other byproducts of the oil palm were processed by women.

Ripe palm fruits were the essential raw materials for vegetable oil. The nuts were separated from the stem, boiled until they softened, and crushed in deep mortars before the oil in the fruit coat could be extracted. In Agbor and Umutu women mashed the nuts with their feet to achieve the same goal. The well-pounded or mashed nuts were scooped into a receptacle and mixed with water to disentangle the twigs. These and particles of cracked nuts were removed before the remaining mixture was boiled, leaving only the oil, which was kept for domestic use or for sale. These methods of producting oil are still in vogue in Anioma. Women in Ndosimili produced more oil than either of their counterparts in the Aniocha and Ika areas, but there was a serious decline in oil production there during the civil war.[87] Palm nuts, the end products of the palm oil production, were cracked manually to extract the kernels. These were dried in the sun and fried in the early hours of the morning or late in the evening when the weather was cool and the chances of the exercise causing a fire accident less likely. The oil that seeped out of the pores of the kernels in the course of frying, called *udeaku* or *uriaku,* was collected and used as body unguent, hair lubricant, and as first aid for minor ailments including simple colds and wounds.[88] Palm nuts served other purposes such as fuel and were used in the production of herbal mixtures by ritual specialists. Women in Umutu were adept at producing body unguent also from the coconut fruit.

The essential ingredient for soap production was the stem of the palm nuts. Once the nuts were removed, the stem was cut up and dried in the sun. The trunks of freshly harvested plantain or banana tree and the tree called *ulu-oyibo* or *elele* in Aniocha were collected, shredded, and also dried in the sun. The dried materials were burnt to ashes, then collected, mixed with water, and sieved to remove the rough parts before boiling the remnants. A thick substance remained after the water had evaporated. To this was added the oil extracted from the palm nuts, the combined substance and the mixture was also boiled. The soap that formed afterwards was used for bathing. Soap for washing cloths was made in a slightly different manner. After boiling the liquid ash, part of the mixture was set aside. Bleached palm oil was added to the mixture and boiled for a second time. Soap made this way was used for many purposes. Soap making was widely practiced in Onicha-ugbo, Agbor, Umutu, Ashaka, and Ossissa. The byproducts of the oil palm tree and the sale of kernels and palm nuts were of great benefit to women, providing them with employment and an income. Women were able to integrate the processing of palm fruits into their domestic activities, and this pattern continued after the war.

The next most important engagement besides farming was trade. This assessment is based on its scale and the number of women involved. Exchanging commodities either for money or for other items was occasioned by a number of reasons: It was the venue for disposing surplus farm yields and for buying or acquiring needed items. Women dominated local trade until after the 1940s, while men controlled the long-distance trade within the same period. Trade has been considered a feminine activity probably because it did not call for much of a display of physical strength, except of course requiring women to carry heavy loads to and from markets over long distances. Today more women in Anioma regard trade as their main occupation and farming as a secondary option because they feel that farming was physically taxing and not very lucrative.[89] But the reverse was true before the war.[90]

Since nearly everybody farmed before the war, large surpluses were not easily disposed of until the growth of urban towns and population shifts to these towns increased the demand for farm surpluses. Women had specific places in the markets, where they converged for exchange purposes. In Anioma, four-day or eight-day periodic markets were the norm until the 1930s, when daily markets sprang up in many towns.[91] The market place was of immense importance to the social and economic life of a town. As a social institution, it provided a venue where buyers and sellers met to discuss problems of common interest. Trade was carried out on the basis of the indigenous culture and belief systems of the people and to satisfy both their material and spiritual needs. Women moved from market to market to exchange their goods, and towns within a walking radius traded with one another. Before motor transport became very common, goods were moved by head portage and traders moved together to avoid molestation and theft. Trade contacts were sustained with the Igala, Ijaw, Urhobo/Isoko, and the Itshekiri before the war.[92] Excluding traders from Warri who came to buy white chalk, other trade associates supplied the various towns in Anioma with fish, livestock, beads, and ivory.

Besides working as traders, women functioned as ritual specialists before the war, but there were more female midwives than female ritual specialists then. In most towns, indigenous medicine was the preserve of men, yet women with mystical powers, as it was regarded, were recognized. Female ritual specialists operated in Okpanam, Obamkpa, Aboh, Onicha-ugbo, Akwukwu-Igbo, Isheagu, Issele-ukwu, Utagba-ogbe, and Alisimie. In Okpanam, the knowledge of herbs and their uses was so diversified that men acquired knowledge about them from more knowledgeable women.[93] Even until recently, some men in Okpanam consider it insulting to their professional ritual specialists if their wives visited modern medical centers.[94]

Indigenous medicine, as a profession, was the means of keeping the people in good health. The establishment of modern medical services in Nigeria at the beginning of the twentieth century did not result in the extension of health services to every part of Anioma before the war. The *National Atlas of the Federal Republic of Nigeria* listed four small-scale dispensaries and maternity centers and three general hospitals as existing in Anioma before 1974.[95] This obviously implies that before 1960 many people in Anioma depended on ritual specialists, who doubled as soothsayers, diviners, and fortune-tellers, as well as on local midwives for medical care.

A prospective female ritual specialist received a certificate of practice by joining the *dibia* cult after learning by divination or soothsaying that she was called into the profession and on completion of the apprentice period. (*Dibia* is the general name for ritual specialists, soothsayers, diviners, and fortune-tellers.) The leaders of the *dibia* cult in all towns were men, and they supervised the initiation of new members, which included the payment of an entrance fee, sacrifices of goats or fowls at a prescribed shrine, and other rituals. The initiation conferred on a new member all priestly functions and the ability to see things invisible to nonmembers but not the knowledge of herbs. This, the initiate learnt from other professionals sometimes for a fee and sometimes not.

Midwives had no formal initiation ceremonies. Usually mothers passed on their knowledge to daughters they observed to be gifted or capable of functioning in that respect. The midwives assisted in child delivery and provided pre- and postnatal services. They carried out male and female "circumcisions" and administered herbs for mild ailments. They were responsible for body scarification, which was common in Anioma until the 1930s. In the Ika area they formed a special guild known as *okonwene*. The ritual specialists had a wider range of responsibilities and were acclaimed for their ability to cure all ailments, to influence the destiny of people, and to foretell the future.[96]

Women habitually engaged in the production of many articles. Clothes and pottery wares were among the goods turned out by female manufacturers in Anioma. Indigenous female weavers produced the handwoven cloth worn by the people in the precolonial and colonial periods. Weaving was widespread in Ubulu clan, comprising Ubulu-okiti, Ubulu-ukwu, and Ubulu-uno; Ezi, Idumuje-ugboko, Ebu, Issele-ukwu, and Onicha-ugbo—all in Aniocha. In Abavo, in the Ika area; and in Akoku, Aboh, Umutu, Ebedei, and Onicha-ukwuani, in the Ukwuani area, women wove on a moderate scale.

Weaving was done during leisure hours after the women had returned from their farms. They mostly produced white cloths made from cotton fibers.[97] Cottonseeds were planted close to the compounds and in the farm areas. Fibers from harvested cotton were essential in cloth production. There was no formal division of labor in weaving, but many women engaged the assistance of their children in picking and blowing the cotton fibers. Six discernible stages were obvious in cloth production. The first was the picking and carding of the harvested cotton. Next was the manual spinning of the cotton into thread. Weaving would not commence until the weaver had obtained the quantity of thread required to make a complete wrapper. The third stage was folding the thread to a length corresponding to that of the material to be woven. The fourth stage was washing, boiling, starching, and drying the bundles of thread. Washing ensured that the finished product would be neat and alluring, for once the bundles were woven into cloth they were rarely washed to avoid their losing their stiffness and freshness. The final step was the actual weaving, using an upright loom that could either be small or large. The smaller looms were used for making small-sized items like shawls or towel-sized wrappers, while the larger looms were used for making items of standard clothing.

Women wove their clothes by interlacing the threads in opposite directions on the loom. Weaving was a slow and time-consuming process. It took a fast and dedicated worker six weeks to produce a complete wrapper. Women wore four pieces and men five, the extra piece to accommodate their girth. The pieces were joined to make two pairs of wrappers for the use of either a man or a woman. All handwoven wrappers were made in different shades of white and were used and worn for all ceremonial purposes. Designs were woven in accordance with the taste of the client or what was in vogue at the time of production. Until processed dyes became available, designs involving a combination of colors were worked in with local dyes obtained from the leaves and barks of certain plants.

There was a wide market for handwoven cloths in Anioma before the war. The entire population depended largely on female weavers for their clothing needs. A short piece, between twelve and fifteen inches in length but forty-two inches wide, looking more like a towel, was used by men for working the farm and by women for securing their babies behind their back. Local bags or sacks used generally by men and by professional hunters, smiths, ritual specialists, as well as materials for adorning masquerades were made by female weavers. In Akoku special cloths were produced and used during the burial of the oldest man in the town and for second burial ceremonies.

The availability of imported threads for weaving during the colonial period adversely impacted the weaving industry. Gradually, weavers resorted to imported threads for their products. The patronage of foreign yarns denied the younger generation the opportunity of preparing the threads themselves. The industry further suffered competition from cloths made in northern Nigeria, particularly those produced in Lokoja and Okene, where weavers benefited from the efforts of the colonial government to entrench the indigenes in cotton growing through the auspices of British Cotton Growing Association (BCGA).[98] Cotton growing had been a flourishing industry there in the precolonial period, the inhabitants—like the Anioma—using locally-grown cotton in the manufacture of high quality cloths. The goal of BCGA in northern Nigeria, therefore, was to convince farmers that cotton could be treated as the main or primary crop, but with the ultimate purpose of producing the raw material for British cloth manufacturing industries.

Colonial efforts to promote cotton growing resulted in its abundance in northern Nigeria. This in turn stimulated increased production of local cloths by the people, whose excess products found their way to Anioma. The relative cheapness of the cloth from the northern region enticed many to patronize them instead of the more costly varieties produced in Anioma. This and the large imports of European textiles in the country during the period led to a decline in the Anioma cloth weaving industry. Nonetheless, weaving is still a notable activity among women in Ubulu-ukwu and its environs.

Basketry, the art of making objects from bamboo fibers taken from the stem of raffia palms, was another aspect of weaving for Anioma women. Products made this way—baskets, hats, mats, and brooms—differed in type and in design. The baskets were used for hunting, fishing, storage, and as mock coffins. After the war plastic products began to compete with basket products, which lacked their degree of durability.

Pottery making was not as diffused as weaving in Anioma. It was the famed occupation of women in Isheagu in Aniocha, but it was also practiced by women in Amai, Eziokpor, Utagba-ogbe, and Ossissa—all in Ukwuani. Producing pottery wares required the use of a knife, an empty sea shell, a flat wooden spoon, a small cylindrical stick, twisted broom-sized bamboo, and a piece of cloth. The clay collected was first dried in the sun, then pounded in a mortar, and sieved with a not-too-porous basket. The fine particles were soaked in water until they thickened. Potters kneaded the clay together with their bare hands, all the while adding crushed potsherds to it. When the needed consistency was obtained, lumps of clay were molded into large rings. Using the neck of a broken pot, potters molded a new product by placing the rings of clay one on top of the other. With the wet cloth, they smoothened the inside of their products and dried them in the sun. Without waiting for them to dry completely, the women worked the surface. Some wares were perforated with a pointed stick that made interesting designs on the partially dried surfaces.

Another aspect of pottery production was the drying of the products in the sun. This always preceded the firing. Clay vessels that were only sun-dried would later soften, and become porous, particularly if used for storing liquids. Firing at high temperatures for ten to fifteen minutes rendered the clay immune to deterioration. Fired wares were dipped inside a liquid substance prepared with the bark of a wild tree called *umina*, and the leaves of another plant called *ibubeshi.* Local potters used this solution to seal the pores of their wares to prevent water or other liquids from percolating through them. Although pottery products were widely used for a variety of purposes, their fragility necessitated their constant replacement, which meant that producers were kept busy. As late as the 1960s, these fragile wares were preferred by the people to imported enamel wares.

An uncommon female occupation in Anioma was mining kaolin (*nzu*). This was practiced in Ozanogogo in the Ika area and in Ukwunzu in Aniocha. In Ozanogogo it was the chief occupation of women in four out of the seven quarters of the town.[99] The chalk was dug out in lumps from the soil, dried in the sun, then broken into smaller particles, and softened in water. Muddy chunks of chalk were cut into small pieces that were carefully molded into desired shapes and smoothened before drying them in the sun. Traders came from surrounding towns to buy chalks in Ozonogogo. It was considered a superior product, as it was whiter than similar products from Ukwunzu and from Igbanke in the present Edo State. The importance of white chalk is rooted in Igbo mythology. Igbo populations used it as a religious object and in rituals and herbal mixtures. It was also used for drawing body decorations. People rubbed it on themselves as a mark of purity and some licked it, believing in its power to give them a "good" mind. Some persons would grind it to powder and blow it into the air as a good-will gesture to cherished friends and family members.[100]

These economic pursuits were by no means the only economic engagements of women in Anioma before the outbreak of the Nigerian civil war. The women in our area of study were not exposed early to western education as their male counterparts. The Christian missions that came to Anioma towards the end of the nineteenth century established mission schools for the people. Despite encouragement from expatriate missionaries, parents started sending their male children to school after seeing the benefits of Western education in former slaves returning from the West. But females did not receive the same advantage because of the notion that it was unrewarding to educate girls who would eventually leave the family once married.[101] Very few families sent their daughters along with their sons to school. By establishing training centers for women, mostly the wives of their clergy, the Church Missionary Society (CMS) that pioneered Western education in Anioma did not give full encouragement to female education after elementary school. Training the wives of the clergy was to equip them to support their husbands' ministry and to use them as examples of hard-working Christian women.[102] Some women who benefited from the training centers initiated similar projects for young girls, teaching them sewing, domestic science, and home management just as they themselves had been taught. The training centers provided jobs for the matrons, as the patrons were called, but the centers declined in importance from the 1950s when the Western regional government launched the free primary education scheme. In spite of the slow start Anioma women had to get an education, by 1966 a small but significant population of trained female teachers, nurses, and midwives had emerged. The education of women eventually received a boost after the war.[103]

Studies on the Igbo have shown different levels of female advancement especially in the economic and religious spheres. Comparing the position of women during the precolonial period with that of the colonial period or with that shortly after independence, some authors[104] have asserted that Igbo women enjoyed considerable influence and independence in the precolonial period. Margaret Green observed that the women she studied, those east of the Niger, were the "chief breadwinners" and were "powerful women".[105] Judith Van Allen, writing about the Owerri Igbo of the Aba Women's War fame, concluded that "strong male domination was imposed on Igbo society both indirectly, by new economic structures, and directly, by the recruitment of only men into the Native Administration."[106] Kamene Okonjo and 'Zulu Sofola[107] extolled the dual sex or coruler concept of governance in Anioma as a mark of the enhanced female political status. These authors blamed the colonial experience for the decline in Igbo women's social and political status. There is enough evidence in support of their assertions. However, the position of women in Anioma in particular varied considerably within the three subsections. In Aniocha, the seven towns that claim Benin ancestry[108] had female chiefs who were respected in the society during the precolonial and early colonial periods. In other towns in Aniocha, lacking such a prominent female figure as an omu, and where the institution developed late, women were of lesser status than men even if they were distinguished and wealthy traders. In the Ukwuani and Ika areas, the principle of male domination was very marked, with women being less visible in public.[109] In all three sections of Anioma, women suffered from discrimination in the society. Ironically, women themselves sometimes encouraged their subordination by complying with discriminatory cultural practices against their own sex.[110]

The relatively peaceful existence of Anioma women was hampered by the incidents leading up to the civil war and the crisis itself. That ominous affair had the positive effect of challenging women to alternative economic activities besides those already considered, as the life of an average Anioma woman was hardly uneventful on the eve of the war. For the society to function, as this chapter has shown, a peaceful and undisturbed atmosphere was necessary. This was the case for the first five years after Nigeria's independence, before the nation was jarred by the internal political crisis in the country, exacerbated by the announcement of a coup d'etat, fifteen days into 1966. From that time onwards the country's political situation ceased to be idealic for Anioma women.

Chapter 2

FROM INDEPENDENCE TO WAR

THE 1966 DISTURBANCES

Nigeria's independence in 1960 did not guarantee political stability for the country. Political ineptitude and gross mismanagement of public office strengthened the sense of ethnic consciousness among the various peoples of the country; hence peoples of different ethnic backgrounds perceived their identity primarily in terms of their ethnic origin. The seeds of ethnic consciousness were sown and nurtured by the British colonial administration.[111] The division of the country into three distinctly dissimilar and unequal regions as mandated by the Arthur Richards' Constitution of 1946 upgraded erstwhile administrative units to semisovereign states. The Richard's Constitution bequeathed to the Northern Region a territorial expanse larger than both the Eastern and Western Regions put together, allowing the north to enjoy more political power than the remaining two regions. The constant struggle for the scarce and unequally distributed resources of the nation, which began before the attainment of independence, continued.[112] The political situation from 1960 until 1965 generated much insecurity in many parts of the nation, culminating in the violent overthrow of Nigeria's first civilian administration.

The reasons given for the coup at the onset appealed to the feelings and expectations of many people from all parts of the country,[113] but this satisfaction turned sour a few months afterwards when a retributive massacre was carried out in northern

Nigeria against the Igbo, including those from Anioma. Besides the Igbo, a relatively small number of people from other parts of the southeast were also massacred in northern Nigeria. The coup planners did not anticipate such a profound consequence of the January purge for it put the ailing country in a worse situation than was previously the case. The peace and self-confidence of the Igbo on both sides of the Niger were shaken by the pogrom against them executed by the Hausa-Fulani, assisted by individuals from the Western Region. The killings led to the desertion of the Igbo from the disturbed areas back to Igboland. The nonliterate women in Anioma concluded that there was a war against the Igbo. They were not alone in this assumption. James Oluleye, a military officer from the Western Region, also described the mayhem generated by the coup as a war between the northerners and the Igbo.[114] The chief mode of transportation for those fleeing the massacres was the railroad, which had a terminus at Enugu, the capital of Eastern Region. Anioma refugees benefited from the free transportation provided for the Igbo fleeing northern Nigeria by Lt. Col. Chukwuemeka Odumegwu Ojukwu, the military governor of Eastern Region.[115] Even as the news of the killings filtered down to Anioma communities women left in search of their relatives in other parts of the country. Some Anioma women had previously lived in different pasts of the Northern Region or had traveled there as long distance traders and had contact with northerners. Their competence in the Hausa language encouraged their rescue missions, which simultameously put them at a risk; although most of them were well rewarded for their efforts.[116]

Following the disturbances, most Anioma returnees previously residing in northern Nigeria, out of panic and deep sense of insecurity, came back without the bulk of their belongings. Their family members were relieved that they had escaped death, but as their stay became prolonged and uncertain a subtle rivalry ensued between local inhabitants and returnees over the scarce resources in the rural areas. Most family members were not willing to share family land and other meager resources for an extended period of time. Among the elements the returnees were forced to put up with was occasional ridicule from their relations regarding their plight, particularly their misfortune in returning to Anioma without their belongings. Ironically, many of the inhabitants erroneously believed that their returnee relatives had come home without their belongings simply because they had none, having failed to utilize the opportunity of living in the cities to better themselves and not really because they left them behind in the rush to escape death.[117]

The forced change of environment made adaptation difficult for many female victims of the pogrom, and without husbands and other male relatives adjustment in their chosen place of refuge was an additional hardship for those who were bereaved. In most sections of Anioma, the absence of social amenities such as good roads and good housing was disconcerting. Nonetheless, the forced relocation afforded the bereaved women the freedom of mourning their dead in a less turbulent environment.

No census data exist with information on the sex, profession, and educational backgrounds of the returnees and the percentage of the victims from Anioma. The official record of the Midwest Region, which became Midwest State in May 1967,[118] claims that fifty thousand (50,000) people of Midwest origin were displaced as a result of the disturbances,[119] a figure regarded as an underestimate by one observer.[120] From oral sources, though, the majority of Anioma women affected by the trauma were traders, farmers, and housewives. The term housewives in this context refers to those whose occupation would be described as full-time home managers. The bereaved among them resumed their economic engagements shortly after the conclusion of the one year mourning period for their dead family members.

The widows were generally sympathetically received, but their condition was ultimately vitiated by the cultural treatment of widows in Igboland. They were not as fortunate as their Eastern Region counterparts who had also lost their husbands in the pogrom but benefited from government assistance in the form of a flat sum of £5 per widow. This financial assistance provided bereaved women east of the Niger with some capital to invest in a trade, helping them cope with the challenges of widowhood. To make it even easier for these women, the government of the Eastern Region paid every child who lost a parent in the disturbances ten shillings per month for a period of six months.[121] Similar benefits were not extended to widows in Anioma by either the Midwest government or the federal government until almost the end of the war, when war orphans were offered a scholarship to complete their postprimary school education.[122]

Displaced female children and adolescents of Anioma origin easily fitted into the educational system available in their respective local areas. By December 1966 many had been admitted into schools in Anioma,[123] while some from Asaba, Ibusa, and other towns closest to the Eastern Region continued their secondary school education in the Eastern Region,[124] which had more female secondary schools than Anioma.

The secession of the Eastern Region as the Republic of Biafra in May 1967, blamed on the inability of the federal government to protect the lives and property of the Igbo after the 1966 massacres, equally led to a string of events that negatively impacted Anioma women. The people of Anioma sympathized with the plight of the Igbo living east of the Niger. Their commiseration derived from their shared ethnic origin and their mutual experience in other parts of Nigeria during the 1966 disturbances. The presence of the Ika Ibo Association, representing Anioma at the Consultative Assembly convened by the military governor of Eastern Region to discuss the fate of the Igbo following the massacres, amply demonstrated Anioma's support for the Igbo in the east.[125] The Ika Igbo Association determined that in the event of the disintegration of Nigeria the Anioma would merge with the people of the Igbo heartland.[126]

A grassroots' identification with the Biafran cause also developed in Anioma and was expressed through letters to newspaper editors and publishers. Letters from the indigenes of Anioma to the government of Biafra offering to enlist in the Biafran army appeared in the *Biafran Sun*. Excerpts from the article "What Happens to Ika Ibos" by Umunna Iwegbu from Ogwashi-ukwu provides an insight into the feelings of the Anioma people about the conflict between the federal government and the Eastern Region, the latter accredited with representing the interest of the Igbo.[127] The letter reads:

> With the proclamation of Biafra, the Midwest Ibo are asking about their position and future.... Events since 1966 have proved that Ika Ibos, like the people of Biafra, have no protection and no security under the Nigerian government. They have suffered humiliation, spite and victimization and were as much the victims of the 1966 pogrom as the people of Biafra.... It seems, therefore, that the Ika Ibos have been condemned to a perpetual status of minority without basic rights guaranteed in the Midwest Region of Nigeria. Now that it is clear that what the 500,000 Ika Ibos would continue to get in Nigeria is perpetual servitude, the solution to their problem lies in a merger with the Republic of Biafra....

Women, like the men, were also emphatic about their support for Biafra. One newspaper article, "Ika Ibos Cross over to Protest," reported that "hundreds of Ika Ibo women from the Midwest crossed to Biafra to join a demonstration by Ika Ibo women in Biafra for a merger of the Ika Ibo section of Nigeria with Biafra."[128] The open support for Biafra in Anioma caused Lt. Col. David Ejoor, the state military governor, to reprove the Anioma for endorsing and applauding every utterance and action of the Biafran leader. In addition, he banned, by an extraordinary gazette, the publication, circulation, and possession of the *Ika Ibo Newsletter*, a monthly publication that expressed the views of the Anioma, declaring the "printers and publishers as an unlawful [group] dangerous to the good government of the Midwest."[129]

BIAFRAN INCURSION INTO THE MIDWEST

The civil war began in July 1967 with the federal invasion of the Eastern Region, now Biafra. Biafra was unprepared and ill equipped for such aggression. The reverses sustained by the Biafran army two months after the commencement of hostilities motivated the decision by its government to invade the Midwest and Lagos,[130] as both were not more than a day's drive from each other. Commanding the Liberation Army, the Biafran invading team, was a Yoruba, Lieutenant Colonel Banjo. The choice of a Yoruba was to give the invasion some credibility to Yoruba-speaking people, through whose territory the Biafran troops would pass before reaching Lagos, and whose support the Biafran government desperately needed. Colonel Banjo, however, had his own reasons for taking part in the scheme, not being enamored with the Biafra struggle.[131] Banjo, who was implicated in the January 1966 coup, was aware that the head of state would only want him incarcerated; a fate he escaped when the military governor of the Eastern Region released him from the Enugu prison. Joining the Biafran army and accepting to lead the Midwest-Lagos invasion was his own idea of fighting his way back into Nigerian territory.[132]

It was with little difficulty that Biafran soldiers led by Lieutenant Colonel Banjo crossed the Niger Bridge that separated Biafra from the Midwest on 9 August 1967, only one month after the federal invasion of Biafran territory. The bridge was both poorly barricaded and poorly defended by the officers of the Midwest Area Command. This was in spite of the public assertion of the unit commander and of the state military governor that the Fourth (Midwest) Area Command was "strong enough to defend and preserve the territorial integrity of the [state]."[133] The residents of Asaba, the Midwest town closest to Biafra, awoke on the morning of 9 August to discover that Biafran soldiers were occupying all the strategic areas in the town, namely, the John Holt beach, the post office, and the Catering Rest House. The Liberation Army marched through Anioma in what was described as a strange collection of cars and trucks. Their weapons included machetes, clubs, and homemade guns.[134] On arriving in Benin City, the Liberation Army dispersed to other parts of the Midwest and before dusk that day the length and breadth of the state had been overrun without any resistance whatsoever. A section of the army proceeded to Ore in the Western Region, where it split into two groups. One group moved towards Ibadan through Ife, and the other made a bid for Lagos through Ijebu-Ode.[135]

The Biafran's entry into the Midwest resembled a triumphal march. To Anioma youths of both sexes, Biafran soldiers were heroes. The older women, recalling the trauma of the previous year, were also enthralled with their presence. A similar reaction towards the Liberation Army's presence was not observed among the non-Igbo groups of the Midwest however. Lieutenant Colonel Ejoor, the state military governor, responded to their arrival in his territory by abdicating his office. A majority of the non-Igbo military officers and civil servants followed his example and went into hiding as the Biafran forces approached Benin City.

Military officers of Anioma origin dominated and controlled the Fourth Area Command in the Midwest. They were later accused of complicity with Biafrans and of handing over the state to the invaders without putting up any resistance. It was not generally believed in the Midwest that Anioma military officers handed over the state to Biafrans on a silver platter, but no one challenged the government's stand on the issue at the time. Decades later, Major Samuel Ogbemudia, a non-Igbo officer, absolved his Anioma colleagues of blame, arguing that the federal government's failure to provide the Midwest with sufficient arms for sustained combat against a determined aggressor left officers of Anioma origin no alternative but to abandon their state to the Biafran army.[136] Besides, the killing of Igbo officers in September 1966 destroyed whatever confidence Anioma officers had in non-Igbo combatants, strengthening their preference for an alliance with their fellow Igbo to working with the non-Igbo.

Biafra's incursion into the Midwest and its subsequent control of the state affected the conduct and scope of the war. That, and the attempted march to Lagos, jolted the federal government and all the peoples of Nigeria except the Anioma, who strongly supported the Biafran cause. Biafra's assertiveness led to the modification of the initial federal military strategy against secession. What the federal government initially believed would be a police action expanded into total war. The incursion resulted in the incorporation of Midwest State into the boiling cauldron. The federal government went as far as extending the economic blockade it had imposed in April 1967 from the Eastern Region to the Midwest.[137] Added to these, the invasion upset the ethnic and political balance of the Midwest and heralded the beginning of another horrifying epoch for the people of Anioma but most especially for its female population.

The immanent differences in the state came to the fore in the reaction of the different ethnic communities to the economic blockade and the hardship it generated. The Edo, Urhobo-Isoko, Itshekiri, and Ijaw—all non-Igbo groups—blamed their sufferings on Biafrans, whom they regarded with mistrust. The Anioma held the federal government responsible for their trauma. The solidarity between the two Igbo groups on the two sides of the Niger was such that when Biafra subsequently disconnected its electricity supply to towns in Anioma on 13 July 1967 it did not make the affected Anioma communities denounce the Biafran government nor deplore its secession. On the other hand, the age-old fear of Igbo domination, rekindled by Biafra's entry into the Midwest, helped to douse any sympathy entertained for the Biafran cause among non-Igbo groups in the state.

The mistrust of Biafrans outside Anioma was exemplified in the irregular military action taken against them by the non-Igbo of the Midwest. Samuel Ogbemudia, who replaced David Ejoor as military governor of the state, credits himself with the daring task of forming, on 18 August 1967, a secret resistance drilled in guerrilla tactics from among "loyal Midwesterners who despised and intensely hated the occupation army."[138]The military uncertainty in the state provided him with the opportunity of putting into practice his knowledge of guerrilla warfare in favor of the federal cause.

The guerilla group, which had a total membership of seven hundred and eighty (780), among them one hundred and eighty (180) "pretty girls," as they were described, operated at night. It was the job of the pretty guerilla girls to infiltrate the Biafran forces for information and to assess the strength of their army, weapons, stores, and food. Many of the girls succeeded in gaining employment as cooks and casual workers with the Biafran troops. Such opportunities facilitated their work and enabled them to loot the stores of their unsuspecting enemies, returning to Ogbemudia with grenades, rifles, and ammunition, which were used to fight the Biafrans. From Ogbemudia's testimony, the girls were highly successful in making life uncomfortable for the Liberation Army.[139]

There are conflicting accounts regarding the attitude of the Biafran soldiers towards the peoples of Midwest State during their stay there. Indisputably, the Biafran soldiers were benevolent to the Anioma but cautious and wary towards the non-Igbo until, as some believed, the animosity of the non-Igbo caused the soldiers to treat them with more severity. There were claims that the Biafrans mistreated the Edo and the Itshekiri, and that they exacted brutal vengeance on people from northern Nigeria found in the state during their tenure. However, the extent of the abuse on the Edo and the Itshekiri cannot be determined given the absence of any factual evidence.

In *The Nigerian Civil War* (1972), John de St. Jorre discusses the possibilities that led to the uncomplimentary attitude of Biafran soldiers towards the non-Igbo groups of the Midwest. He explains that upon the arrival of the Liberation Army in the Midwest they made some genuine attempts to win the hearts and minds of the non-Igbo peoples, for given their limited resources they realised it was the only way of consolidating their grip on the state. Consequently, "they behaved well, bought rather than stole, cajoled rather than commanded and treated the local population humanely...."[140] In spite of all these, it was apparent that all Mid-westerners did not accept the Biafrans. The non-Igbo remained fearful and hostile and interpreted the Biafran presence as an occupation instead of, as the Biafrans saw it, as a liberation.

Writing later, Fola Oyewole, a member of the Biafran army in the Midwest, contradicts St. Jorre's views on the Biafrans' treatment of the local groups:[141]

> Troops of the Liberation Army did not behave in a manner likely to improve their relationship with people of the area they occupied....Men of the 18th Battalion based in Warri were notorious, looting anything they could turn into cash. Abandoned commercial houses were indiscriminately broken into and emptied by looters.... Vehicles, bags of salt, and provisions of all sorts were favoured commodities. Some of the things were either sold on the spot at give away prices or sent to Biafra to be sold later.

The contrasting opinions expressed by the two writers on this issue should not be dismissed as untenable or grossly exaggerated. Oyewole's comments seem to be based on his observations of the Biafrans' reaction to the hostility of the local groups, possibly, towards the end of their six-week stay in the state, although some Biafrans could well have manifested such hostility soon after their arrival. Nevertheless, as St. Jorre asserts, and as oral testimonies posit, the animosity mostly characterized the latter part of their stay.

Within two weeks of the Biafrans' arrival, the hatred of the non-Igbo of the Midwest for them and for the Igbo as a whole became obvious to indigenes of Anioma residing in the non-Igbo sections of their state. Some of those interviewed reported that friends informed them of the existence of plots against the Igbo in those places.[142] Awareness of the impending danger motivated another gradual migration of the Anioma people but this time from Benin City, Warri, Sapele, and Ughelli, the major non-Igbo cities of the Midwest. Although for a while Biafrans remained in control and the federal government made no move to deal with their challenge, the people of Anioma who relocated to their towns appeared in the long run to have acted in the wisest way possible. The arrival of federal forces on 20 September 1967 intensified the exodus of the Anioma from the non-Igbo towns. This time, civil servants of Anioma origin adopted the strategy of their non-Igbo colleagues when the Biafran army first entered the state and started commuting to work in Benin City from their rural communities or from towns in the Ika section of Anioma, which are closest to Benin City.

Until federal forces reclaimed the Midwest from the Biafran troops, the people of Anioma continued to show their support for Biafra. Necessary provisions were ferried to Biafra through Asaba seemingly in complete disregard of the economic blockade. In addition, Anioma communities contributed food to Biafran soldiers in the Midwest. The intensity of their support was especially obvious from the attitude of the Asaba, who relaxed their decades-old intolerance of soldiers and accepted Biafran troops in their town. For more than six decades before this period, the people of Asaba had regarded soldiers as barbarians. The women particularly abhorred them because of their libidonous habits, which once led many of their number into scandalous relationships that aroused the anger of the rest of the town. The general poor opinion of soldiers held by Asaba indigenes antedated the Nigerian civil war and has its history in the days of the Royal Niger Company (1886–1899), which first established a constabulary and a prison in the town. The brutality, high-handedness, and lasciviousness of the soldiers of the Royal Niger Company, also observed in the soldiers of the two World Wars temporarily lodged in the town, earned those in the military profession the ire and disgust of the Asaba's civilian population. An indication of their disdain for the military was their use of the word *soldier* as a curse in the town.[143] It became a very serious matter to associate an Asaba woman with that word. To fling the word *soldier* at any woman in the town was equivalent to accusing her of licentiousness or adultery, an indictment that would automatically label her as defiled and in need of ritual purification. The accused sought redress by insisting on being ritually cleansed of the pollution and by being absolved of blame by her accuser. To appease the accused, the accuser would present her with a wrapper, and only then could she be absolved of the guilt of infidelity. If this is not done, the accused risked being divorced by her husband.[144]

The attitude of the Asaba towards soldiers was sanctioned by the elders of the town and upheld by the entire community. Thus, prior to the outbreak of the Nigerian civil war professional soldiers were not highly esteemed in Asaba and, up till that time, it was not an enviable move for a woman to marry someone among their ranks. There was no other town in Anioma besides Asaba where such an antipathy for soldiers was observed. This may have accounted for the presence of so few senior military officers from Asaba before 1970, although Asaba had relatively more soldiers than some other less-developed towns in Anioma.

The climax of the Biafrans' incursion into the Midwest came in the formal declaration of the Midwest as the Independent and Sovereign Republic of Benin by Major (M.D.) Albert Okonkwo, the Biafran-appointed administrator for the state and an indigene of Ibusa in Anioma. The announcement, made on 20 September 1967, preceded the arrival in Benin City of the Second Division of the Nigerian army by merely a few hours. Announcing the Midwest as the Independent and Sovereign Republic of Benin, afterwards known as the Republic of Benin or the ROB, was to suggest that Lt. Col. Odumegwu Ojukwu had no territorial ambitions other than being the liberator of the oppressed people of the country. How true this was remains conjecture. The declaration was no doubt bait to the southern states of the federation to support Biafra and, if possible, to assert their independence from Nigeria. Had this plan succeeded, it would have led to the states of the federation "pulling apart a little" in a confederation as recommended by Odumegwu Ojukwu in January 1967 at the meeting of the Supreme Military Council held at Aburi, Ghana.[145]

Before Biafra's declaration of secession, Yakubu Gowon, the head of state, in a May 1967 broadcast, informed the nation of his determination to use force against any part of the federation that attempts to secede. He explained that the force might result in civil war, in which case "it will just be added to the list of civil wars that happened in other places and at other times."[146] It was in keeping with this statement that a new Division of the Nigerian army, the Second Division, was hastily raised, and on 25 August 1967 its commander was charged with the responsibility of flushing out Biafrans from parts of the West and the Midwest.[147] Clerks and cooks were among the volunteers recruited into the Second Division, which was formed when Biafran forces were enjoying a respite in Benin City in the course of their march to Lagos. The administrative headquarters of the new division was Ibadan until Benin City replaced it in the course of the war.

Two other divisions of the Nigerian army—the First and the Third—existed before the formation of the Second Division. The First Division had already been to work against Biafra since 6 July 1967. Soon after it was supported by the Third Division, which was charged with securing the riverine areas of the Midwest State, as well as the Southeastern and Rivers states that were carved out of Eastern Region earlier that year. The Second Division, therefore, was charged with protecting the West and of salvaging the Midwest for the Nigerian government. The injunction to Lt. Col. Murtala Mohammed, the general officer commanding (GOC) the Second Division, to reclaim the Midwest from Biafran control involved a combination of factors. The first consisted of campaigns in the non-Igbo areas of the state and its purpose was to push Biafrans out of those areas. The second (to be discussed in the next chapter), which was the thrust of the order, led to the militarization of Anioma. To ensure humane conduct during the war, the head of state distributed an operational code to his military commanders to guide their prosecution of the war and their treatment of civilians. The Code of Conduct, as it was called, proffered the following conditions:

- Under No circumstances must pregnant women be ill-treated or killed;
- Children will NOT be molested or killed. They will be protected and cared for;
- Youths and school children must NOT be attacked unless they are engaged in open hostility against Federal government forces. They should be given all protection and care;
- Hospitals, hospital staff and patients should NOT be tampered with or molested;
- Soldiers who surrender will NOT be killed. They are to be disarmed and treated as prisoners-of-war. They are entitled in all circumstances to humane treatment and respect for their person and honour;
- NO property, building, etc., will be destroyed maliciously;
- Churches and mosques must NOT be desecrated;
- No looting of any kind—a good soldier never loots;
- Women will be protected against any attack on their person, honour, and in particular against rape or any form of indecent assault;
- Male civilians who are hostile to the Federal forces are to be dealt with firmly but fairly. They must be humanely treated;
- All military and civilian wounded will be given necessary medical attention and care. They must be respected and protected in all circumstances;
- Foreign nationals on legitimate business will NOT be molested but mercenaries will NOT be spared—they are the worst enemies.[148]

From all indications, Lieutenant Colonel Gowon was determined to treat the national crisis as a family affair. Besides providing a code to guide the prosecution of the war, he publicly acknowledged and explained to the nation that the responsibility for healing the wounds of the war in the future was the duty of all Nigerians.[149] Major Samuel Ogbemudia of the Midwest admitted that Gowon had given him a copy of the code for the military operations in his state and warned him personally that civilians should not be killed.[150] This was before his appointment as the military governor of the Midwest. Gowon's instructions did not prevent Ogbemudia, as he affirmed in his book, from encouraging members of his guerilla team to carry tales to federal troops about the Biafran army that would incite the former against the Biafrans. Provoking the federal army this way would seem convenient under the circumstances, but the strategy had an untold effect on the Anioma because of the failure of the federal army and its commanders to distinguish between the Biafran army and the people of Anioma.

EXTENDING THE WAR FRONTIER TO THE MIDWEST

Federal soldiers with the Second Division began their military operations in the Western and Midwest states early in September 1967, but their progress was very slow. The troops' destruction of two bridges on the Ore–Ijebu Ode road and also on the old Ondo road, both in the Western Region and close to Lagos, halted the Biafran army in their advance to Lagos. In the course of Biafra's retreat, they, in turn, destroyed more bridges in the attempt to stall the pursuit of the federal army. The various ethnic groups again interpreted federal military campaigns in the Midwest differently. The non-Igbo considered it liberation from the unwanted control of the Biafrans; but the people of Anioma regarded it as an invasion by a hostile army.

The exodus of the Anioma from the non-Igbo areas of their state, which commenced in the early days of the Biafran occupation, was intensified with the Biafran retreat. A good number of the Anioma succeeded in leaving their places of abode days before the arrival of the federal troops. What made the period of Nigerian reoccupation of the Midwest traumatic for the Anioma

Map of Midwest State

was the full-blown animosity towards them. James Oluleye, who commanded the Second Division in the Midwest towards the end of the civil war, noted the determination of the non-Igbo to exact vengeance on the Biafrans for violating what he regarded as the neutrality of the Western and Midwest states.[151] In reality the Biafrans created more enemies for themselves and for the people of Anioma by their occupation of the Midwest. The intended retribution against them spilled over and engulfed the Anioma and other Igbo civilians in the Midwest.

The enmity for the Igbo was displayed in a number of ways. Without waiting for the arrival of the federal army in Benin

City, most especially the Edo and the Urhobo/Isoko, rose up in arms against their Anioma neighbors. No law enforcement agent came to the rescue of the hunted people as they had done during a similar rampage in Benin City in November 1966. (Then some non-Igbo were reacting to Lietunant Colonel Ojukwu's order evicting all non-Igbo residents in the Eastern Region after that year's pogrom on the Igbo.) In the subsequent development, the rioters carefully hunted down the indigenes of Anioma, killing a large number of them but reserving some for the federal troops to kill. Unsuspecting workers of Anioma origin found in the outskirts of Benin City were stoned or clubbed to death by local youths of Edo and Urhobo/Isoko origin who organized themselves against those escaping from the terror unleashed on their ethnic group. Some Igbo caught fleeing were thrown into the Ikpoba River. Giwa Amu, the then Midwest solicitor general, remarked on seeing hundreds of unarmed Igbo civilians shot on sight in Benin City, describing it as a fleeting period of lunacy.[152]

The arrival of federal soldiers in the Midwest was celebrated with disorder and anarchy. Operating under the protection of the army, unruly crowds visited hospitals in Benin City, where the majority of the senior medical personnel were of Anioma origin. They also gained entrance into the Benin City prison and other government establishments, including the Nigerian Institute for Oil Palm Research (NIFOR) and killed any Igbo found in these places. Their mission was to decimate indigenes of Anioma. Anioma victims of this rampage had their property, market stalls, shops, workshops, and residences looted by the rabble. In some reported cases, the daughters and wives of the victims suffered various assaults and abuses even after their fathers and husbands were killed.[153]

The people who lost their lives in this storm in their state of origin were among those who expressed their confidence that their personal relationships with their non-Igbo neighbors with whom they worked and among whom they lived were enough credentials for their protection.[154] No amount of reasoning could convince some of the soon-to-be victims to leave the non-Igbo areas and to return to their own communities before that violent outbreak. It would seem that the arrival of the federal troops and the ensuing unrest provided an opportunity for the Urhobo/Isoko to avenge the death of Festus Okotie-Eboh, the federal finance minister killed during the 15 January 1966 coup organized by Chukwuma Nzeogwu. What the Urhobo/Isoko did was not entirely unusual since they acted in the same manner as the Hausa/Fulani did during the 1966 pogrom in which they avenged the deaths of Ahmadu Bello, the sardauna of Sokoto; Tafawa Balewa, the nation's prime minister; and Brigadier Maimalari among others. The Urhobo/Isoko were not punished for taking the law into their own hands, the same privilege the Hausa/Fulani enjoyed after exacting vengeance on the Igbo.

The killings in Benin City and other parts of the Midwest did not escape the attention of senior federal military officers. Major Ochefu of the Third Division, who led the 63rd and 32nd battalions assigned to clear the riverine areas of the Midwest, reported to his superiors that his team had little to do in those places because the local people, the Urhobo/Isoko, did the fighting using their local weapons.[155] Lieutenant Colonel Olusegun Obasanjo, the army engineer attached to the Second Division, affirmed in writing that federal soldiers spent some time in Benin City but claimed that they were flushing out rebels hiding in some houses.[156] The truth, based on interviews in Benin City and in Anioma and on eyewitness accounts, appears to be that those driven out from Benin City and other non-Igbo towns were mostly civilians of Anioma origin and other Igbo. Some of these people escaped death by trekking the long distance from Benin City to their hometowns, picking their way through thick forests. All the while federal soldiers ran into the woods in pursuit of the anxiously escaping individuals, mistaking them for Biafrans (the Igbo from east of the Niger).[157]

The following eyewitness account of the retreat of Biafran troops and the arrival of the federal army in Warri testifies to the treatment meted out to the people of Anioma by people of non-Igbo extraction in the Midwest.[158]

> Benin fell [to the Nigerians] on Saturday.... People ran into the streets shouting and cheering and began rounding up the 600 or so Ibo left in Warri. Ibo stores were looted and the police just stood idly by, though the police chief did try and intervene.... On Friday the killing of the Ibo began. It was done principally by the civilians especially the Urhobo... though occasionally some of the Yoruba and Midwestern soldiers—but not the Hausas—joined in. The massacres were completely indiscriminate. Men, women, and children were hacked to death and I reckon between 250 and 450 Ibo died in Warri.

The atrocities against the people of Anioma were indications of deep-seated animosity. The Edo, Urhobo/Isoko, as well as the Itshekiri did not avenge themselves on Biafran troops for occupying their state or for violating their neutrality; instead they manifested their hatred for their Anioma neighbors. What could possibly be responsible for this anti-Igbo feeling? Interviews and discussions with the Edo revealed that other ethnic groups in the Midwest felt intimidated by the Anioma people and the Igbo generally.[159] They saw Anioma men as rivals for being better educated and for occupying most of the important positions in the Midwest government. At this time the literacy level in the country was highest among the Igbo and the Yoruba. The Anioma were felt to be greedy for advancement and unabashed in doing menial tasks as long as these provided the gateway to their advancement.[160] This opinion of the Anioma held by the non-Igbo was exacerbated by the assassination of the Finance Minister Okotie-Eboh, who was an Urhobo. The yearning to be on par with the Igbo and to avenge the death of the minister found an outlet with the arrival of the federal army in the Midwest and was expressed in the destruction of the Anioma. Thus, the soldiers who came to drive out Biafrans and reclaim the

Midwest for the Nigerian government were left with little to do. The clash in the Midwest, which was to be between the Nigerian and Biafran armies, evolved into a contest between the Nigerian army and Anioma civilians.

The political and military situation in the Midwest between the months of September and October 1967 led to the migration of individuals and families from Anioma to Biafra. The massacres in the Midwest helped convince many in Anioma who were disconcerted and terrified by them that they would fare better in Biafra than in their own state. The anxiety and feelings of insecurity compelled many to relocate to Biafra. Some of the Anioma men who escaped into Biafra from that time onwards helped swell the fighting force of the seceding republic, while the women also assisted in the war effort in various ways.

Chapter 3

ANIOMA AS A THEATER OF WAR

RECLAIMING ANIOMA

The goal of the federal military operations in the Midwest was to wrest Anioma from Biafran control. The campaign to free Anioma was preceded by the broadcast of Lt. Col. Murtala Mohammed, the commander of the Second Division, the contents of which heightened the apprehension of people in Anioma regarding the federal army. Murtala Mohammed announced in Benin City that the liberation of the Midwest, with the exception of towns between Agbor and Asaba, had been achieved. He tersely warned that whoever stands in his way to liberating Anioma would be crushed. The broadcast was concluded with an appeal to the people of the Midwest to help trace the Biafran soldiers in their midst.[161] This addendum seems responsible for the witch-hunt of Anioma people in their very localities.

The first phase of the military campaigns in Anioma went on simultaneously in the Ika and Ukwuani areas from 28 September 1967 but under different battalions and divisions of the federal army. The Third Division liberated the Ukwuani area and at the completion of the exercise handed over Ukwuani to the Second Division, which controlled all of Anioma from 1 October 1967 until the end of the war. Military operations in the Ika and Aniocha areas, completely executed by the Second Division, were more intense than those of the Third Division that operated in Ukwuani.

From the Ika area the federal soldiers arrived in Aniocha. Their military operations in Anioma were carried out between 1 and 10 October 1967. The exception was Illah, which was reclaimed on 11 November 1967. Eyewitnesses of the operations in the Ika and Aniocha areas agree that different brigades visited the towns one after the other. Diverse approaches were adopted in establishing a federal military presence in Anioma towns. The most common was by long-range gunfire, popularly called shelling. Only a few towns—among them Akwukwu-Igbo, Okpanam, Ewulu, Isheagu, and Illah—were fortunate enough to escape any form of long-range bombardment. Federal troops captured Akwukwu-Igbo, Ewulu, and Illah somewhat peacefully, sometimes in the dead of the night as in Akwukwu-Igbo.[162] In other less fortunate towns, shelling often resulted in death, some by stray bullets, massive destruction of infrastructure – people's homes, property, and public structures, displacement, and suspension of public services.

Very few people thought of digging trenches for themselves and their families before the federal soldiers arrived. The Agbor families that considered constructing a trench worthwhile were motivated by the sight of Biafran soldiers retreating from the Midwest prior to the arrival of the federal troops.[163] The meticulousness of such people informs the extent to which they appraised the situation they were likely to find themselves in after the Biafran troops' withdrawal. In spite of the profound support for Biafra many people objectively guessed that the Biafran position at the time of their retreat was precarious, and that the Liberation Army's ability to maintain its hold on any part of the Midwest, at least, was only a probability.

Certain features of the war were observed in all sections of Anioma. The strange and menacing sound from the bombardments frightened many women, confirming their apprehensions about the advancing troops.[164] Women who witnessed the arrival of the federal troops in their towns reported that the shelling and shooting were in sharp contrast to the manner in which Biafran forces moved into the Midwest.[165] The arrival of the federal soldiers instilled not only fear but uncertainty and confusion in the people, causing many to desert their homes and sometimes their community. Every conceivable secluded and inaccessible area served as a place of refuge. Many indigenes of Aniocha and Ukwuani residing in Boji-boji, as well as primary school pupils let out of school because of the shelling, sought temporary shelter in the palace of the Obi of Agbor.

There were different reactions from the local people and also from the retreating Biafran soldiers to the federal troops' advance into Anioma in late September to October 1967. Women for the most part sought refuge elsewhere. In most towns in Ika and Aniocha where shelling commonly preceded the advancing federal army, women were confused by the noise from shelling, mistaking it for a distant Dane gun used in announcing the commencement of a second burial ceremony in all parts of Anioma. The noise from shelling always provoked a stampede of both people and animals, particularly once it became clear to the former that it preceded the federal army.[166] A bomb fell inside a church building in Ubulu-ukwu disrupting the service. In the stampede that followed a young mother of Yoruba origin, married to an Ubulu-ukwu indigene, dropped her newborn baby in the bid to save her life. Mother and child eventually survived the war. In Ewulu, Ufuegbunam Olise jumped into Ewulu Lake, hoping to swim to safety. She had difficulty in swimming with her baby on her back. Her child fell in the lake and drowned.[167]

Women more than men abandoned their homes at the sound of shelling. They either made temporary homes in the bush and farm areas or took refuge in communities yet to be visited by troops, thereby constituting a group of internal refugees. While many women were displaced by the war, there were those—men and women—who remained in their homes and still survived the shelling and stray bullets. Within this latter group, some were not so fortunate. For example, in a family of eight, a father and the six children were set ablaze in their car by federal soldiers, leaving the mother as the only survivor.[168] Many women who sur-

Federal troops shelling seen from Asaba

vived the military operations did so by methods of evacuation, although they encountered new dangers away from home. Such a situation was not peculiar to women in Anioma and was also observed with displaced women in many parts of the globe. Displacement, the uprooting of home and hearth, as Nicole Dombrowski calls it,[169] has become one of the ways in which women, children, and the elderly survive military invasions. It was usual for women fleeing their homes to forget a few essentials like food items and cooking utensils. Some even left their children behind. The suddenness of their flight and the sense of danger clouded their thoughts. These women suffered severely when their stay away from their homes was prolonged.

Anioma women constantly moved from one part of Anioma to another during the federal campaign to reclaim the area. The fortunes of the war, military operations by federal troops, and the women's assessment of places of relative safety determined the incessant movement. Most women were so upset during the early stages of the federal occupation that at the sound of a gunshot they would troop into the bush and other hiding places. This also occurred in Onicha-olona in Aniocha, which was not visited or occupied by federal troops. In some cases women returned from their hide outs only when assured by subsequently displaced women that there was relative calm in their towns[170] or when community leaders announced that a troop commander had promised not to molest the people.[171] In the confusion surrounding federal penetration, a sixteen-year-old youth was at pains appreciating the fears of those around him and the consequences of the federal troops' incursion into his community that October. He described the incident as "strange, exciting, and adventurous" and was amused to see old women and men frantically running about and falling in the process.[172]

The Biafran army retreating from Anioma did not permit the federal army easy access to the area. Their destruction of the Abudu Bridge linking the non-Igbo areas of the Midwest with Anioma prevented a smooth advance into Boji-boji, the gateway to the Ika area, by the 6th and 7th brigades of the Second Division.[173] Biafran troops also destroyed the Oboshi Bridge connecting Ogwashi-ukwu with Ibusa and other towns in Aniocha. At Umunede, another important commercial town in the Ika area, the federal army encountered yet more resistance from Biafran soldiers. In this case, both the retreating Biafran troops and the advancing federal troops came upon a deserted town.[174] Umunede later became an important corridor, as the Second Division's headquarters in Anioma, and remained so till the end of the war. From that location, other units of the federal army received reinforcements and supplies until the capture of Onitsha, the closest Biafran town to the Midwest.

Attempts by the Biafran soldiers to obstruct the federal advance into Anioma towns had devastating effects on the local people. In Agbor, Ogwashi-ukwu, Ibusa, Asaba, and Aboh, the Biafran efforts, though gallant, ultimately failed to achieve its goals. The federal commanders with better-equipped and numerically superior troops regarded the Biafran military interference with displeasure and reacted by viciously clamping down on the local people. Efforts by some local rulers to appease the federal commanders who arrived in their towns and to prevent undue massacre of their subjects became tainted by Biafran military offensives.

Most local leaders organized receptions for the "visiting" federal troops in the hope that it would convince battalion commanders of their loyalty and protect their people from the rage of the soldiers. They taught their subjects to welcome the troops with shouts of "One Nigeria," indicated by pointing with one thumb. It is uncertain whether the brutality meted out to the Anioma in the non-Igbo sections of the Midwest in the previous weeks informed the decision to organize receptions for the federal troops. These efforts met with various degrees of success. In Utagba-uno in Ukwuani the battalion commander promised that the local people would not be molested but in spite of his assurances some of the men, including a well-known ritual specialist, were arrested and accused of aiding Biafra's resistance by providing Biafran soldiers with food. To clear themselves, the leaders of the community sent provisions to the federal troops, explaining that they were naturally hospitable and not given to discrimination. Their action secured the release of the captives.

The federal commanders did not show similar leniency in Boji-boji, Ogwashi-ukwu, and Okpanam. Federal soldiers demanded a welcome from the people of Okpanam but not before killing three of the four boys who, out of curiosity, went to see the soldiers on their arrival. The boys were caught, tied up in stakes, and shot. One survived the execution and was released from the stake the following day by the second batch of soldiers that visited the town. The welcome was deemed appropriate when the men of the town assembled with their dance groups, gifts of food items, livestock, and wine, for the soldiers. The items were originally meant for the Biafran army but became handy for the arrival of federal troops. The gesture did not prevent the soldiers from seizing as much livestock as they could, abducting women indiscriminately, and using sacred buildings in the town as their *rendezvous*. The use of sacred structures was offensive to the leaders of the town, who craftily made their concerns known to the soldiers and later introduced them to professional commercial sex workers to entertain them and possibly end the abduction of their women. The opinion was expressed by one of the local leaders that their response to the abduction of women kept the soldiers from wrecking untold havoc in the town.[175] Federal soldiers' penchant for killing and seizing people's livestock was reminiscent of the soldiers of the Royal Niger Company stationed in Asaba before 1899 who, as Asaba oral tradition recall, "constituted a great menace to Asaba people, catching goats, fowls and cows at will for their food and pleasure."[176] It was locally interpreted to be the soldiers' way of complying with the strategy of total war advocated by Lieutunant Colonel Gowon.

In the case of Ogwashi-ukwu, despite being received with the usual chant of "One Nigeria" and a parade of local leaders, the federal army was far from impressed. The harmony anticipated by the Obi of Ogwashi-ukwu[177] from the commander was stillborn because of the Biafran troops' attack on the federal army shortly after their arrival. Indiscriminate killing of men and a house-to-house hunt for Biafrans and their collaborators ensued and continued intermittently under the name of bush combing until the end of the war. Bush combing affected schooling when eventually it became routine in 1968, causing students to alternate their residences between their homes and the bush. Since the Anioma like other sections of the Midwest was in territory under the Nigerian government, they were legally not Biafrans. But, it did not escape the federal soldiers that they shared strong bonds with Biafrans. Thus, the recurring demand to single out the Biafrans among them was not an insensible one and usually implied Biafran soldiers and active Anioma supporters of Biafra, for federal soldiers regarded Biafran sympathizers as Biafrans.

More elaborate steps were taken by the local rulers of Agbor and Owa[178] who controlled the Boji-boji area to ensure the safety of their subjects prior to the arrival of the federal soldiers. The obi of Agbor instructed ward chiefs to hide the people of Anioma who were not indigenes of Agbor and to do all they could to prevent loss of lives. Certain chiefs were assigned to claim their subjects in cases of questionable identity, while the people were told to chant "One Nigeria" as soon as they caught sight of the federal troops.[179] The various wards in Agbor were organized to welcome the federal soldiers with gifts. The soldiers gave little room to either the obi of Agbor or to his subjects to display their preplanned hospitality largely because of the clash with Biafran soldiers on the outskirts of the town. The following narrative from an eyewitness of the federal arrival in the Boji-boji area reveals the cruelty of the federal troops on the local people.

> On September 30 [1967], we started hearing the sound of shelling. Between 6 and 7 p.m. the Nigerian soldiers had arrived. By the next day the town resembled a ghost town, except for very few of us. Three men, including myself, were arrested.... I was told to say my last prayer... Afterwards, a soldier said move! As I took a step, my mother ran out and started shouting '*na my pickin!*'. The soldier turned round, seeing her facial marks, he said, "Yes, you are from Benin!".... That was what saved me.... For the next two days they shouted for people to come out of hiding but without any success. After four days another contingent arrived, led by Captain Idahosa, a Bini [Edo].... From that time on they started killing people's domestic animals and raping women. No young girl could come out of hiding.... The soldiers committed a lot of atrocities...[180]

Rape was not a crime perpetrated only against adult women. Little girls were as much the victims of this weapon of war as their older sisters and mothers. To illustrate with a few examples from the Boji-boji area alone, a girl not yet fourteen years of age was raped by four soldiers one after another. Sympathetic villagers, too petrified by the soldiers to rescue her from the ordeal, later took her to a hospital for treatment. In instances where the soldiers seemed too busy to engage in this abusive behavior themselves, they made use of scapegoats. On one occasion young boys of primary school age, on their way from school, were ordered to rape their classmate, the same age-bracket as the boys, while the soldiers amused themselves with the sight.[181]

The sexual abuse of women is a regular feature of wars, and it is understood to have personal dimension and often public and political aspects. In Anioma it was one of the dreadful humiliations of the civil war that reduced women to objects of war and humiliated their men. Soldiers act out their contempt for male civilians by sexually abusing their women, showing the helplessness of civilians to protect their women during crisis. Atina Grossman affirmed that women are the booty of every war, the unrecognized and uncompensated targets of war crimes.[182] Rape displays the perpetrator's contempt for his victim. It casts doubt on women's integrity and makes them strangers to themselves. The 1949 Geneva Conventions regarding the protection of civilians in war explicitly prohibit rape, enforced prostitution, and any form of indecent assault.[183]The widespread recourse to rape by soldiers during armed hostility has been cited as proof that sexual violence is endemic to military culture and the recurrent sexual abuse of women by soldiers all over the globe is evidence that those trained to fight wars are not best suited to protect the human rights of women and female children.[184]

The assaults on Anioma women made them very insecure during most of the war. It effectively inhibited the freedom to move about and to express sympathy for the Biafran cause. To avoid mistreatment, young women disguised themselves as old women before leaving their homes. Some preferred to leave home accompanied by a newborn baby or a toddler to give the impression that they were married or were nursing mothers.[185] Yet that did not always guarantee immunity from assault for all women, because some soldiers had few scruples about seeking intimacy with married women. Such efforts by women in Anioma parallel those of German women who masqueraded as men or as ugly women disguised by layers of clothing and faces smeared with dirt and ash, all to escape being abused by Russian soldiers after the defeat of Germany in World War II.[186] Universally the majority of women resort to various antics in order to escape sexual abuse, yet it has remained an intractable problem during crisis situations.

The soldiers who entered Agbor did not only molest women; they also harassed men. When the local people refused to come out of hiding, they promised not to harm them but requested to be formally welcomed. Some fifty local men who assembled for that purpose were dressed down with insults by the soldiers and nearly lost their lives.[187] The rulers of Agbor and Owa did not give up their attempts at pacifying the battalion commanders. They invited them to their palaces and sent them gifts. The Obi of Agbor repeated a claim earlier made during the 1966 disturbances that the people of Agbor were not Igbo but the descendants of migrants from Benin.[188] In spite of this assertion, which aimed at securing better treatment for his subjects, people were killed indiscriminately in the area soon after they came out of their hideouts in response to the soldiers' coaxing. Those who suffered most either remained in the area during the early stage of the hostilities or returned after leaving their hiding places before January 1968.

A reign of terror marked the arrival of the federal soldiers in Ika and Aniocha. The situation in the occupied towns was described as chaotic, while the presence of federal soldiers symbolized for the people pain, disillusionment, uncertainty, and mutual distrust of individuals. There was unrestrained destruction and massive looting of the local's property, mostly to homes vacated by those who had taken refuge in the bush, in neighboring towns, and in Biafra. No town was spared this feature of the war. Ibusa had the highest number of military officers in Anioma who moved to Biafra with the Biafran Liberation Army in September

Okwechime's House in shambles

1967.[189] The federal army destroyed the houses of these officers including the home of the mother of Major Albert Okonkwo, the administrator of the ill-fated Republic of Benin. Journalists with the Second Division took pictures of the demolished buildings and published them soon after the military operation in Ibusa. Captions of their report read as follows.

> After the shelling by federal troops, above picture shows what remained of the house of Col. Mike Okwechime, at Ibusa, near Asaba. He was one of the [Igbo] officers who betrayed the Midwest State on August 9 to the rebel regime of Emeka Odumegwu Ojukwu.[190]

In many towns people were caught and held by the soldiers for being "Biafran," that is, a Biafran supporter, collaborator, or loyalist. Later in the conflict, some members of the community masterminded intrigues culminating in a "witch-hunt" to persecute or harass their real and imagined enemies and rivals. Incidents of subversion, even involving women, occurred in all sections of Anioma but especially in Aniocha, causing those with undisguised sympathy for Biafra to move to places where they were not so well known or to towns with minimal federal pres-

SUNDAY TIMES, October 15, 1967 Page 7

HERE USED TO BE OKONKWO'S VILLA AT IBUSA

• YES, indeed, a villa that is no more. The costly price of treachery. On this spot was once the fashionable villa of Col. Albert Okonkwo. Ojukwu's Man Friday as administrator of the still born "Republic of Benin". It once stood at Ibusa eight miles from Asaba, the home town of Okonkwo.

Here Used To Be Okonkwo's Villa At Ibusa

YES, indeed, a villa that is no more. The costly price of treachery. On this spot was once the fashionable villa of Col. Albert Okonkwo. Ojukwu's Man Friday as administrator of the still born "Republic of Benin." It once stood at Ibusa eight miles from Asaba, the home town of Okonkwo.

ence in order to avoid victimization.[191] All incidents of looting, widely indulged in during the war, will not be blamed on the federal soldiers alone. From the incidents in Asaba, which will be seen shortly, indigenes of the occupied towns participated in the looting but not soon after the arrival of the federal troops in their towns.

Not all the towns in the Ika and Aniocha areas experienced the war in the same way or in the same magnitude. The least affected towns included Otolokpo, Ute-okpu, Ute-ogbeje,

Abavo, Ozanogogo (Ozarra), Onicha-olona, and Issele-ukwu. Ozanogogo was spared much of the distress that accompanied federal occupation by a well thought out ploy. The federal contingent that first arrived in Ozanogogo was met by the senior citizens of the town. They converged at the town's civic center to welcome them. The leaders of the community presented the federal soldiers with food items, livestock, and palm wine, while the old women entertained the troops with dances, expressing much excitement that the soldiers had come to liberate them. The federal troops appeared reasonably impressed with the treatment they received. There is no recollection of anyone being shot in the town, and there were no soldiers stationed there to supervise the people after that initial visit. One probable reason for the latter could be Ozanogogo's location, away from the township areas. Then, perhaps too, the soldiers acted out of deference for the old women of the town. Whatever the case, most features of the emergency were not felt in Ozanogogo, but schooling was suspended as in other towns, and the teachers, including members of the American Peace Corps, who left the town before the arrival of the federal army did not return to it until the end of the war. The pupils also willingly kept away from school. Even though federal soldiers intermittently visited Ozanogogo from other stations during the crisis, it still served as a haven for refugees from the worst hit towns.[192] The soldiers' leniency on the people of Ozanogogo did not imply that they completely relaxed their guard with them. They were very conscious of the inbred hatred of the local people, no matter how disguised; hence, there were instances of federal soldiers asking members of the community for water or wine but insisting that the people taste it first.

Anioma communities and border towns accessible from the major gateway connecting Asaba with Benin suffered more than others from the federal soldiers' efforts to reclaim Anioma. Persons who accidentally ran into the soldiers lost their lives. Some were pensioners and civil servants, women and men, from different parts of Aniocha summoned to Asaba to collect their unpaid salaries on 2 October 1967. Many were unaware that the federal soldiers had overrun the entire area. Quite a number of those who complied with the injunction died on their way back to their towns, and their bodies were strewn along the roads. This incident illustrates the lack of coordination between the political and military arms in the Midwest State at the early stages of the war. The federal army subverted a state government directive causing the death of civilians. An unperturbed federal soldier did not attach any importance to civilians dying from stray bullets, as he called it, but advised the survivors to ignore the unburied corpses and inform those still hiding to return to their homes, promising that they would not be handled roughly.[193] Although the sight of the unburied bodies contradicted his pledge of safety for those in hiding, some believed him.

The process of reclaiming Anioma from Biafran control was neither easy for the local people nor for the federal soldiers. The latter were in an unfamiliar terrain and among people who prior to the militarization of Anioma did not show by their action that they were completely loyal to the Nigerian government's commitment to One Nigeria. Violence was the federal army's way of ensuring effective control of Anioma. Varying numbers of people died in many towns as the federal troops were settling down in Anioma, and as their stay lengthened, the soldier-civilian relationship further deteriorated. People were incarcerated for such trivialities as holding a box of matches or a portable radio set. In Ossissa in Ukwuani, a soldier mistook an optical case for a walkie-talkie and beated the owner severely.[194] In the same town men stayed longer in hiding to avoid conscription into the federal army, while women were sometimes denied permission to leave the locality to trade.[195] The soldiers confiscated the bicycles of some women and the cars of some men in Utagba-ogbe in Ukwuani. Roadblocks were mounted in Anioma villages, where residents were interrogated and sometimes ill treated by the soldiers. Federal units prevented the communities they supervised from freely mixing with their neighbors and possibly interacting with Biafran soldiers in the process. *Afia eze*, the major market in Utagba-ogbe, located by the bank of the Ase creek and served various towns within that radius, was closed down in order to enhance the soldiers' ability to check traffic in and out of the town through that location and to dissuade Biafrans from coming in to trade in the area.[196]

From time to time federal soldiers issued a series of orders to the people that were meticulously obeyed. Recalcitrant indigenes were beaten or disciplined in other ways for neglecting any of the commands. One of the injunctions was the observation of a period of curfew, from six o'clock in the evening until six o'clock the next morning, during which hours any form of illumination in the people's homes was outlawed; late cooking and listening to radio transmissions (regarded as noise[197]) were prohibited. In parts of Ukwuani, women were informed of the commencement of the curfew with repeated shouts of "quench." In Ossissa, some were disciplined for ignoring the warning.[198] In Okpanam, three huntsmen who broke the curfew and went hunting were shot.[199] Community elders were unanimous in their assertion that the soldiers made many people victims of circumstance.

Families with military officers became targets of the soldiers' aggression. The federal officers demanded that those military officers be produced. In nearly all cases, the wanted officers had joined the Biafran army, and their relatives left behind in Anioma were either forced to remain longer in hiding to avoid molestation or to change their names to avoid detection. The wife of Colonel Nwajei, who was at Ibusa while her husband was in Biafra, faced constant interrogations from the federal army commander and also endured the suspicion of her neighbors in Ibusa. They blamed her for the federal attack on their town. Her problem was compounded by her ethnicity, being originally from Nembe in Rivers State.[200]

Federal soldiers constantly nursed the fear of betrayal to Biafran troops by the local people, a situation that might lead to the infiltration of a contingent of the Biafran army at any of their unguarded moments. That, ignorance, and sometimes sheer mischief occasionally exacerbated their suspicion, harassment, and intimidation of civilians. Of all classes of the community, old women were the only ones relatively free to move about—constrained only by the menace of stray bullets—during the early period of the war. Female adolescents and adult women were partly restrained by threats of physical molestation. On the whole, women lived in fear as would any people under a siege. Generally, the Anioma barely tolerated the soldiers, who, though despised, had admirers among little children. These were fascinated by their guns and in Ossissa sometimes visited them. Considerate soldiers found time to entertain the children by dismantling and reassembling their weapons for their amusement and sometimes invited them to eat with them. Their benevolence towards these infants turned to unconcealed anger and aggression when bigger boys came around.[201]

Intimidation and harassment of civilians by the federal army during their settling-in period in Anioma was not experienced in every town. Issele-ukwu provides an interesting case study. The absence of excessive violence in relations between the soldiers and the people of Issele-ukwu was attributed to the far-sightedness of a local Baptist minister – the Reverend Samuel Martins.[202] Rufus Osemena, the Obi of Issele-ukwu, left for Biafra before the federal soldiers arrived, leaving the leadership of his town in the care of the *iyase*, the local spokesman. Many people vacated their homes, but Reverend Martins' strong appeal for them to return was heeded by a considerable number of individuals, particularly women and children.

Reverend Martins first established contact with the commander of the Second Division at Umunede before the arrival of the soldiers in Issele-ukwu. Afterwards, he organized the Issele clan—comprising Issele-ukwu, Issele-mkpitime, and Issele-azagba—to contribute food items that were sent to Umunede for the soldiers. As the federal army advanced towards Issele-ukwu, preceded by their mortar and artillery shots, Martins, in the company of the elders he mustered and a group of anxious women and their children coming at a safe distance behind them, met the soldiers at the outskirts of the town. It was reported that the rapport he established with the army days earlier was all the commendation he needed for the soldiers' patient attention to his address. Reverend Martins' efforts were handsomely rewarded. Issele-ukwu was not exposed to bush combing by the federal soldiers searching for "Biafrans," their associates, and accomplices. This was in spite of the people's commiseration with the seceding republic, ebulliently shown in the sacrifices of their able-bodied men in the Biafran army.

Reverend Martins acted as a buffer between his community and the soldiers. Victims of unjust intimidation reported their mistreatment to him, which he in turn brought to the attention of the unit commander. His intervention in soldier-civilian matters made federal soldiers quartered in Issele-ukwu very cautious in their treatment of women than soldiers in other places.[203] This does not suggest that the soldiers in Issele-ukwu did not misbehave in other ways. Besides looting, women were randomly ill-treated, but none openly reported a sexual assault. Within days of the federal troops' arrival the women were able to return to their own affairs, all the while taking care not to provoke the soldiers. The experience commonly shared by women in Issele-ukwu regarding the war was the prevalence of hunger and the unavailability of necessary provisions.

In spite of the efforts of Reverend Martins, many in Issele-ukwu attributed the tolerant disposition of the federal soldiers to the efficacy of a special charm made by their omu. They also believed that the same charm prevented the concentration of a large number of soldiers in the town. In Onicha-ugbo, the people claimed that the Mkpitime goddess, the guardian of the town, came out from the river and waved the soldiers away. People held to these views during the crisis because of the psychological torment of the war; but it has been common practice among Igbo traditionalists to interpret issues from a religious perspective. Their imaginations were stirred by grandiose stories handed down the generational line of the ability of the omu to fight wars using mystical powers. While the veracity of their belief is open to question, it is clear that the people needed to anchor their hope and confidence on an extraterrestrial being. It suited their psyche better to believe that a god protected them from harm than to give credit to a mortal for his diplomacy, as was the case in Issele-ukwu. The possibility of a person dying could not be denied, but if it happened, their hope in that savior would be dashed.

The interaction between the Nigerian troops and the local people during the war was not always tinged with hostility and intimidation. In Illah, soldiers and civilians related with mutual suspicion until the soldiers relaxed their attitude and made friends in the community. Whenever there was a lull in the fighting, the soldiers allowed a détente. There was rapport particularly between the soldiers and women who could speak Hausa and languages spoken in the Middle Belt and those whose daughters they dated. Thus, from being aggressors some became protectors of such families. This development was not restricted to Illah. Other occupied towns enjoyed varying periods of respite. Such occasions encouraged the people of Utagba-ogbe to build a house for the units stationed in their town, using communal labor and local materials. This became an addition to the civilian houses the soldiers forcefully occupied. The leaders of the town hoped by doing so to impress the soldiers and ensure continued cordiality in their interactions.[204] What they did not initially know was the military logistics by which different battalions visited the town during the war. Nevertheless, the community communicated to the combatants their preference for peaceful coexistence instead of military hostility.

One town that suffered terribly from federal soldiers during the September-October military operations in Anioma was Asaba. Federal soldiers on their way from Okpanam, a walking distance to Asaba, encountered the toughest resistance from the 12th battalion of the Biafran Liberation Army under the command of Col. J. O. G. Achuzia. This was the same battalion that had attempted the invasion of Lagos two months earlier.[205] The majority of those who fought in the 12th battalion, including their commander, were of Anioma origin. Intense fighting between the opposing forces raged for two days until the combined strength of two federal battalions — the 6th and the 7th, dislodged their few, poorly equipped, and determined opponents.[206] The coming of the federal army to Asaba did not elicit such a stampede among women as in other towns. Most of the women were confident that the Biafran army, which up till this time maintained a provisional headquarters in the town, was capable of repulsing the federal troops. They were also of the opinion that the federal soldiers would not vent their aggression out on civilians and were seen joking about the situation, making such off-hand comments that they would not vacate their homes for anyone.[207] Confident of their safety, Asaba women did not seek shelter elsewhere. Many were indifferent and complacent to any danger until the federal soldiers dislodged the Biafran troops and gained control of the town.

The stance of the men differed from that of the women. The Asagba of Asaba, his chiefs, and elders had met before the arrival of the soldiers to discuss the impending federal "visit" and agreed to accord the troops a welcome as was done in other places. Adequate preparations were made for the reception, and the men were levied to that effect. The people were informed of the various parts they would play and were also advised to chant and show the sign for "One Nigeria" when the soldiers arrived to convey their friendliness to the troops.

With the federal success over the Biafran troops in Asaba, the victorious army shelled the town with ferocious intensity. The complacent women as well as the men took to their heels. Obi Odiachi, the Asagba, quickly left Asaba for Biafra. Frantic mothers rounded up their children and along with nursing mothers and pregnant women made for the Niger Bridge to Biafra. There was quite a crowd that sought escape through the bridge, causing the impatient ones who could afford the cost to ferry themselves and their families across. Some women left one or two of their children behind. Patricia, a girl of fifteen, sent on an errand by her mother a short distance from their home, returned to discover to her dismay that her mother had left for Biafra. Patricia was found by one of the federal soldiers and became his companion until the end of the war. Many children lost track of their parents and relations in the uproar, while displaced persons from other towns who had taken shelter in Asaba were forced to seek refuge elsewhere. Asaba women who tenaciously held on to the notion that soldiers would not touch civilians without provocation remained in the town. They, however, hid their male children in places considered inaccessible to an outsider but not without the precaution of disguising them in girls' garb to preclude their conscription or death in case of unforeseen developments.[208]

There was a total suspension of essential services in Asaba following the commotion. Asaba indigenes were not given the opportunity to hold the welcome reception they had planned for the federal troops because of the confrontation with the Biafran army, but a few days later the battalion commander requested a reception from the leaders of the town. Asaba indigenes who took shelter in other towns and those hiding in the bush heard the announcement for the program and assumed that normalcy had returned to their town. On the day of the reception, men and women, all beautifully dressed in their handmade white cloths, converged at the Eke market square, the venue for the occasion. The variant quarters in the town were represented, with the sectional heads leading each group. Some refugees from other towns joined their hosts for the ceremony. In the course of the dancing, soldiers separated the women and children from the men. Soldiers holding whips kept watch over the women. Without any warning to the unarmed dancing groups, gunshots rang out. Strategically stationed but well-concealed machine guns were uncovered and used to decimate the male dancers. Women and children became unwilling spectators at the death of their husbands, fathers, sons, and other male relatives. The soldiers guarding them prevented them from running about in frenzy. A few, unable to contain themselves, ran out from where they were and were killed. One of the old women caught hold of a soldier who had killed her husband and insisted on being killed and, of course, was killed. A much younger woman, Comfort Obianeze, reported her shock when she saw her husband and only child lying helplessly, both dead. The welcome ceremony had swiftly turned into a nightmare.

The men who attempted to run away were unsuccessful. Bullets from the rapid-fire guns of the federal soldiers caught up with them. The sounds of the shots were drowned amidst the agonizing cries of the wounded and dying and the terrified wailing and whimpering of the women. Corpses littered the scene everywhere. The women observed that most of the time soldiers not directly involved in the shooting were smiling, as if deriving joy and satisfaction from the carnage.

Very few of the men who attended that event escaped death in the rampage. Azuka Iwebi was one of them. The bodies of dead men, which fell over and concealed him, saved him from death. At night, assuming that the soldiers had retired, he crawled from under the heap of corpses and carefully made his way home, where his wife hid him under a bed for two weeks.[209] A few other dancers escaped death through the intervention of a woman from the Hausa community in Asaba. Peter Okobi, who was among those taken to a road intersection, away from the main reception area, recalled that the lady collected money from them and handed it as ransom to one of the soldiers in charge of his group. The soldier accepted the bribe and dismissed the dancers before his colleagues could rejoin him. Onianwa Omezi, an elder in the town, said that he left Asaba shortly before the incident after being informed by a federal soldier of Anioma origin of the plot to kill those who would attend the ceremony.[210] The event was not completely shrouded in secrecy. It was nevertheless a well-planned retributory scheme by the federal army on Asaba.

The massacre of male civilians in Asaba continued the following day while the bodies of those already killed awaited burial. For a few days afterwards, any male seen on the streets was shot. Some managed to sneak out of the town secretly with the assistance of some federal soldiers. Such soldiers were few, and their efforts saved only a few individuals. The soldiers later resorted to visiting the people in their homes. Many who escaped the public execution of 5 October 1967 eventually met their death at home. Among them was Apuogo, an eighty-year-old blind woman who was set ablaze inside her house.[211] She was asked to leave her home for a camp but being blind was unable to do so without assistance. The soldiers disbelieved her blindness and set her home ablaze with her inside. Okwuebiejo, another blind old man, shared the same fate. Other victims were Ogoegbunam, a girl of six who was shot along with her equally young nephew as they were having lunch in her father's house; and Emmanuel Akwule, a medical doctor killed inside the General Hospital at Asaba in complete disregard of the head of state's military code that hospital staff should not be molested.

In the house-to-house hunt federal soldiers killed people indiscriminately. Some were accused of supporting or hiding Biafrans. The soldiers announced their intention to kill a victim with the remark: "Go and give Ojukwu a letter." This was identified as one of their facetious expressions in that early period of their stay in Asaba. Many individuals ordered to go and give Ojukwu a letter attempted carrying out their mission unfortunately to their graves. Various excuses and means were given as reason, and employed, for killing men in Asaba. Some were ordered to dig their own graves after which they were shot in such a manner that their bodies fell into the holes. In Asaba the impression remains that all families sustained at least one casualty from that gory incident. It is known for certain that in many families all the males were exterminated.

If unverified tales were lavishly spread during the war anywhere, it was in Asaba, where people needed an explanation for what happened there, which was unparalleled by the situation elsewhere in Anioma. Some, therefore, claimed that orders were given for every male child above four years of age to be killed. Others held that the soldiers came with a master list of those to be executed in the town. The authenticity of the rumors that were widely reported has not been proven. The rumors were the product of the people's search for an interpretation of their perplexing experience.

The insistence of one of the chiefs that a soldier had intimated to him a plot to kill every living thing in the town[212] may not be attributed to the Nigerian High Command, although it coincides with the testimony of Onianwa Omezi. It is possible that the federal soldiers in Asaba decided to avenge the challenge by the Biafran forces before their arrival in the town. What occurred in Asaba does suggest that the federal soldiers nursed murderous intentions towards the people. Whether they came with a list or received an injunction to execute all males, they displayed the undisguised purpose of decimating all the men of the town. If they had a list and stuck to it they might not have killed as many as they did. Olusegun Obasanjo who was with the Second Division in Asaba, dismissed the event with the following words:

> An unfortunate event involving some fifty civilians took place in Asaba without the knowledge or approval of senior or superior officers. Troops of 8th brigade ... carried away for execution those civilians whom they suspected to be spying on them on behalf of the rebels after the federal troops had suffered heavy casualties from a surprise attack by the rebels.[213]

His account is a gross misrepresentation and is not corroborated by information from eyewitnesses to the incident. What happened in Asaba leaves much to the imagination and beclouds the real assignment of the soldiers of the Second Division. Plausibly, in a bid to reclaim Asaba Division, which then comprised the entire Aniocha area, the soldiers misunderstood their assignment and narrowed it down to Asaba town, which was merely a small part of Asaba Division. The women of Asaba expressed this probable coincidence with this satirical song:

> Olu n'aza Asaba
> Igbo n'aza Asaba
> O lue ka agha bulu
> Onye akpolu onye Asaba o ju;
> O lue ka agha bili
> *Onye akpolu onye Asaba okwe!*[214]

A loose translation of the song will read:

> Distant communities claimed patrilineal links with Asaba
> The entire Igbo group also claimed links with Asaba
> While the war raged
> Anyone called an indigene of Asaba denied it;
> But, when the war ended
> It once more became fashionable to claim links with Asaba!

Obasanjo's claim that the killings occurred without the knowledge and approval of senior or superior federal officers is suspect, because if that were so the superior officers would have become aware of it on the first day and called a halt to the carnage on subsequent days. The purposeful killing of civilians all over Anioma was against the injunction of Article 4 of Protocol II to the Geneva Convention of Human Rights (1949). The document reads: "all persons who do not take a direct part or who have ceased to take part in hostilities...are entitled to respect for their persons." The same document prohibits "violence to the life, health, physical or mental wellbeing of persons."[215] It is also recorded in the International Law of War that an officer must try to prevent violations by his troops of crimes bordering on genocide and against humanity or bear responsibility for such acts even though unaware of their commission.[216] It was, therefore, the responsibility of the Second Division commander and his brigade commanders to monitor the actions of the soldiers under them. Assuming that the superior officers had no regard for Gowon's military code for the prosecution of the war, they were still bound to ensure that any crime against humanity, such as that which occurred in Asaba, was not indulged in. Obasanjo's report of this incident was perhaps designed to exonerate the brigade commanders.

The number fifty given by Obasanjo is a minuscule of the exact figure and shows the danger of relying on official documents in proffering figures for military casualties in Nigeria. Official estimates of casualties during the war were based essentially on guesswork, sometimes purposely distorted. Hence, relying on such figures could be misleading as seen from Obasanjo's account on the carnage in Asaba. In the first instance, federal commanders did not keep records of those slain in direct combat, and this excludes individuals who died from stray bullets and from other lasting effects of the war. In the case of Asaba, the leaders of the town, from the list they compiled of the dead and missing, claimed that over a thousand people were killed. However, John de St. Jorre suggests a casualty rate of about 800 men and children.[217]Many homes in Asaba were burnt down, and the federal soldiers wantonly looted people's property. But what many women detested most was the intrigue that ensued after the massacre. Fellow indigenes were accused of co-operating with federal soldiers against others by pointing out houses of those in sympathy with Biafra to be looted or destroyed by the soldiers. John Osu, a Biafran deserter who joined the Second Division of the Nigerian army as an intelligence officer that October, blamed the looting on local thieves and hooligans, and the massacre in the town and subsequent killings on sabotage. Men and women were implicated in these crimes. Reports of interactions with Biafrans, he claimed, alarmed the federal soldiers, making them act as they did.[218] The survivors of the carnage in Asaba, mostly women and old men, were eventually herded to designated refugee camps.

Osu's excuses for the federal army are debatable for a number of reasons. It was widely acknowledged that much of the looting occurred while the survivors of the carnage were in refugee camps under the daily surveillance of federal soldiers. Although the local people later took part in the looting, completely holding them responsible for it is untenable especially when the injunction in the Code of Conduct against looting and malicious destruction of people's property was for soldiers and not for civilians. To allow civilians to manipulate and use them to wreck havoc on people's property was evidence of a lack of professional discipline in Nigerian soldiers.

The news of the massacre in Asaba spread so rapidly all over Anioma that women in Illah, the last town to host the federal army in 1967, were strictly cautioned by their leaders on the proper conduct to adopt during the emergency. One interesting warning they received was to avoid moving in the company of men to minimize the degree of casualties in the town. By the time the soldiers visited Illah, a month after the executions in Asaba, their thirst for blood had abated. Their training and rehearsal for crossing the Niger River into Biafran territory kept them very busy. They therefore summoned the people and assured them of their safety as long as they remained quietly in their homes, avoided trouble, exposed infiltrators from Biafra, and complied with the curfew.[219]Maintaining the Federal Hold on Anioma

It was one thing to flush out Biafrans from Anioma but another thing altogether to ensure that they remained out. For the latter, the battalion commanders of the Second Division needed to maintain effective surveillance on Anioma until the end of the war. Units of soldiers were stationed in more towns, and places without resident soldiers were visited from other towns. This strategy did not intimidate Biafran soldiers, who continued to attack federal bases in Anioma throughout the war. The Biafran military surprises were more widespread in Aniocha and in the riverine areas of Ukwuani. While the infiltration was distressing to the federal troops, they also exacerbated the sufferings of the Anioma, with each attack resulting in the federal army avenging itself on the local people. Ogwashi-ukwu, Ibusa, Isheagu, and the riverine area of Ukwuani were victims of such retribution in April 1968 during the Easter holidays.[220]

Indigenes of Anioma who had grown weary of federal soldiers assisted Biafran troops in their attempts to push out federal soldiers from Anioma to lessen the threat on Onitsha, the Biafran town closest to Anioma in the first quarter of 1968. In Ibusa, people were startled when they heard a distant gunshot that Easter Monday. The noise led to pandemonium. The story of what happened in the Umuisagba section of the town that fateful day was recounted by one of the women.

> The morning after Easter, we heard a gun shot. Within minutes people were running about for shelter. We ran because we heard what happened in other places. We left behind the elderly and the mentally deranged who could not understand what was happening and who did not run. These ones were eventually killed.... We spent a long time in the bush and at other hiding places. Recollections of what happened in Asaba made us unwilling to return. The soldiers accused us of hiding Biafrans to kill them. They came to the bush where my family was and detonated a bomb, which killed a woman and her four children.[221]

The federal troops pushed back the Biafrans, but the local people became casualties in the clash. A single family lost thirty persons to the incident.[222] In the ensuing military operation St. Thomas' College, one of the best schools in Anioma, was bombed on alternate days by the Biafran and federal air forces. Economic trees in the town were cut down and domestic animals were either shot or became booty for federal troops. People of Ibusa, famed for breeding cattle, insist that they lost their stock in this military exercise. The deaths and destruction that attended the April 1968 attack exceeded the effect of the federal incursion in October 1967. After the mayhem, female survivors were moved to one of the refugee camps in Asaba while the two postprimary institutions in the town were transferred to Onicha-olona and Issele-ukwu respectively.

At Ogwashi-ukwu, Faustina Oko was among those who died in response to the April attacks. She was the only woman executed purposely for allegedly spying on federal soldiers on behalf of Biafran troops.[223] Any understanding that may have developed between the federal soldiers and the Ogwashi-ukwu people broke down as a result of the April attacks. The federal unit discontinued its program of distributing food items to alleviate the people's food problems. There was almost a total breakdown of soldier-civilian relationship in all the affected towns; and hardship became pronounced, generating further displacement as people sought refuge in less hostile places.[224]

The aggression on Isheagu was not only because of the Biafran attacks but also because of its economic importance as the pivotal trading point between Biafra and Anioma. Reports of a thriving trade with Biafra stirred the interest of the federal army in the town in December 1967, when the soldiers seized a lot of goods awaiting transportation to Biafra and arrested some of the traders. The Biafran infiltration during the Easter 1968 weekend provided federal troops with the opportunity to break that trade relationship. The death of some federal soldiers and their hosts in Isheagu, supposedly at the hand of some Biafran soldiers, led to a gradual desertion of the town by the local people who were eager to escape retribution. Surprisingly, there was no reaction from the federal army; rather they assured runaways of their safety, asking them to return.[225]

The people recalled hearing some weeks later, on the night of 1 May 1968, heavy shooting that lasted till daybreak. As soon as the noise died down, federal soldiers went round the small town and picked up the men who were all executed, leaving two survivors. The younger of the two men was ordered to bury the dead. The women were moved to Ogwashi-ukwu, and the town was razed by fire. It remained unoccupied till the end of the war.[226] The battalion commander who led the operation was certain that he had succeeded in destroying trade with Biafra,[227] but that was not the case, as will be seen in chapter 5. About four hundred men were reported by the local people to have died in Isheagu in April 1968.[228] In the case of Ogwashi-ukwu the federal government estimated the victims to be about 200.[229] The people, however, claim a higher figure. In Aboh in Ukwuani, many people were in hiding for a considerably long period because of the endless clashes between the federal soldiers and the Biafrans, which lasted until 1969. Thirty years after the war Isheagu still appears a dismal and dejected place, and the people remain very suspicious of strangers. Many of the inhabitants are quick to remind themselves of the civil war whenever they see strangers in the town—one of the lasting effects of Isheagu's horrifying experience.[230]

To avert retribution from the federal army after the Easter holiday and subsequent Biafran challenges some towns in Anioma tried in several ways to appease the federal field commanders. The leaders of Issele-ukwu donated twenty pounds towards the Armed Forces Welfare Fund, expressing their appreciation to Lieutenant Colonel Ally, the brigade commander at Asaba, for containing the Biafran attacks. Women in the Ika area and those in Ossissa in Ukwuani adopted a similar strategy, giving forty-three pounds and one hundred pounds respectively to the same Armed Forces Welfare Fund.[231] The federal occupation of Anioma put women in a particularly difficult position. Although many women were against the federal aggression on Anioma and some actually fought against it, some tried to identify with the federal goals in the hope that it would minimize the threat to their communities.

Instances of further military clashes in the Ika and Ukwuani areas, with the exception of Aboh, were few when compared to Aniocha. Nevertheless, a Biafran air raid on Umunede in December 1969 resulted in the death of a ten-year old boy and the destruction of people's houses.[232] In addition to the danger from air raids and Biafran military surprises, squabbles between federal soldiers often meant doom for the people. A whimsical matter like the misunderstanding between some soldiers over mutual interests in a lady that occurred in Asaba in 1968 led to the death of some civilians, one soldier, and the destruction of some homes.[233] Similarly, at Umunede, dispute between an army officer and a policeman caused the death of Igwe Obu, killed on her way from the farm by a stray bullet from one of the contestants.[234] Federal forces never succeeded in cutting off the link between Biafran soldiers and their Anioma collaborators. In Aboh and Utagba-uno, most especially, federal soldiers lived in close proximity to Biafran soldiers till the end of the war.

A SHOCKING INVASION

The trauma of the war affected women variously resulting in their sustaining diverse social and psychological wounds. Matthew Ofuani blamed the death of his mother on the war. His testimony reads:

> The war was responsible for the pre-mature death of my mother. The fighting in Ogwashi-ukwu made her terrified at the sound of a gun. She lived in agony for many months, afraid that her sons would not survive the war. Each gunshot intensified her pain. My father's efforts to encourage her were fruitless. She died suddenly in 1968.[235]

In addition to the psychological torment the war brought, the loss of family members left bereaved women in acute emotional pain. Comfort Obianeze, whose husband and only child were killed in Asaba, was, thirty years after the incident, still expressing her bitterness and helplessness over their deaths. The intensity of her pain made her incapable of continuing an interview with me. The session was called off shortly after we started and this was in spite of the many days it took to persuade her to tell her story and the efforts expended to that effect. The effort to recall the past seemed to revive both the incident in her memory and all that she lost from that event. At one point she broke off and for some moments muttered to herself that if her son had survived he would have been a grown and accomplished man by now.[236]

The death of Anioma men in Anioma and in Biafra left a vacuum that was difficult to fill, initially, in the lives of the bereaved women. The death of husbands and sons involved other things besides emotional loss. Some of these were the loss of economic support and a degree of social legitimacy.[237] Women's relative lack of economic power and opportunities in Anioma society was responsible for their dependence on their male family members for economic survival.[238] Their economic plight became aggravated by the death of the men in their lives. For the old and feeble, their levels of privation become particularly heightened.

The absence of Anioma men during the federal occupation left the women unprotected, enhancing the chances of soldiers having access to as many as they could. Sexual assault from federal troops was the most dreaded experience of women in Anioma during the war. No community was exempt. The majority of women who took shelter in the bushes and farm areas did so to widen the distance between them and the nearest federal soldier. They were aware that Biafran stragglers and guerrilla bands roamed these places, but they preferred them to running into federal soldiers who, the women reported, subjected them to all forms of disparaging treatment.[239] Life in the bush was less than ideal, and this we see from the accounts of Anasthesia Okonmah and Augustina Okogo, then aged twenty-three and nineteen and from Ibusa and Isheagu respectively, who found themselves in different hideouts during the crisis.

Anasthasia Okonmah's account was as follows:

> I ran to a very thick bush near Oko. We carried nothing with us. There was nothing to feed on, no salt, no fish, and no market. We ate anything, including rodents and snails. We built thatched houses and made beds from bamboo sticks or we slept on the ground. We scrubbed ourselves with sand because

> there was no soap. We had no change of clothes, so we looked and dressed haggardly but nobody laughed at the other. There was no joy in such a condition. After three months I escaped to Issele-ukwu where the situation was a bit better. Friends helped me with clothes until I earned enough money and bought my own.

Augustina Okogo had a similar but slightly different story to tell about her life in a bush on the outskirts of Isheagu:

> During the war we used tact in order to avoid trouble. Young mature girls were the targets of Nigerian soldiers. I was interested in saving my head to the point that I ran until I outran my family.... There were no houses in the bushes. If it rained for a whole day, the rain will fall on us for the whole day. Giant stinging ants bit us without remedy. Sometimes we ran to nearby communities to be assisted with food items, but if we heard the sound of shelling we run away again. We had no food to eat, no soap, no cream. Many of us were afflicted with scabies and only got cured after the war.

Irrespective of such degrees of privation, many people survived the hostilities. The experiences of displaced women in Anioma parallel what other displaced women elsewhere have expressed of their situation. Referring to the more than thirty years of civil war in Guatemala, a Mayan woman reports: "Most of us left the communities and hid in towns and cities, mostly in the capital, in order to safeguard our lives. Since then, we have been living in fear and a lot of suffering." In 1990, another Mayan described the lives of displaced people thus "We are the ones who are in need. We are like a plant, which has been snatched away and not yet planted.... We are like the dog who's waiting for a bone that never comes."[240]

Displacement puts women in an ambiguous situation; little wonder that the displaced in Anioma felt that their lot was worse than that of their colleagues who were not displaced. Displaced women were not welcomed everywhere. Asaba and Ibusa women who sought refuge at Oko, a nearby town, were requested as a prelude to their acceptance to take an oath at the town's shrine that they would not attract federal soldiers to the community. The displaced women could only decline doing so. A few weeks' later, federal soldiers visited Oko and resettled the indigenes at Regina Mundi, one of the refugee centers in Asaba.

Women who were not displaced were not insulated from problems. Situations exposing them to abuse by federal troops were many. Daily chores like fetching water and firewood and the pursuit of a means of sustenance provided opportunities for such mistreatment. A number of young women had the notion that refusal to accept a soldier's advances or to gratify a sexual demand would bring death and, therefore, did not put up a determined struggle when cornered or abducted. Likewise, the fear instilled in the people by the sight of a gun prevented most men from intervening in favor of female victims of sexual abuse. They could not be entirely blamed. Some men recalled being threatened with death for making such attempts. One known proof of this was Chuks Momah, who was shot at Asaba when he tried to rescue his wife from a soldier in October 1967. Such antecedents incapacitated persons who wished to step into a matter involving a soldier and a captured woman.

The only case of interference mentioned in the course of fieldwork occurred in Okpanam over the use of sacred places as *rendezvous* by federal troops. The interference by the leaders of the town was more to salvage the town's sacred structures from desecration and not primarily to prevent the abuse of women, although they attempted this by introducing the soldiers to female professional commercial sex workers and requested that they meet them anywhere but away from the sacred buildings. It is uncertain that the soldiers demanded sexual partners. Most likely, the leaders of the town thought it safe to provide them with some. Whatever the case, their sacred buildings, most of which were make-shift structures, were preserved but the ranks of prostitutes in the community were swelled when other women joined the business after seeing the material benefits that accrued from it.

Most of the women in Asaba who remonstrated that soldiers would have nothing to do with civilians did little to prepare for any eventuality. The arrival of the troops took them unawares and sent them scampering away from their homes with their possessions improperly secured. Much property was lost in the looting and destruction that occurred in Anioma. Craftswomen in particular lost their professional equipment and, consequently, their main sources of sustenance. Not all the women were indifferent to securing their possessions. In Illah, Madam Ijomah, a middle-aged uneducated woman, hid her valuables in a bunker dug for that purpose and covered with a stone slab. She disguised the spot by using it as a garbage dump and a public latrine for children.

The carnage in Asaba involved women in a peculiar but distressing manner. The responsibility for burying the dead devolved on them. They were not asked to do so but the federal soldiers' apathy to the mass of lifeless bodies that littered the town moved the women to act as they did. Admittedly, not all the men were killed in the town, but the survivors went into hiding. Without the men to help, the women took over the job of burying the dead. There was little time for self-pity. As many as could, dug shallow graves for their dead ones. These female undertakers dispensed with most of the cultural burial practices and buried the victims anywhere close to where their bodies were found. The burials were as decent as they could possibly be under the circumstances, but only in the efforts to hide the corpses under the soil and not on how properly they were undertaken. In some instances, they were so haphazardly done that a few limbs were seen sticking out of graves. Those women who could not lift their dead relatives dragged them on the ground to their graves while some used domestic trucks to convey the corpses to their final resting places, unconsciously setting precedence for the survivors of the 1994 genocide in Rwanda.[241]

The emergency burials lacked the trappings of a standard and culturally approved ceremony in any part of Igboland but particularly in Anioma where burials were big events. There were no gunshots to herald the incidents or to announce to the spirit world that sons and potential ancestors were on their way to join other ancestors. No processional marches by mourners graced the events. The women undertook this sordid responsibility with as much emotional detachment as possible. Not all Asaba women were so brave as to participate in the burial exercise. Those who could not stand the torture left their dead for any sympathetic person to dispose of. Such corpses subsequently benefited from the services of a caterpillar driver, provided by the federal army, who, with his land-moving vehicle, dug mass graves for the unburied bodies as a complement to the efforts of the women. Until Asaba women buried their dead, it was unknown in Igboland that women could function as funeral undertakers. Yet in spite of the collaborative work of the women and the caterpillar driver, there were bodies that escaped burial and decomposed where they fell. The bravery women displayed in burying their dead unaided did little to soften the harshness of the soldiers on them. The involvement of a caterpillar driver challenges the fallacious claim of Colonel Olusegun Obasonjo that some fifty civilians were killed in Asaba.[242] The corpses of some fifty civilians are not too numerous to require the services of a caterpillar driver after the efforts of the local people to bury their dead.

Another confusing and unnerving experience of the war was the confinement of women in refugee camps. Three institutions were chosen for that purpose and these were situated in Asaba.[243] Although the majority of the inmates were from Asaba, these institutions at different periods during the civil war became the official homes of refugees from Ibusa and Oko. In 1969, similar camps were opened at Ibusa where Ibusa refugees were transferred. Women whose houses were not destroyed were grossly agitated over their confinement. The freedom of the bush appeared more alluring to many except that food rations came at specified intervals to those in the camps while their counterparts in the bush had no such benefit. Refugee status imposed on the inmates was not a guarantee for total safety. The inadequate attention given to the refugees and exposure to inclement weather conditions led to the death of some elderly ones. People were occasionally picked from the camps and shot on the claim that they were collaborating with Biafrans. One such attempt, which would have led to the death of many men and women, was arrested through the intervention of Father James Colon, an expatriate Catholic missionary. John Osu, the federal troops' Intelligence Officer, again explained the reason for the confinement of the local people in camps within their own community.

> We sent them to refugee camps to protect ourselves and to protect them. In the camps the chances of mischief were reduced and we needed to keep them off to watch out for Biafran soldiers. Their confinement made it easy for us to know when outsiders entered the town. If we had not taken that step many more would have been killed.[244]

His testimony contradicts the soldiers' claim that inmates were collaborating with Biafrans from the camps and indicates that the soldiers had no cogent reason for brutalizing the civilians they isolated to protect. It is possible that the accusation was a hoax for killing the Anioma whom the soldiers assumed were, like the Biafrans, their enemies. Anioma women remember these soldiers for the massacres, their atrocities, and their indiscriminate and gratuitous brutality. A number of women contacted to share their experiences preferred not to recount their ordeal during that war.

The federal military unit in Asaba provided raw food—usually donated for the civilian population by church organizations like the Misericordia Heart of Mercy and Caritas—for the refugees, who would improvise cooking utensils mostly out of empty and discarded tins. Some women moved into the camps with portable stoves but for the majority sticks picked up within the camp premises or books from the colleges served as cooking fuel in place of kerosene. The federal government imposed kerosene scarcity in the areas of occupation to prevent kerosene from being smuggled to Biafra, where the federal government suspected that it was used in manufacturing explosives. Women who had access to kerosene through the help of some federal soldiers were always wary of the prying eyes of other soldiers to avoid being caught with the liquid.

RUMOR DURING THE EMERGENCY

The tension of the war and the cloud of uncertainty that hung over Anioma found expression in rumor. Rumor has been described as "a reaction against bureaucratic monopoly of information."[245] They are not always objective reports of something that happened but hyperbolic representations of a given reality as perceived by those who lived through them.[246] The participants in the dissemination of improvised news to which rumor belongs form a conglomerate of people who react to the news in different ways and also contribute to the distortion of the story either consciously or unconsciously.

In the course of the civil war, rumor became a substitute for news from institutional channels. It provided a camouflaged means through which the local people expressed their feelings. Men and women unconsciously strove to excel as leading rumormongers. Women functioned more as secondary transmitters since they relied often on men for information. Fragments of news gleaned from Radio Biafra, the preferred station, were passed on freely by those who listened to the broadcasts. Incidentally, most of what Radio Biafra transmitted was for propaganda purposes. At certain points during the war it became fashionable in Anioma for a woman to be in possession of the latest news and especially from Radio Biafra.

After the subjugation of Anioma by the federal army story highlights among rumor peddlers revolved around the activities of the soldiers in the occupied areas. No clear line of demarcation was drawn between the feasible and the unreal. Both the actual and the possible became merged, and some recipients of the rumors seemed incapable of separating the essential from the nonessential. In all the towns in Anioma, some of the informal news items circulated had no origin to any radio station but were speculations that appeared real. A recipient would misunderstand a story and in an attempt to relate it would reproduce it out of context thus confirming the universal opinion that certain stories end up expanding into a colossus of invented facts.[247] Inevitably, the stories heightened women's apprehensions and intensified their fears. Nonetheless, some interviewees contended that the rumors did have some advantages. The most important was to heighten their awareness of danger and motivate actions that would guarantee their safety. Catherine Agbon, from Otolokpo in the Ika area, was one of the women who attributed her knowledge of the political crisis in the country and the brutality of Lt. Col. Murtala Mohammed, the first GOC of the Second Division, to rumor. The news led to her flight from Boji-boji to Otolokpo, a town never visited by federal troops throughout the war. Even though much of the information disseminated as rumor may be incomplete they were not entirely inaccurate and baseless.

Many women in Anioma, if not all, depended on rumor during the crisis. There was constant exchange of information between different groups of displaced women. Consciously collating news became the surest way through which the displaced in the various hideouts kept abreast of happenings in their towns. Asaba women at Achalla Ibusa provide a good illustration of this. At intervals they dispatched one or two individuals to assess the extent of the calm in their town and how conducive it would be for a returnee.[248] Their action helped some persons to determine the best time to leave their hideout and move back to their homes.

Rumor during the war can be linked with the indigenous system of disseminating information orally; only this time the stories were not traced to a town crier but to a radio station and to military personnel. In emergency situations a preoccupation with rumor and rumor mongering is unavoidable. Women who are mostly indifferent to news become sensitized to it during ambiguous moments in order to maintain their bearings. Information is necessary for planned action, but false information can have grave consequences. Tamotsu Shibutani explains that what makes decisions in unsettled times so important is that crises are crucibles from which many innovations emerge, and that new modes of action often get their initial direction in attempts to cope with emergencies.[249] The authors of *Oral Communication: Message and Response* hold the view that sharing information has a therapeutic effect on human beings.[250] These explanations throw light on why women in Anioma had an ear for all kinds of stories and acted on any kind of information during the war.

Chapter 4

WOMEN DURING THE OCCUPATION

Anioma indigenes felt little threat in the six weeks of the Biafran army's control of the Midwest. This was one result of the solidarity between the two Igbo groups. The other was the enlistment of Anioma women in the Biafran militia and their activities in aid of the survival of the Republic of Biafra when eventually they moved there. The constraints experienced in Anioma because of the economic blockade imposed to hasten Biafra's expulsion from the Midwest were considered mild in comparison to the privation felt during federal control. The impacts of these two phases of the war on Anioma are considered in some detail in this chapter.

BIAFRA CONTROL OF ANIOMA

The control of Anioma by the Biafran Liberation Army led to two major developments with spiraling consequences: the enhanced trade relations between the Anioma and the Igbo east of the Niger; and the influx of Anioma men and women into the Biafran militia to form the Republic of Benin (ROB) unit of the Biafran militia from which Anioma women in the militia derived the name ROB women. A trading alliance had long existed between the Eastern Region and the Midwest, but, beginning in April 1967 when the economic blockade was imposed on the Eastern Region, this expanded into distinctive trading involving Biafra and Anioma. Trade between the two regions blossomed under Biafran control of the Midwest and continued until the end of the war. Since it spanned both the Biafran and federal periods of occupation of Anioma and also fits in as part of the women's survival strategies during the federal occupation, its consideration is reserved for treatment in the next chapter.

ANIOMA WOMEN IN BIAFRA

Biafran military officers, during their stay in the Midwest, formed a paramilitary group in Anioma that would later be called the Biafran militia. It was established as part of the recruitment drive for the Biafran armed forces. The need for a paramilitary group was voiced in Biafra as part of preparations in case of increasing deterioration into armed conflict of the stalemate between the Eastern regional government and the Nigerian federal government.[251] It was the intention of its initiators that the militia, initially called the civil defense, would serve as a medium for educating civilians in civil defense activities. Anioma men were encouraged to join the Biafran army, but the women were needed in the militia along with some educated persons who did not want to be under army commanders with less formal education than themselves.[252] The group was organized along military lines to satisfy its objective of assisting the Biafran army, but it remained separate from the Biafran armed forces throughout the civil war. The duties of the militia were specific and revolved around security within Biafra and, for a while, in Anioma. With its focus on internal security, it freed the Biafran army for military engagements against federal forces. Later, the Biafran army would depend on the militia to supplement its forces and as a source of reinforcements.

The Biafran organizers of the militia appealed to the different departments of the Midwest civil service and to market women for entrants into the group. Their targets were able-bodied young men in the state civil service and traders. The cooperation of the local leaders in Anioma was solicited in starting civil defense groups in their towns. Since there was no specification given concerning the group of civil servants preferred, there was also no

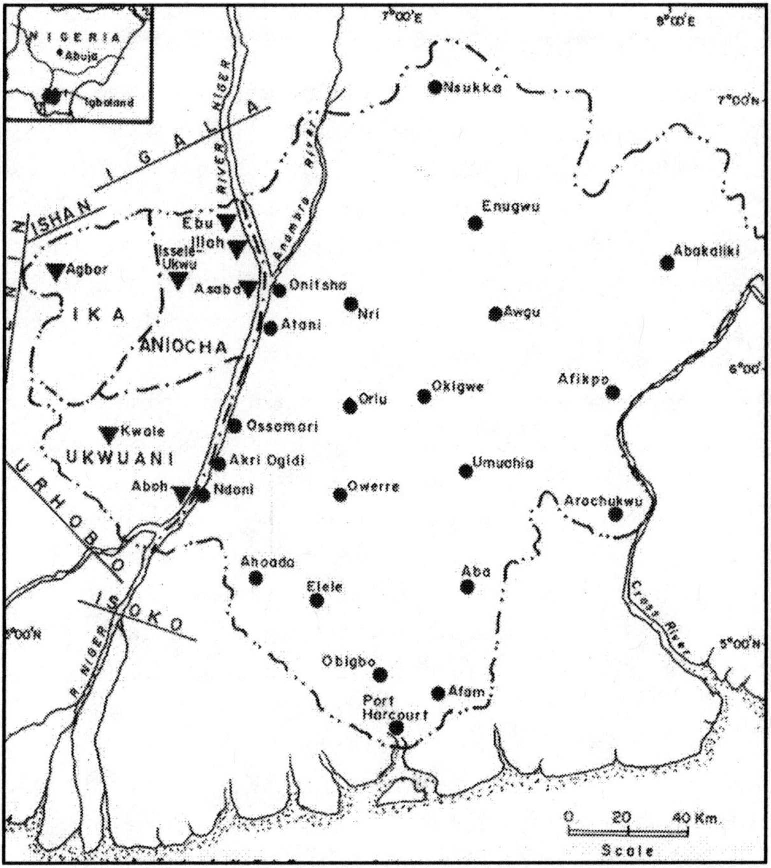

Igboland, east and west of the Niger River

discrimination against the first crop of females who responded to the appeals.[253] Later, women all over Anioma were specifically requisitioned to join a group and the recruitment that started in August 1967 continued until the federal army arrived in Anioma a month later.[254] All over Anioma teenage girls and young female adults, some of whom were married and with children, responded to the appeals; but the majority of those who later went to Biafra to join similar groups there were from Aniocha, where a training center was established to train Anioma recruits. In the Ukwuani and Ika areas, civil defense was no more than a grassroots' affair and operated only at that level. These groups disbanded in the wake of the federal reconquest of Anioma.[255]

Biafra, which territorially and numerically was no match for Nigeria, needed all the support it could secure to wage successful campaign against a stronger foe. This awareness was behind the appeals for Anioma youths to enlistment in the civil defense. Their favorable response to the Biafran entreaty was as a result of Anioma's support of, and its contribution to, the Biafran dream for political independence from Nigeria, commonly called the "Igbo dream" both in Anioma and in Biafra.[256]

Women joined the militia from a number of motives that were as varied as themselves. The most important reason was the opportunity it afforded them for revenge. B. Nwandu, who was eighteen years old in 1967, saw it as an outlet to avenge atrocities meted out on the Igbo and the deaths of some members of her family in Kano, where she lived until October 1966. She recounted how she escaped being lynched by a mob during that year's disturbances by hiding in the ceiling of her parents' house.[257] Other women, from their testimonies, joined the militia for the following reasons: "as an indication of their solidarity with Biafra," "to invest their efforts in the survival of the new republic and the rise of the Igbo nation," "to save their lives," and "to defend their fatherland." Some joined for love of adventure but a few young girls with no opinion of their own, obviously because of their age, followed their older siblings and friends into a group. One such girl, Edith Dibie, thought that by joining the militia she would meet her brother who was already an officer in the Biafran navy.[258]

More women joined the civil defense out of a sense of patriotism and a desire for social justice than for adventure. Their reasons for enlisting in the Biafran militia were similar to those of Vietnamese women in the 1960s who joined their country's revolutionary war from such motives as "to unify their families separated by the division of the country into North and South" and "to avenge the death of their loved ones as well as the rape of their sisters by the United States' troops."[259] The action of Anioma women also had a parallel to that of Chinese women who, beginning in the 1930s, joined communist organizations, and eventually the army, just to participate in a revolution, which to them meant freedom from exploitation and the acquisition of a sense of identity.[260] In addition, such ventures find similarities with the Tigrayan women in Ethiopian who joined the Tigrayan revolution to put an end to a life of poverty and exploitation.[261] In many ways during the emergency, Anioma women discovered their capability for activities that they had rarely been encouraged to do. Their performance in a male-dominated sphere like the militia challenged the contempt they had so often encountered in every-day life because of their gender.

Civil defense training involved physical exercises, psychological indoctrination, and the inculcation of a disciplined and structured behavioral pattern on the trainees. All these were meant to adapt the members to the prevailing conditions during warfare, which the organizers considered to be unfamiliar to civilians. The Asaba (Technical) College of Education was the improvised training center for the militia and at the end of the training the members were deemed qualified to act as a buffer between civilian populations and the military. Among the things women learnt were the proper way to take cover during air raids, how to move out of a besieged area, self defense, life-saving devices necessary in emergency situations, and practical drills intended to enhance their level of vigilance and alertness.[262] Only a few selected women were taught in advanced training sessions how to put a gun to good use. The main focus of the drills was on building the endurance level of the members and instilling military discipline in them. Biafran army officers handled this latter aspect of the training. On the whole, recruits into the militia acquired knowledge of military procedures and operations that constituted part of the training for an infantry soldier. Instead of the required six months training for a military draftee, a requirement that was not met during the war, members of the militia had theirs condensed into three weeks. They barely completed their training when the news of the movement of federal troops into Anioma forced their relocation to Onitsha in Biafra. Not all the women who participated in the training crossed into Biafra. Those who remained behind were reabsorbed into the civilian population of Anioma.

Militia members from Anioma were referred to as the ROB members throughout their stay in Biafra and their existence as a unit. The name, as stated above, was derived from the title *Republic of Benin*, which was Biafra's designation for Midwest State when it took over the area in August 1967. The ROB remained separate from other militia groups within Biafra although all the groups were organized in the same way and operated in a complementary fashion. As a unit within the Biafran army, the militia had no specified supervisor or coordinator of its own. It was split into smaller units of near-battalion strength each. These were further subdivided into platoons, each with a leader who could be either male or female. Few platoons had female leaders. Rufus Osoemena, the obi of Issele-ukwu, who was honored with the title of major in Biafra, became the self-appointed superintendent for the ROB arm of the Biafran militia. This was in addition to his official original assignment with the Biafran Refugee Commission. He rallied the ROB members together and made sure that they were well taken care of and reasonably integrated into Biafra.[263] They, like himself, were from Anioma. His efforts brought relief to R.O.B. members who had not previously been to the Eastern Region and who felt a bit lost in that environment.[264]

The chief responsibility of the militia in Biafra was ensuring internal security. They achieved this by manning checkpoints. The ROB had done this in their towns in Anioma before moving to Biafra. They were on the look out for strangers whom they would apprehend and send to either the local rulers or to the army units for interrogation and further action. Women who took part in this exercise were always paired with male militia members or soldiers at a ratio of two men to one woman. The men, unlike the women, were armed with machetes, clubs, and sometimes a gun. They were assured of visibility at night through the use of hurricane lamps. In Anioma, people recalled that some members of the militia abused their opportunity of serving their communities, as their duties were understood at the initial period, using it as a means of settling grievances and of intimidating others.[265] Similar accusations were voiced of militia members in Biafra. Biafran members of the militia were seen brandishing their weapons and menacing people, sometimes those who were not Igbo.[266]

The female members of the militia dominated the group from 1968. As the fortunes of the war began to alter and with need, the male members were drafted into the regular fighting force, leaving women to fill the functions for which the militia was formed. The majority of the Biafran soldiers involved in military campaigns against federal troops in Anioma in 1967 and the surprised attacks on federal bases in Anioma towns from 1968 were from the ROB unit. It is difficult to give an accurate figure for the ROB women since no record was kept of their enlistment, but going by the information gleaned from the female participants, it is estimated that at most about a hundred females from Anioma were paramilitary personnel in Biafra. The participation of women in the Nigerian civil war was modest if compared with female participation in the military or as revolutionaries in Vietnam before the 1960s and in Tigray in Ethiopia, Eritrea, and Zimbabwe after the 1970s.[267]

With the exit of the ROB men, drafted for military operations in Anioma, the ROB women were assigned to different Biafran battalions and brigades, where the commanders determined what use to put them to. Some battalion commanders kept them busy with odd tasks in their administrative headquarters but others rejected them, considering them a distraction to their soldiers. Those who were given responsibilities worked as telephone operators and aides to quarter masters, issuing supplies to soldiers and new entrants into the army. In their capacity as telephone operators, they helped to coordinate combatant units in different locations and to pass information about enemy troops' movement to Biafran army officers.[268] Other areas where the services of the ROB women were utilized in Biafra were in the hospitals, sickbays, and refugee centers. They assisted in carrying wounded soldiers to hospitals, helped the few regular medical staff in administering first aid, and distributing relief materials to refugees on behalf of the Biafran Red Cross. Militia girls under fifteen years of age were exempted from these duties. The same consideration was shown to them during their training period, when they were excluded from taking part in the most strenuous exercises. Thus Edith Dibie, who joined the civil defense in Anioma in anticipation of meeting her brother, described her life in the ROB as consisting of "eating and changing camps."[269]

Some ROB women, who found themselves under battalion commanders who were not in favor of having women in their units, kept busy with self-assigned tasks. Most became spies for Biafra, relaying whatever information they gathered to friendly officers. Their role in espionage was not especially necessary. Espionage was the responsibility of the Biafran Freedom Fighters (BOFF), an all-male group whose members were specifically trained for that purpose. But, instead of a life of idleness, inactive ROB women assigned themselves the job of moving in and out of Biafran-held areas in search of information that might be useful to Biafran military officers. This, they felt, was a way of contributing to the survival of the Biafran Republic. In some instances, spying served self-fulfilling purposes; being used to solicit favors from either Biafran or Nigerian officers. The female spies were confident that they would escape detection and the majority did. As some explained, federal soldiers rarely shot women at sight unless on provocation or when the woman in question acted suspiciously and as an enemy.

The self-appointed spies enhanced their chances of success with their tattered clothes, portraying themselves as innocent peasants going about their normal daily activities. They went in pairs, relying on the assistance of their Nigerian-soldier boyfriends to move about relatively freely in federal zones. Military intelligence is inseparable from warfare; so as they believed, these women directly participated in the execution of the war.[270] The information relayed back was needed especially in the formulation of plans for combat operations. The risk was grave for the women, since if caught they would scarcely be accorded the same privileges a soldier would receive as a prisoner of war.[271] Their fate would not have significantly differed from that of Faustina Oko, executed in Ogwashi-ukwu in 1968 for allegedly spying on federal troops for Biafran soldiers.

The ROB women's participation in espionage was not unusual. In instances of armed confrontation, contending aggressors have often used women in this way. The "pretty girls" who worked for Major Ogbemudia in the Midwest against Biafran troops provided a localized model for the ROB female spies later in the conflict. What may be considered peculiar might be that the ROB women took the initiative to function as spies, which again is not unheard of. As far back as two centuries ago American women served as self-appointed spies during the country's civil war, providing their military leaders with indispensable logistical information. Their actions were so varied that some helped prisoners of war to escape.[272] Tigray female revolutionaries in Ethiopia first acted as spies for the Tigray People's Liberation Front (TPLF) before they were allowed to join the fighting as regular combatants.[273] Although military combat in Biafra was largely limited to men, the presence of self-appointed female spies is evidence of how the war encouraged female assertiveness.

Besides searching for information, the spies received food donations from federal soldiers, part of which were shared with Biafran soldiers.[274] This aspect of their clandestine activity became especially useful when the food situation in Biafra deteriorated and rations for the army became very irregular. Their efforts would seem to have gone unnoticed by the Biafran government and its armed forces, none of which publicly acknowledged them. Yet a number of Biafran soldiers recall the camaraderie that existed between them and some female militia members and the assistance they received from them.

ROB female platoon leaders helped in coordinating other female members of their groups by assigning duties to them, thus making sure that the girls maintained acceptable conduct while in camp. Two such platoon leaders prepared weekly activity rosters for their group members, which involved keeping their surroundings clean, posting girls to checkpoints in less endangered areas, and appointing them to other outside duties. According to their standard protocol, the platoon leaders were to receive directives on weekly responsibilities from the battalion or brigade commanders to which they were assigned. Occasionally, too, Major Rufus Osoemena informed them of areas in need where they might be of help. When no directive came, they used their initiatives. Part of what they did on their own was teaching life-saving skills to female refugees who flocked to their camp, attracted by the sight of other women in military uniforms.

Only female platoon leaders were officially given and allowed to carry rifles. The weapons were for their defense but also to distinguish them from their subordinates. Some did not find it easy moderating the activities of all their female group members. Adventurous ones were particularly hard to control or to force into conforming to what others considered appropriate female behavior. Such persons intermittently challenged the authority of the platoon leaders to censure their liberty and would often leave camp to accompany regular soldiers on campaigns. A former Biafran soldier gave the following testimony about three such women. The first two he referrs to were from Anioma, while the last was a Biafran.

> I know about three women in the Biafran army. They were gallant soldiers and went with us to the front. One of them was from Ubulu-ukwu, the other from Ogwashi-ukwu, and the third from Orlu. They were unmarried girls.[275]

Contrary to the perception drawn from the above account, female members of the militia were not officially sent as combatants with regular soldiers. They were also not formally dispatched to spy for the Biafran army even though Biafran officers rarely dismissed the information that came in through them and were not known to have discouraged their efforts. The women who fought with the soldiers did not go against the reason for the establishment of the militia and their personal convictions for enlisting in the group. All members of their sex did not appreciate their desire for self-fulfillment nor did the men who came into contact with them; hence, they were regarded and described as "stubborn girls who rebelled against the norm by doing what they were not asked to do."[276] One tenable argument against their conduct would be that the female militia members were not qualified by their training to take part in combat, but, from all indications, these women wanted a taste of the experience that they were being denied by their insulation from combat duties. For some of them, the association with regular soldiers resulted in their use of narcotics and alcohol, habits socially considered as unbecoming for women.[277] Thus, in many respects they challenged communal images of women in Igboland. On the other hand, their ability to live off the trenches with male soldiers proved false the assertion that women must always be protected and are incapable of enduring extreme privations, an allegation made against members of their gender in Anioma during and after the war.[278]

For a militia member to become a regular soldier in Biafra, she needed to complete the formal military training required of regular soldiers, and this did not happen. The platoon leaders who were given further training were few and made up an insignificant proportion of the female militia members. The Biafran army did not wish to take responsibility for combat women and therefore isolated them from the fighting. Actually, senior military officers in Biafra held the notion that the war had not gotten to the level that women should be asked to fight.[279] That notwithstanding, women were found in different commands, decked in combat uniforms and carrying guns, and acting as officers or as other ranks just like men. What differentiated them from soldiers was that Biafran army officers did not recognize their zeal for service and did not treat them in the same manner as they did the regular soldiers. For instance, unlike the soldiers the female militia members were not on the Biafran payroll and if found taking part in combat could be disarmed and sent back to camp.[280]

The failure of the Biafran military leaders to publicly acknowledge female militia members did not deter some officers from commending their efforts. They were described as "representing the inflexible and determined courage of most Biafrans, which was manifest during the war," and, "if the truth be known, their efforts by far surpassed those of the men especially in the field of intelligence, mob control, as well as the battle field."[281] The reference to the battlefield is somewhat exaggerated considering the number of militia women who took part in actual combat. Yet the tribute reveals that the impact of the women was felt by those who were afraid to recognize their efforts towards the survival of Biafra and the success of its military operations.

Tina Okwuashi was one of the women referred to in the extract on the preceding page and acclaimed by many as a gallant soldier. She never fought in a battle, according to her own testimony, but was a platoon leader who played a significant role as a language translator for Biafran army officers. Language difficulties posed a big problem for Biafran commanders during the war, because of the presence of many war prisoners from different ethnic and linguistic groups.[282] Often federal soldiers caught by Biafrans relapsed into their local languages and dialects as a protective mechanism. By so doing, they avoided any communication in English or in any of the three major languages spoken in the country—Yoruba, Igbo, and Hausa—thereby frustrating the efforts of their captors to glean useful information from them. As a way out of the problem, officers sought individuals who could assist in getting information from war captives. Tina Okwuashi was fluent in the three major Nigerian languages and could also communicate reasonably well in English, Idoma, Urhobo, and Edo. Her ability to speak six indigenous languages made her an asset to the Biafran army. Coincidentally, a considerable number of federal soldiers were from Idoma- and Edo-speaking groups. Getting information from a captive was a task anybody could perform but searching out an individual gifted in any of the less well-known languages of the country was definitely time consuming. Tina Okwuashi filled this role with her competence in five languages spoken outside Biafra, three of which belong to minority groups.

The militia as a unit lacked a formal process by which members were rewarded for their commitment and hard work. Promotions were given arbitrarily. This was attributed to the absence of a central coordinator for the organization.[283] Ranks in the militia in reverse order were recruit, cadet, corporal, sergeant, sergeant-major, and lieutenant. No ROB woman attained a rank above sergeant. Nevertheless, none of the women interviewed expressed any regret about joining the group even with its limitations; rather they expressed deep convictions that the training they acquired and the privileges they enjoyed more than made up for the risks and other organizational setbacks in the group. ROB women did not battle against hunger to the same degree as the civilian population in Biafra. However, there were very strong rumors that within the military and militia, people were served human flesh when animal meat became scarce in Biafra. Up till the first quarter of 1969, militia members were relatively well fed and taken care of in spite of the menace of Kwashiokor, a condition caused by protein deficiency, in the enclave. Their lack of access to any form of financial benefit did not expose them to extreme cases of lack and want. They were able to maintain those family members they brought with them from Anioma to Biafra from their individual supplies and whatever relief materials they received through the Biafran Red Cross.[284]

One of the enduring effects of the women's involvement in the militia came from their training and conditioning in daily physical exercise. Former ROB members acknowledged the profound impact of the exercises on their physical well-being. The training on the whole, they pointed out, made them aware of their unexplored abilities. Some expressed the belief that their courage in the face of challenges came from the training. A recurring confession from past members on the benefits of their involvement in the militia was their immunity to any form of intimidation. The stories were not all ones of success, for on the other side of the scale were those who ended up as alcoholics and addicted to narcotics.[285] Few ROB women died during the war. One well-remembered casualty was Rosemary Ofune from Ubulu-ukwu, who died from health complications. Biafran soldiers described her as a brave warrior, while her surviving female colleagues remember her for her fearlessness and adventurous spirit.

A turning point occurred in the experiences of the ROB female members in 1969. The situation in Biafra that year was more than many could bear. As Biafra shrank in size, the level of privation and suffering became quite severe. Daily supplies for the army and the militia were very irregular, and hardship and hunger became the norm. From July 1968 the Nigerian federal government had accepted starvation as a weapon of war. Anthony Enahoro, the Nigerian information minister, held a press conference at the United Nations headquarters in New York, describing starvation as "a legitimate weapon of war," a view also expressed at different points during the crisis by Obafemi Awolowo, the commissioner for finance, and by Hassan Usman Katsina, the Nigerian army chief of staff.[286] From 1968 it was obvious to all within and outside Nigeria that the federal government was poised to compell Biafra to surrender through starvation. Biafrans felt the brunt of this policy, which by 1969 had indeed worsened the level of undernourishment in Biafra. For members of the ROB, life was more difficult for those with dependents and the result was a gradual desertion from March 1969. Most ROB women returned to Anioma, which in comparison with Biafra was relatively less militarized. They avoided detection from federal troops scattered in the liberated areas of Biafra and all over Anioma by disposing their militia uniforms and identity cards in the Niger River, after using them to gain free passage to the riverbank. The majority of them were easily reabsorbed into the civilian population in Anioma without incident. But Tina Okwuashi was arrested and detained soon after her arrival in Onicha-ugbo for her role in Biafra. She regained her freedom almost nine months after termination of the war.

FEDERAL RECONQUEST

For twenty-eight months of the thirty-month span of the civil war the federal soldiers held sway in Anioma. The period saw a series of changes in Anioma communities. Anioma had over many centuries developed a defined culture with definite customs but these were disrupted by the war. The major social and cultural disruption involved, and stemmed from, the absence and subjugation of the elderly, who in Igbo society were and remain the custodians of the culture and the chief determinants of the social norms. Some of the local leaders, drawn from different political strata in the society, were among those who died in the war. Others who survived federal incursion in their localities were temporarily displaced by the war while such local rulers as the Obi of Ejeme-aniogo, Obi Rufus Osemena (Issele-ukwu), and Obi Oyetenu (the Asagba of Asaba) escaped an uncertain fate by taking refuge in Biafra. The war and the dictatorial control of Anioma by the federal army raped the system of local administration in Anioma. As a result of the massacres and the displacements gaps existed in the governmental hierarchy of most towns.[287] The women, who out-numbered the men, could not step into the vacated positions because they lacked credibility for such an action. Local administration in Igboland had never revolved around women and the few privileged female leaders such as the omu in the male-dominated political caucus in Aniocha derived their authority from the consent of the men.

The federal soldiers displayed very little respect for the local rulers who survived their incursion. The rulers were not accorded the honor commensurate with their social standing nor treated in a manner different from the rest of the people during the federal occupation. Major Samuel Ogbemudia, the Midwest military governor, created a situation in which the local elite in Anioma were treated shabbily and occasionally embarrassed by the soldiers of the Second Division. His extraordinary gazette of 26 October 1967 provided for the establishment of the Rebel Atrocities Tribunal of Enquiry, headed by Justice Omo Eboh, to look into the atrocities alleged to be committed by Biafrans in the state. Part of the tribunal's terms of reference was "to enquire into the role played by public officers and other civilians in respect of Secessionists' activities before and during the Secessionist troops' occupation of the state."[288] All the local rulers of Anioma were arraigned before the tribunal on charges of conspiracy against the state and collaboration with Biafrans.

The sitting of the tribunal, from December 1967 until September 1968, necessitated the constant absence of these rulers from their communities. The harassment they encountered from federal soldiers during their trips to Agbor, where the tribunal met, made it difficult for them to regularly appear before the court. Even after Major Ikwuazu from Anioma was assigned as their escort in response to their complaint over the harassment and a military vehicle was dispatched for their use federal soldiers' high-handedness towards the local rulers was not completely arrested.[289] The soldiers disregarded the federal government's declaration in March 1968 that it shall "direct ... attention to the physical safety of every Nigerian no matter his state of origin."[290] In the long run, the findings of the tribunal were never disclosed to the public but apparently formed the basis on which the people were treated during the postwar rehabilitation process.

The omu were not summoned to appear before the tribunal, unlike the women suspected of collaborating with Biafrans. Yet, like the male chiefs, they were not insulated from the harassment of federal troops as indicated by the death of Mgboshie Okolie, the omu of Asaba, during the crisis. Mgboshie was clubbed to death in her home and physically mutilated afterwards by two federal soldiers from the military unit stationed in her town. All over Anioma, members of the community noted the general disregard with which federal soldiers treated the ruling elite during the emergency, completely contravening the custom of the people and the declaration of the head of state.

After the commencement of military operations in Anioma, Major Ogbemudia appointed two sole administrators for Anioma, one for Asaba and Ika divisions and the other for Aboh. The sole administrators replaced the three divisional officers who controlled the administration of the three sections of Anioma before its military subjugation.[291] The appointments placed the sole administrators at the apex of the divisional administrations, to work closely with the battalion commanders in their divisions. As a result of this arrangement, local rulers suddenly found themselves subservient to the military commanders and the sole administrators, taking orders from them and implementing their directives.

The administration of Anioma by military fiat put a burden on nearly all communities but most especially on those with resident units of the federal army. Most military codes formulated by the army to guide civilians during the emergency immobilized the indigenous political structures for the maintenance of peace and order. Consequently, lawlessness became a way of life, and many women felt the brunt of it. Besides the scandalous behavior of the Nigerian soldiers, some Anioma youths and even adults preyed on other members of their communities during the war and a lot of vices found the opportunity to blossom. Crimes of every description were rampant. Stealing was so widespread that local residents could not contain the menace. The local rulers in Aniocha in particular did not see the relevance of making a representation to that effect to the federal commanders whom they regarded as rivals and enemies,[292] and the officers, for their part, did not show much interest in the welfare of the people.

Their interest in Anioma was focused on their own safety and individual gain in addition to the responsibility of holding the territory for the Nigerian government.

The new order posed various problems for different communities. Many cultural practices were abandoned. Social and biological rites of passage and periodic communal festivals were accorded little importance. Aspects of the religious observances of the people were dispensed with. Whatever involved noise or caused the people to be seen outside their homes at night was not allowed. The different *otu-omu* groups in Aniocha and other female associations in Anioma could not freely carry on with their social and religious functions. Also setting off of any form of firearms for any purpose whatsoever, including burials, was forbidden to the people. Given all the inquisitions, the preoccupation of Anioma women, in particular, was how to live through the crisis and not with the unaesthetic aspects of life.

Under the circumstances, men and women found it difficult to adhere strictly to cultural habits. For instance, Madam Anyafulu, who died in Asaba in 1968, was denied the honor of a burial ceremony. The unfriendly relationship between the federal soldiers and the local people made it risky for her children to accord her such a rite. Her son, who left his hideout for that purpose, was scolded by other relatives for risking his life.[293] Prior to that incident, some had lost their lives trying to accord a dead female relative a proper burial. The bereaved husband was one of the victims. He had rallied some people together to assist and accompany him return his wife's corpse to her natal family for burial, as was the custom. The entourage was met by federal soldiers who shot at the mourners on the grounds that they had the time to bury one single woman, while Nigerian soldiers were dying daily in a war caused by the Igbo and were not receiving the same honor.[294] Many people who died during the war, like Madam Anyafulu, had their burial ceremonies performed after the hostilities.

Marriage ceremonies had always attracted a lot of fanfare among the people of Anioma. People married in the course of the war, but the celebrations were deprived of the usual trappings of noise and merriment. The federal soldiers' aversion to noise robbed life of color and compassion. Women in particular were restrained from giving spontaneous expression to their feelings both on joyful and mournful occasions.

The exigencies of war tended to disrupt households. It was quite common for father, mother, and children to find themselves in different locations. The hardship and difficulties that accompanied the Nigeria–Biafran conflict in many towns worsened its already depressed psychological impact. Women who could not cope with the challenges were obliged to enter into new relationships. Those who held to their marital vows had a difficult time and faced more egregious challenges. Many married women were denied any form of economic assistance because of the absence of their husbands. A number of households came under the headship of women, most of them proving themselves capable organizers of their homes. (In the same manner, some female adolescents were forced by the crisis to shoulder the responsibility of caring for themselves, their aged parents, and younger siblings. In most cases, this was achieved at great emotional and psychological cost to those affected.) In spite of the laudable efforts of many mothers, the family units did not all have a holistic impact on younger members. The clash between cultural observances and the combination of a new order and a hostile environment undermined the efforts of these women. Besides, the conduct of the soldiers who served, albeit briefly, as the ruling class encouraged certain lifestyles that were unacceptable to the people from the standpoint of their social norms. The conflicting interests therefore contributed in weakening the moral base of many families, and some women could not single-handedly ensure orderly and disciplined behavior from their dependents. This proved to be a very burdensome responsibility. Mothers of adolescent girls encountered much pressure from federal soldiers interested in their daughters.[295] They equally battled against the enticing benefits of yielding to the soldiers' demands.

The provision of social amenities was hampered by the war. The destruction of bridges rendered many roads in Anioma unusable and made movement difficult. Roads in very bad condition were not repaired until after the emergency. Schooling was affected by the presence of soldiers in many towns. Girls ten years of age or less could go to school when eventually classes resumed in 1968, but any sign of pubescence put a hold on their studies. Many suspended their education because of this interruption and some either lost the two academic years over the time the war lasted or dropped out from schooling completely.

Certain educational institutions did not function during the crisis. Some schools in Agbor were turned into military camps and for a while served as training centers for soldiers who did not complete their training before the advance of their division. In Aniocha schools served as military barracks or as hostage camps. A number of schools that were neither used as barracks nor as refugee camps remained closed throughout the war. St. Patrick's College, St. Thomas, St. Augustine, St. Rose, St. Brigids, Oboshi Grammar School, and Asaba Girls Grammar School were closed down because of their proximity to the war front. Their students were transferred to other places. It was towards the end of the war when the federal army felt more certain that they have successfully overrun Biafra and was set to win the war that these schools were reopened.

The attitude of the federal soldiers towards the people of Anioma differed from place to place. A few towns were treated humanely while others suffered terribly. The actions of the soldiers, to a reasonable extent, depended on official policy during the war and the inclinations of the unit commanders. Even though the Second Division was notorious for having the highest number of unprofessional soldiers, the presence of Biafran soldiers aggravated situations for townspeople where their presence was felt for any number of reasons. The federal government was less stringent on some areas like Agbor and Igbodo in the Ika area and in most nonriverine towns of Ukwuani than other places in Anioma, particularly those in Aniocha. Schools in Agbor resumed earlier and remained opened until the end of the hostilities. Most students in Aniocha who were able to relocate to Agbor started school there or at Igbodo.[296]

A limited number of hospitals operated in Anioma during the war.[297] No private dispensary or maternity functioned in the course of the crisis except a few church maternity centers and dispensaries in the Ika area and the Nigerian Red Cross Mobile Medical Team from Lagos, which visited a few towns in the Ika and Asaba Divisions in 1968.[298] Government hospitals functioned primarily as military hospitals, with their attention focused on wounded soldiers. Still, those civilians who had the courage to visit them received medical attention. But, since hospital care encompassed such large area few civilians benefited from their services. Government hospitals that functioned during the emergency suffered from both scarcity of drugs and paucity of personnel. The Midwest commissioner for health, J. M. Erugha, attributed the inability of his ministry to provide drugs for the hospitals during the hostilities to the absence of vehicles. He claimed that the state's official cars were seized by Biafran soldiers in the course of their retreat from the Midwest and sent to the Eastern Region.[299] Failure to ensure adequate supply of drugs was compounded by the poor handling of drugs that occurred during the emergency. Some of the available drugs were smuggled out of the hospitals and sold to individuals. Most of the smuggled drugs ended up in Biafra.[300]

The hospitals' level of performance is discernible from an official report stating that in Agbor about eighty infants out of four hundred and twenty registered births died from lack of proper healthcare between January and May 1968.[301] The figure was definitely higher in Aniocha towns, which recorded the highest number of deaths in Anioma and in Midwest State during the emergency, but the military operations precluded keeping similar records in the area. The child mortality rate in Agbor goes to confirm the observation that during civil wars in Africa child mortality is three to four times higher than the continent's average,[302] and that up to 90 percent of the casualties in war around the world are civilians.[303] Most children died from preventable and easily treatable diseases like diarrhea and malaria. The major cause of their deaths was not just the war but the lack of medical attention. In general, civilian casualties in Anioma certainly surpassed military casualties in Midwest State during the war.

The few church missions' medical centers were not spared the scarcity of drugs that besieged Anioma during the hostilities. Being mostly maternity centers, their clients were primarily women. Poverty and insecurity prevented those in need of their services from patronizing them. Moreover, recourse to modern medical practices had not yet become very popular among uneducated women in Anioma by this time. Thus, out of habit, fear of federal soldiers, and the long distances to the nearest hospital or maternity, many women continued to have their babies at home. During this period of hostilities most women interviewed gave birth outside the hospitals and maternity centers, relying on the assistance of friends or on the indigenous professional midwives and sometimes under very crude and unhygienic conditions. For some, periodic relocations hampered their being attended to by even the local midwives. For most health problems, women relied on herbs, local remedies, and indigenous medical practices.

Missionary bodies played important roles in Anioma during the civil war. Mention has already been made of Reverend Samuel Martins, the Baptist minister who acted as a buffer between the civilian population of Issele-ukwu and the federal military unit stationed in that town.[304] Many in Aniocha and Ika areas remember the local and expatriate missionaries of the Church Missionary Society (CMS) and the Roman Catholic Mission (RCM), the earliest of such groups to be established in Anioma for their charitable and humane acts during the war.[305] The Roman Catholic church had largely Irish reverend fathers who had lived among the people, especially in the Ika and Aniocha areas, for many years and who insisted on remaining in their localities during the crisis although British missionaries were evacuated. Ukwuani had no expatriate missionaries and was regarded as spiritually defenseless during the hostilities.

The most prominent wartime missionary in Anioma was the Reverend Jimmy Conron, who was stationed in Asaba. During the Asaba massacres of October 1968, he went round the town consoling the bereaved and administering the rites of the church to those who requested it. Others were Father Mcdonaugh, Father Cardogan, who worked in Ubulu-ukwu; Father J. S. Stephens, who was stationed in Okpanam; and Canon Echenim of the Church Missionary Society or Anglican Church. Unlike the Roman Catholics, the Anglican Church operated only with local clergy. The sight of local persons moving about in militarized areas wearing cassocks generated much suspicion among federal troops, most of whom regarded them as pretenders. Because of this, local Anglican clergy were extremely careful in their activities to avoid being mistaken for Biafran soldiers or labeled Biafran supporters. The Anglican Church also limited the number of their clergy who were visible during the crisis to avoid such confusion. Thus, Canon Echenim had the responsibility for much of Aniocha, which was a very daunting task for just one person. Female missionaries were not as visible as men largely for safety reasons. After December 1967 the Irish sisters and other nuns who remained in Anioma were found mostly in Agbor where there was less harassment of civilians, unlike in Aniocha. They assisted by offering accommodation to refugees and working in the hospitals.[306]

While the missionaries saw to the spiritual well-being of the people, international church organizations took care of the physical aspect. Misericordia (Heart of Mercy) and Caritas, both Catholic religious organizations, sent tons of food, drugs, and clothing to Aniocha for war victims and refugees and to schools in Agbor and its environs, which were reopened after the subjugation of the Ika area.[307] Misericordia offered scholarships through the Catholic church to Anioma war orphans to support their secondary education during the war.

When Father Conron died in Ireland years after the war, his missionary order notified the people of Asaba, who mourned him profoundly, recalling the ways he helped them during the war. The following was said of him in appreciation of his services to the local people during the war:

> There's nothing like having a man who will give you water when you need it, who will give you a piece of cloth to cover your nakedness, who will even help you to bury your brother, mother, and father when you are crying. Father Conron did all these for us. He gave us shelter and he gave us food.[308]

Chapter 5

WOMEN AND SURVIVING THE WAR

SURVIVAL STRATEGIES

War tests the limits of human endurance. Crisis was once described as "mountaintop experiences" that lead to the discovery of a person's latent strength, which would otherwise remain dormant.[1] The assertion appropriately mirrors the reaction of women in Anioma to the challenges posed by the Nigerian civil war. The commencement of military operations initially induced inertia, borne out of fear, in most women; but the feeling did not linger, because the absence of the men altered in particular the economic scale and made women an important economic factor throughout the emergency. Those who had hitherto rarely taken an independent action without the input of their husbands and other male relatives were forced to do so by both orthodox and unorthodox means.

Two categories of women were discernible in Anioma during the war. Those were the displaced, some of whom took refuge in the bush and in farm areas, and those who remained within their communities. From these two groups a third group emerged, composed of women who intermittently altered their places of residence by moving from their homes to the bush and *vice – versa,* according to the shifting fortunes of the war. The number of women in each of these categories was reasonably high. The women were in places that they hoped would ensure greater relief from the consequences of the raging conflict. Certain benefits accrued to each group from their places of residence, just as there were attendant disadvantages too. It is uncertain that the advantages favored one group more than another. What is obvious is that a strong determination existed in women in all categories to survive.

The majority of the displaced women residing in the bush and farm areas were idle for quite a while during the war. At the onset of their displacement they neither pursued a profession nor engaged in any worthwhile profitable activity. What concerned them most was establishing enough distance between them and the federal soldiers. They depended largely on charity for sustenance and therefore adopted begging as their common activity. They sought help from people who came to the bush for a respite, to attend market sessions, or to tend their farms. Occasionally they would visit nearby communities to ask for assistance from people they met on the assumption that those not displaced were in a better economic situation than they.

Displaced women did not organize themselves for the purpose of begging, but it was discovered that all who lived in the bush, at one time or the other, depended on charity.[2] Begging was not considered demeaning, nor was it confined to a particular age group. Soliciting aid was seen by the women involved as transitory and the gains were transient. The individuals approached for assistance rarely ignored the interim beggars. The desperation prevalent at the time made the people willing to help each other. Aid came in the form of food items and sometimes a few coins, but such aid was hardly sufficient. Food was scarce throughout the war that donors could dispense with only a little from what they had. Sometimes the women would arrive at an abandoned settlement presumed to belong to farmers from the Igbo heartland, east of the Niger, and avail themselves of whatever useful items the original inhabitants left behind.[3] In the Ndosimili area of Ukwuani in particular displaced women were able to fish from their hideouts using their baskets.

Proceeds from begging were supplemented with the rewards from bush combing, a totally different activity from the bush-combing exercises of the federal army discussed in chapter

3. Women's bush combing was to search for food, especially edible leaves growing in the wild. Mushrooms, tortoise, snails, and rodents emerged as important food items. The people, particularly children, had been familiar with these alternative food sources long before the war but hardly exploited them. During the crisis such items became major sources of food. Displaced women who took refuge in the bush prepared their meals with whatever was available. Some rarely made use of local condiments and ingredients for food preparation.[4] Their greatest problem was the unavailability of salt. Salt famine prevailed throughout Anioma. Women in riverine communities or close to the Atlantic improvised by boiling natural salt water to extract the salt in it. In Aniocha, the acute scarcity of salt led some to substitute ash for salt.[5]

When it became obvious to the displaced women that the conflict was not likely to end soon, many devised better coping strategies. The majority engaged in farming. The occasional setback was their periodic relocation. Even then they managed to visit the old farms from their new places of abode to take some produce. Those who migrated to communities other than their own also made attempts to secure uncultivated portions of land, however small, for farming. Farming was the primary engagement of most women during the war, yet there was a general decline in agricultural activities in Anioma because of the hostilities and the military operations.[6] Hunger and the inability to practice specialized crafts confirmed women as dedicated farmers. Much pilfering of farm products occurred in those months of inactivity. The federal troops arrived in Anioma just before the year's harvest period, with the result that most farms were not harvested, being left to the mercy of bush rovers who included soldiers. Biafran soldiers, cut off in Anioma, raided people's farms; but in Ossissa, Utagba-ogbe, and Ogwashi-ukwu women also complained that federal soldiers looted and destroyed their farms.[7]

Military hostility, fear of molestation, and restriction prevented women from going to their farms before their towns were brought under effective control of the federal army. The process took some days in a few inaccessible towns to accomplish but a number of weeks in others. In all of Anioma the subjugation of the towns was effected in the first three months of the war. Women in towns with resident federal soldiers farmed close to their homes and in farming areas within their towns. The practice of going to distant farms was seriously checked, and for safety reasons women visited their farms in groups. They were careful to avoid breaking curfew. Usually they worked with a sense of trepidation and always had their ears alert to strange sounds. The faint sound of a gun had them scampering away for shelter. Yet with all their caution casualties still occurred, as the case of Igwe Obu from Umunede revealed.[8]

Farming was irregular and hazardous. Whatever disrupted the truce period and put the federal soldiers on their guard adversely affected it. One of the features of wartime farming was that the farmers poorly tended to their farms. The lingering climate of insecurity rendered farming strenuous and less rewarding than it should have been. No new crop was introduced in Anioma during the war, but the women preferred fast-yielding crops. Thus, yam relinquished its pride of place to cassava, which became more widely cultivated at the time.[9] Don Ohadike has demonstrated the shift from yam, a superior and male crop, to cassava in 1917 after a series of political and economic calamities that resulted in the absence of men, who until then were the sole cultivators of yam in Igboland.[10] Five decades after those incidents, and in the course of the civil war when men were largely absent from the scene, people in the war-torn areas watched as yam cultivation was once more replaced with cassava and women resumed their role as its foremost cultivators. In other words, the socio-economic and political factors that hampered the cultivation of yam promoted the cultivation of cassava.

Farming in Aboh and Okpai in the Ukwuani area was more difficult than in other parts of Anioma. The constant infiltration of Biafran soldiers into those towns, even as late as 1969, made life much unsettled for women. In Asaba in Aniocha, the situation was also grave. Asaba women and later Ibusa and Oko women kept as hostages in refugee camps and at different periods during the emergency could not farm. The harsh and stringent treatment meted out to the people of Asaba in particular disrupted their economic pursuits for a considerable period. As a result, from time to time the federal army distributed raw food items to those in refugee camps to help alleviate their food problem. When the people left the camps, they required official permits tagged "passes" in order to move about within their home town and to engage in any kind of activity, including farming.

Female farmers did not produce all that they needed. There were always items like cosmetics and clothing whose supply could not be guaranteed through farming. Besides, farm produce rarely lasted from one farming season to the other. What farming could not provide came by way of trade and exchange. These competed with farming for attention during the emergency. Trade during the war came in two forms that existed side by side: local trade and trade with the seceding republic. By its nature and scope, trade with Biafra was at the onset not considered a transborder or crossborder trade. It however became a transaction between members of the same ethnic group who found themselves in different political and geographical areas. Anioma women actively participated in and benefited from this trade.

The federal government's economic blockade on the Eastern Region necessitated a boycott of trading links between that region and other regions of the federation. The Eastern Region utilized the months before the outbreak of hostility to stock up supplies from Anioma. Food items, including meat, were moved in incredible quantities from Anioma to the Eastern Region despite Lt. Col. David Ejoor's commitment to enforcing the blockade in the Midwest.[11] The sealing of the Niger Bridge connecting the Midwest with the Eastern Region did little to check the trade relations between the two Igbo groups, as canoes and boats were employed to cross the River Niger. Equally ineffective were official directives prohibiting travelers going to Asaba from the Eastern Region to carry more than five pounds. The same official injunctions banned foodstuffs from the Aniocha, Ika, and Ukwuani areas from finding their way to eastern Nigeria and directed the seizure of lorries loaded with foodstuffs bound for Onitsha from Anioma.[12]

In spite of all these, Asaba had a site where canoes plied a thriving trade with the Eastern Region. In addition, the old and abandoned marine wharf at Asaba was resuscitated for trade purposes.[13] The trade association between the two Igbo groups continued until the war erupted. The campaign to flush out Biafran soldiers from Anioma and to severe the links between Anioma and Biafra did little to affect this trade. Until August 1967, the trade route was from Asaba to Onitsha. From September of that year, the route became Isheagu–Abala–Oko-ogbele. Three months later, when federal troops were alerted to the magnitude of the trade between Anioma and Biafra, traders were forced to make some modifications in the trade organization. Instead of daylight hours, they resorted to moving at night. They changed most of the foot tracks but still retained the usual route, which took them from Isheagu to Abala and into Oko-ogbele to Biafra. On the whole, Isheagu was left to its own devices, but people from nearby towns, afraid of the danger that trade with Biafra would expose them to, sometimes raised the alarm about trade. The sacking of Isheagu in May 1968, however, resulted in further alteration of the route used. It was crucial to the Nigerian federal government and to its armed forces for this vital economic link between Anioma and the Republic of Biafra to be severed because it hampered the effectiveness of the starvation policy intended to force Biafra into surrender. The sacking of Isheagu was primarily intended to achieve that goal.

Unaware of the extent of the trade relationship with Biafra and the commitment of the people of Anioma to that informal contract, the battalion commander who authorized the military aggression on Isheagu presupposed that he had eventually succeeded in destroying the transborder trade by razing Isheagu and its market. He erroneously concluded that Isheagu was the only place in Anioma for "trafficking in foodstuff and dangerous commodities" between the people of Biafran and the Igbo of the Midwest.[14] Contrary to the assumption of the federal commander, the transborder traders were not subdued; rather they merely shifted westwards to Nsukwa from where they moved to Abala, then to Oko-ogbele and on to Atani in Biafra. Concurrently, other trade routes existed. In Aniocha, traders moved from Issele-azagba and neighboring towns to Ngbotukpe, then to Oko-anala or Oko-ogbele, and finally into Biafra. There was also the route from Okpanam to Anwai in Asaba, to Eke-mkpu, and then into Anam in Biafra. Many routes existed through which traders from Anioma moved in and out of Biafra, but the majority of them passed through Oko-ogbele or around it. The traders were adept at changing routes at any time to outwit vigilant federal soldiers. In the Ukwuani area, Obikwele and Okpai served as alternative routes to Abala and Atani.

The transborder trade was popularly called the "attack trade" in Biafra, because it took the traders across the frontlines; but in Anioma it was generally referred to as the "night market," the "bush market," or simply "trade with the east." These names did not only indicate that it was a trade contract with the Igbo, east of the Niger, but pointed to other features of the trade: That it was carried out at night and in the bush. Outside Anioma and Biafra, it was called "frontline trading," because of the involvement of soldiers in the northern sector of the trade (that is, between Biafra and northern Nigeria border towns).[15]

From its inception, the participants in the trade were from the three sections of Anioma. The traders spent most of their time (some literally lived) in the bush because it enhanced their chances of moving in and out of Anioma. By 1968, starvation had become a major problem in Biafra and was aggravated by overpopulation. The federal government's economic and trade embargo and the policy of starvation initiated during the war compounded the food situation in the seceding republic. At the same time, following the Biafran attacks of April 1968 on federal units in Anioma, food scarcity, hunger, and hardship became more pronounced from then on in the affected Anioma towns, resulting in more people taking part in the trade with the people of Biafra. It was, therefore, partly in the bid for personal survival as well as to help solve the food crisis of Biafra that many in Anioma took part in the transborder trade.

Although, until the sacking of Isheagu, the number of women in this trade was high, after May 1968 their number was significantly reduced. The women, along with the men, who braved the risks of trading with Biafrans were branded as hardened individuals, which was not a compliment by Igbo standards. Adolescent females took part in the trade in its early stages, serving as carriers and porters. Their duty consisted of carrying items of trade for the traders from collection site to transaction site. This earned them, and their male counterparts, the nickname "job men." For the equivalent of fifty pence (or thirty U.S. cents), the young women walked a distance of fourteen hours daily to transport a cargo of goods each. In those days, the finacial reward per trip was considered worth the trouble. Girls who were unable to walk fast could not cope with the difficulties of the trade and dropped out on the business early, while those who were unaccustomed to walking long distances developed swollen feet after each journey.[16] As federal soldiers tightened their hold on Anioma in May 1968, the trade became very hazardous and the role of these carriers became unnecessary.

Items of trade comprised everything that was needed in Biafra but especially food, salt, cigarettes, tobacco, potassium, batteries, and medicines. Goods were obtained from Agbor, which replaced Onitsha as the major market that served Anioma during the war. The presence of federal soldiers and the establishment of their military base in Agbor were partly responsible for stimulating the rise and growth of a vibrant trading market at Boji-boji and women from different locations in Anioma patronized it using their "passes." However, the restriction on movement and the poor transportation system during the war period limited the number of those who used Agbor as a purchasing center. Women in Ukwuani and in towns around Nsukwa used Nsukwa as their purchasing center. There were, though, women who collected their wares through a house-to-house hunt. Acquiring satisfactory quantities of saleable goods that way saved them the trouble of going to Agbor or to Nsukwa for their purchases.

The place of exchange was often the bush while the medium of exchange was with the Nigerian pounds, then at par with the British pounds. But on 1 January 1968 the federal government made some alterations on the currency notes as a war strategy to nullify Biafra's foreign exchange; which, according to the federal government, was a misuse of the country's currency notes. Biafra responded by minting its own currency and recalling the old money in circulation, replacing them with the new Biafran currency. The Biafran currency was illegal for transactions in sections of the country under the federal government. Meanwhile, federal officials in charge of the circulation of Nigerian currency failed to freely make the new money available. This brought much hardship to the people of Anioma and made many vulnerable to exploitation. Racketeers from Benin and other major cities in the Midwest swarmed Anioma and bought up large sums of the old currency in exchange for very small sums of the new currency. The racketeers succeeded in exploiting their victims because the latter, afraid of the military situation in Anioma, were unwilling to travel outside their immediate environment in search of a place where they would exchange the old currency for the new one on an equal basis.[17] Also, the closure of most banks in Anioma worked to the advantage of the racketeers. All the banks in Asaba, for instance, suspended services throughout the war, while only one bank rendered services to the public in Agbor. People had nowhere to go to exchange their old Nigerian currency.

The federal government had a spectacular economic victory when it effected the change in currency. Substantial sums of Nigerian currency in Anioma and in Biafra, including the reserves that had been in the Enugu and Benin vaults of the Central Bank, became instantly worthless.[18] The currency change had untold impact on the Anioma generally but most especially on the transborder traders. The new Biafran money was of very little value in Anioma. A thousand Biafran pounds was the equivalent of twenty Nigerian pounds.[19] For a while, trade in Anioma was crippled because of the difficulty in obtaining the new currency. Gradually, the situation resulted in the emergence of a class of women who facilitated trade by changing money for traders at a profit. This made it possible for traders without the new Nigerian currency and those with Biafran pounds, which were illegal for transactions in Nigeria, to receive the acceptable legal tender with which they conducted their transactions in Anioma. Scarcity of the new Nigerian notes led to the Nigerian coins being commonly used for transactions, although they were cumbersome. They did however enjoy a far higher purchasing value than the Biafran notes.[20]

The transborder trade was carried out secretly and for women, fearfully too. Female traders most often relied on professional fishermen to sail the Niger into Biafra at night. Any trick that could disguise their activities and grant them safe conduct was resorted to, e.g., using a coffin to transport wares. Traders did not always take their supplies into Biafra. Transactions could take place wherever Biafrans were found. It was also normal for traders to sell their goods in Oko-ogbele or Abala or in any of the border towns to either Biafran traders who ventured that far inside the federally controlled areas or to colleagues intent on getting into Biafra. Traders living close to the exchange centers usually waited until news of the arrival of Biafran traders filtered in before moving out their goods. Besides carting away trade items, Anioma traders assisted individuals wanting to leave Anioma for Biafra or for towns in the Western Region to make good their escape.[21] This often amounted to smuggling individuals out at night.

The transborder trade was of great benefit to Biafra and to the people of Anioma as well. Even though it primarily served Biafra, it was through transborder trade that many women in Anioma had access to needed items and enhanced their economic power. The trade was risky and endangered the lives of its female participants. Those caught by federal soldiers with large quantities of salt, batteries, cigarettes, and potassium or were suspected of sending items to Biafra were severely dealt with. The risks involved in the trade were major deterrents to promising new entrants midway through the crisis. An unknown number of women lost their lives through their involvement in this trade. One well-remembered victim was Okwuaba from Asaba, whose burial ceremony was held in 1991, twenty-one years after the war.[22]

Anioma women involved in the transborder trade had different opinions about it. Some saw it as their means of spiting the federal soldiers, retaliating for their atrocious activities in Anioma, and aiding the young Biafran Republic. Many female traders derived some satisfaction from the opportunity it furnished them to undermine federal efforts to crush Biafra. In effect, what women could not verbalize was communicated by their actions. In spite of the desire for vengeance, some traders genuinely engaged in the trade with the humanitarian intent of helping their fellow Igbo survive the war. Others did it solely for profit and self-interest. The frustrations the federal army encountered in their attempts to arrest and break this trade link between Biafra and Anioma is evident in their repeated but unsuccessful pleas to the Anioma throughout the hostilities to cooperate with them and give up the trade.[23] Federal commanders acknowledged that Biafra's ability to hold out as long as it did was partly due to this trade.

With the exclusion of the transborder trade, local exchanges of goods continued in Anioma during the war. This was done chiefly by women, many more of whom took to trading as a means of coping with the menace of hunger and unavailability of necessary provisions than from choice. The arrival of federal troops initially led to the desertion of the markets and women began to meet in the bush and farm areas for trade. Sometimes they converged in each other's homes to avoid exposure and bomb attacks. The custom in Aniocha by which traders waited for the omu to ceremonially declare the market open for transactions was not strictly adhered to and sometimes, depending on the intensity of the military operations, was not observed at all.

The war did not just result in the relocation of market sites but in changes in their session times. New markets sprang up as a result of war exigencies. The number of women found in any market at any given time was nil compared to what was the case during peacetime. Besides, trade lasted for a few hours, sometimes as little as one hour.[24] Long-distance trade was discontinued. The non-Igbo could not attend markets in Anioma because of military uncertainty. Their Igbo partners were equally unwilling to relate with them after their brutal treatment of Anioma indigenes at the onset of the crisis. Their manifested hostility had a far-reaching impact on intergroup relations in Midwest State in particular. In addition to the unwillingness of Anioma women to trade with the Edo and the Urhobo/Isoko, in most communities in the Ika area up till mid-1968, any form of relationship with other groups in the Midwest was considered an abomination.[25]

The dearth of money led local female traders to revert to the barter system. The reduced numbers of people of Anioma origin in paid employment adversely affected the availability and circulation of money in Anioma. As late as June 1968, T. E. A. Saluti, the Midwest commissioner for trade and industry, expressed surprise that civil servants from Ika, Aboh, and Asaba Divisions (referring to Ika, Ukwuani, and Aniocha areas) had not returned to their places of work.[26] On one hand, the comments of the commissioner confirm that many civil servants from Anioma were not back to work nine months after the commencement of military operations in Anioma. On the other, it revealed the indifference of the Midwest government to the predicament of civil servants from Anioma during the hostilities and the failure to create an enabling atmosphere that would encourage them to return to their jobs. And this was in spite of the head of state's assertion three months earlier that the federal government was "determined to do all in its power to ensure that no Ibo man is molested or intimidated anywhere in this country."[27] Little was done to protect the Anioma who were displaced by military operations and the harassment of federal soldiers. Rather, Major Ogbemudia quickly announced that Igbo civilians of the Midwest who failed to report to their places of work before the end of October 1967 should consider themselves to have voluntarily retired.[28] It was less than a year before the end of the war when the commander of the Second Division gave verbal assurances in Benin City that the army was there to protect all civilians and to encourage people to report cases of maltreatment immediately after the incident to the division's headquarters.[29]

Food was scarce during the occupation, although the degree differed from town to town, and depending on the location and the degree of the federal control. Money with which to make purchases was also unavailable. Many traders found themselves in possession of the same items, thus frustrating trade and exchange. Most of what women sold were the proceeds from their farms, but some sold their personal belongings—jewelry, apparels, and household goods—or exchanged them for other items they needed but had no money to buy. An individual would buy an item like soap and exchange part of it with another item that she was unable to buy for lack of funds. The war converted such commonplace items as milk, salt, and cosmetics into scarce or essential commodities. In a bid to avoid running into debt as a result of the war, the federal government banned the importation of many goods, including commonplace items like butter.[30] One result of this wartime economic policy was the high price of basic food items in places under the control of the federal government. It was common for women in Anioma to hoard salt and later sell it at an exorbitant price. A number of women became rich by selling salt but the degree of their prosperity fell far below peacetime level. Yet, going by the general poverty of the people, dealers in salt appeared reasonably at an advantage.

Trading in salt had its negative side however. Whoever was caught with a quantity above what was approved or considered normal by federal soldiers suffered serious humiliation as punishment. Throughout Anioma, people recalled instances of brutality meted out to women for possessing salt in some appreciable quantity. In Ogwashi-ukwu, culprits were paraded at the town's public square and were ordered to demonstrate to spectators where and how they hid the substance. This usually led to a near total stripping of such women, as most of them were caught with salt concealed amidst their wrappers.[31]

The local traders like their transborder colleagues procured their goods from Agbor using "passes" issued by federal soldiers. It was not in all towns that women were freely issued passes permitting them to move outside their towns. Women in Ukwuani living close to either a creek or a river were for some time not allowed passes because of the suspicion that they would abuse the privilege in favor of the people of Biafra.[32] The confiscation of bicycles belonging to some women in Ukwuani compounded their situation and temporarily deterred other traders from venturing out on theirs. As a result, a trip to Agbor was either made by walking the long distance or by hitching a ride in military vehicles. A number of women shied away from either of the two options, satisfying themselves with goods procured from communities closest to them rather than from Agbor.[33]

Fear inhibited trade. In the markets women sometimes dispersed in a panic, as they had while farming, at the sound of an unfamiliar noise. Sometimes, too, their dispersal was motivated by the presence of federal soldiers. This occurred often in Asaba, where soldiers occasionally visited the market just to seek out women to chat up and others to extort money from. Harassment from federal soldiers was common during their period of occupation of Anioma. They carefully searched women on their way to and from the market, at which points those carrying outlawed items were caught. In many instances, those returning from the market were made to relinquish some of their purchases to the soldiers at the numerous checkpoints. Women who were able to communicate in Hausa suffered less than others.

The civil war and the presence of federal soldiers in Anioma also brought about changes in the trade pattern of the people and in the original location of markets. In Ukwuani, for instance, markets were moved inland from the riverbanks. The Afia-eze market in Utagba-ogbe has since maintained its new site at the center of the town instead of its primeval location on the bank of the Ase creek. The growth of the market at Boji-boji in the Ika area was a reaction to the exit from the town of people of eastern Igbo origin on the eve of the arrival of federal troops in Agbor. From oral testimonies, many Ika indigenes took to trading in an attempt to emulate the Igbo east of the Niger, who distinguished themselves as ingenious and successful traders while in their midst, and to fill the gap created by their absence from that subsection of Anioma.[34]

In Asaba, in particular, a minimarket locally called a "mami-market" was started and held in the evenings in place of the town's major markets. Mostly wives of federal soldiers patronized it. Two items were introduced into the community through the auspices of the soldiers and this minimarket: the cooked and dried hide of cattle nicknamed *kpomo,* which served as meat; and *acha*—similar to millet but with very tiny seeds and prepared as pudding—which was widely grown in northern Nigeria.[35] The condition of Asaba women made the development of the minimarket possible. With their intermittent confinement during the hostilities, wives of federal soldiers started the minimarket as a place where residents could purchase what they needed. Asaba women, on leaving the refugee camps, required passes to take part in the trade.

The militarization of Asaba made life very difficult for the indigenes such that a few desperate women who had passes picked refuse dumps in the barracks in search of discarded food items. Partly decaying tubers of yam, bags of rice, and garri, and other items were retrieved from the garbage heap. The edible portions of the salvaged items became food to these women and their households.[36]

The civil war was a period of insecurity but interspersed with opportunities. The desire to live through the crisis was strongly entrenched in many and was responsible for most of what women did. Hawking and running minirestaurants, not too common in Anioma before the war, were well indulged in. Hawking was preferred in most towns to the normal transactions of the market place because of its propensity to reach a wide range of people. Women made use of their little daughters and wards, often rarely more than ten years of age, to carry their products around, as was the custom in the big cities of northern Nigeria before the war. At their age their mothers and guardians assumed that they would not be easy targets of sexual abuse by soldiers, but this was not always the case. Hawkers operated within their communities and concentrated on fast foods. Soldiers were the primary consumers of their products. The patronage of the civilian community was not as high, for many could not readily pay for the products like the soldiers. The items hawked did not enjoy the wide circulation that had been anticipated. The various hideouts were not penetrated and most displaced women did not have access to necessary items like soap, but this also was partly the result of their poverty.

Minirestaurants and drinking houses sprang up in towns with large concentrations of federal soldiers, notably, at Agbor (in the Ika area), Akwukwu-Igbo, Illah (in Aniocha), and Utagba-ogbe (in Ukwuani). For the most part, women manned these businesses, while a few men also took part in towns where the soldier-civilian relationship was less traumatic for civilians. The chief clients of the restaurants and drinking houses were soldiers. In Akwukwu-Igbo, one of such businesses began by coincidence and at the initiative of some federal soldiers. While on a routine check to ensure that the indigenes complied with the laws that governed civilian activities in the subjugated areas, a group of soldiers attracted by the flicker of a light arrived at the house of Regina Ijeh, a nursing mother.[37] In the process of interrogating the offender they learnt that she grew up in northern Nigeria but was forced back to Anioma by the 1966 pogrom. This information and the knowledge that the lit lantern was for the sake of a newborn baby tempered the harshness of the soldiers. She was interviewed on the spot about her knowledge of northern cuisine and, convinced that she could be trusted, was requested by the soldiers to prepare northern dishes for them. Regina Ijeh's home, from that moment on, was transformed into a makeshift restaurant, and her state of inactivity gave way to a lucrative business that guaranteed a relatively steady income throughout the war, setting her financially above most other women. She enjoyed certain privileges from her work. Her movements were not as circumscribed as that of most women, who needed passes to move about, and who were exposed in spite of their passes to harassment depending on the whims of the soldiers. She could visit other towns to make purchases for her business or sometimes was provided with the food items and ingredients for the meals while she did the cooking, using her balcony as the dining room. She was paid in installments, and from the profit she made was able to sustain her family during the occupation.[38] In Agbor and Illah, women involved in a similar engagement took the initiative and were rewarded with the patronage of Nigerian soldiers. The basic problem they all encountered was the failure of the soldiers always to pay for the services rendered or for what they obtained on credit. Consequently, while these women made some gains from the business, they also forfeited part of their profit.

Another aspect of the food business involved women working as contractors for federal units. Gladys Obi operated in Asaba while Agnes Odagwe did the same at Utagba-ogbe. Neither of the two had been a contractor before. Their jobs required making bulk purchases of food items for the military units quartered in their towns. They provided the initial capital and sold their purchases at a profit to the federal units.

Proceeds from the sale of local gin provided an income for some women during the war. Distilling and marketing this product was not uncommon in Anioma, but they have never been officially approved. The war situation drove female dealers in local gin further underground. All aspects of the production of the gin and its distribution were carefully concealed because of their illegality. In the Ukwuani area, Emu women were the professionals and the famous producers of this drink. Dealers in neighboring towns, using every ounce of discretion, bought from them and marketed the gin in their respective communities, taking care to avoid attracting the attention of law enforcement agents, which might result in their apprehension, although some agents secretly patronized these illegal dealers.[39]

One group of local professionals who thrived all over Anioma during the war was the local medical practitioners. Ritual specialists, soothsayers, and diviners all belonged to this group. Such individuals were highly in demand at the time. The growth of Christianity in the twentieth century was instrumental in decreasing the number of clients who patronized these practitioners by the time the war broke out. The situation was altered dramatically during the crisis. The troubled state of the generality of the people in Anioma gave ritual specialists a fresh allure and resulted in undisguised syncretism. Many professed Christians borrowed aspects of the indigenous religious practices that they thought would be of benefit to them. The female practitioners enjoyed the interest reposed on their profession and on their person during the emergency. Their ministrations were so properly rewarded that on average they found themselves above the poverty line during those difficult times.

The chief clients of the ritual specialists and diviners were civilians anxious to safeguard their lives and those of their relatives and were also federal soldiers angling for promotion. Part of what the ritual specialists did was to prepare charms and herbal mixtures reputed to guarantee the safety of their clients and their wards. The latter were often young men serving as combatants for either of the contending armies. Survival charms were also made on demand for individuals living in endangered sections of Anioma. Gladys Obi, who also was a member of this group of professionals, called the charms she made for federal soldiers "luck."[40] With a sense of self-accomplishment, she announced that she "gave luck to soldiers." This particular charm was to work in such a way as to initiate sporadic progress in their military careers. Another charm served to make the recipients invulnerable to bullets. On the whole, various charms and herbal mixtures were made for clients for different reasons. A peculiar but notable one served to strengthen the relationship between a couple. It was made on demand for women in polygynous marriages who wanted to hold the affection of their husbands; but during the war, unmarried women demanded it to help them retain their partners.

Some female ritual specialists for a number of reasons did not diversify their activities to accommodate unforeseen developments like the accelerated recruitment of soldiers, the existence of a habitat beneficial to disease pathogens, or the instances of individuals pursuing life styles that facilitated the spread of such skin problems as yaws prevalent at the time. For instance, the Iyase-omu[41] of Issele-ukwu deliberately curtailed the number of people who benefited from her services out of concern for her son, who was a Biafran soldier. The fear that he might not survive the war rendered her psychologically and emotionally unstable and unable to bring herself to solve the problems of others. She restricted her services to the preparation of those charms that would ensure the safe return of those fighting for Biafra, including her son, and was careful not to cause the death of any one during the period to avoid retribution from the gods, which she feared might come in the form of her son's death.[42]

Even with their limited activities, female ritual specialists provided healthcare for their patients and battled the spread of diseases in their towns. Gonorrhea, syphilis, and yaws were reported to have come with the federal soldiers and were prevalent in towns with resident units. The menace and spread of these diseases especially was alluded to as the worst effect of the war. Infected individuals in many towns sought relief from ritual specialists and indigenous medical practitioners. Their condition was not only disconcerting, but also equally embarrassing. The social stigma associated with venereal diseases during this period did not encourage those afflicted to seek help in public hospitals. Unfortunately, besides government hospitals that served chiefly as military hospitals, private hospitals and other care-providing centers were for the most not operational. The ritual specialists and indigenous medical practitioners, judging from the assessment of the people, did not perform poorly even though they exploited the greed, ignorance, and fear of those who sought their services.[43]

Commercially, the local manufacturing industry suffered the most during the war. The women in this sector were unable to continue with the production of their goods because of the disruptions and uncertainty of the war period. Weaving and the production of pottery wares most especially received little attention during the crisis. The famed Isheagu potters were either hiding in the bush or were refugees in other towns. The pottery and weaving industries required a less turbulent environment to flourish, but this was nonexistent during the war. With a notable number of the adult population in Anioma without any paid employment it was unthinkable to many people to patronize these professionals. Some women preferred selling their hand-woven clothes in order to meet more pressing needs. In reality, the demand for these products was not sufficient to keep the manufacturers reasonably occupied.

Women in paid employment had a less difficult time. The few female nurses, teachers, secretarial staff, and casual workers who did not give up their work because of the war and those recruited by the Second Division to help with administrative functions in their headquarters and in the hospitals were able to sustain themselves from their salaries. Women who were caught up in places where there was a suspension of civil engagement escaped to less turbulent areas. One of them, Anasthesia Okonmah, after three months in the bush escaped in July 1968 to Issele-ukwu. From her job as a typist she was able to replace the wardrobe she abandoned when she fled Ibusa in April 1968.

Paid employment had its share of distractions but it was a more certain source of sustenance for the emerging crop of female civil servants in Anioma. Locating the headquarters of the Second Division of the Nigerian army at Umunede fostered the temporary employment for some women as casual workers. There were not many female teachers. There were more informally trained nurses than teachers or typists. Most primary schools had only one or two or no female teachers at all.[44] The education of women in Anioma did not begin in earnest until after the civil war. It was therefore after the crisis that more female civil servants emerged in Anioma. For those already in the civil service during the hostilities, the condition under which they worked was less than ideal. They contended with the constant threat of a military clash resulting from Biafran military infiltration, the threat of stray bullets, and the mischievous acts of those who preyed on the fears and insecurity of others. The testimony of Ngozi Ochei, a teacher in Ogwashi-ukwu who went back to work in 1968, gives an inkling into the life of civil servants, at least those in Ogwashi-ukwu, during the war.

> Almost every night somebody would raise an alarm that Biafran soldiers had come. We would all run away and return the next day. The same alarm was sometimes raised during school sessions. In one of such occasions, our headmaster was shot dead.... We lived daily in panic. We were so uncertain of staying alive the next moment that for each hour we lived we thanked God. One day the Biafran soldiers came... and we all ran away from the town.... I had no plans at all for myself during the war. ... At the end of each

> month I would collect my salary and eat whatever I could....[45]

Surviving the war took various forms. In addition to those already discussed there were marriages to federal soldiers and the dating of federal army officers. Part of the reason why some married and unmarried women resorted to such liaisons was the need to end the severe hardship they faced. Excluding the fortune of holding paid jobs, relationships with military men provided the surest means of getting food to eat and being certain of living till the next day. Other advantages attended such relationships. The women involved were freed from the psychological torment that fear and uncertainty imposed. They could move about freely when others were more circumspect. In terms of financial standing, they were better placed and, through their soldier friends, had access to goods that were widely unavailable. No wonder some observers reported that the grass was greener around the soldiers.

Midway through the war more women encouraged and courted such liaisons. In Ubulu-ukwu, a recurring saying among women in relationships with soldiers was "Isele eju m obo aka," meaning "My hands are filled with money."[46] Other women, it was believed, were thus attracted and encouraged to have their own military consorts. Many people in Anioma frowned on such liaisons and condemned the relationships with soldiers as immoral and licentious. Men particularly felt that it was greed and the inability to endure privations that encouraged women to accept the attention from federal combatants, especially people of non-Igbo origin. Some quickly cited this as one example of how the war corrupted their women and contrasted it with the prewar situation when northerners seemed too timid to approach and speak to Igbo girls. Critics of the relationships concluded that hardship caused their women to run after the soldiers, thereby weakening the deference with which women of Igbo origin were treated before the war.

Not all women entered into relationships with soldiers willingly. Other relationships resulted from abduction. Women in either category justified their action with one argument or another. For many it was a means of supporting their families and dependents. Patricia, the girl who was taken by a soldier in 1967 at the age of fifteen and who lived with him as a partner until after the war, saw it as her only means of surviving the war. Contrary to the Igbo tradition, federal soldiers rarely sought the consent of the parents of their female companions before living with them. Most of the unions with military men were no better than cases of two individuals of the opposite sex cohabiting. In many instances it was the female partners who tried to legitimize the relationship by claiming that they and their partners were married. A marital relationship was definitely not the goal for which the majority of the soldiers fixed themselves up so easily with Anioma women. After the war only a few soldiers attempted to marry their wartime female partners in a culturally-acceptable manner, and often they accomplished this by merely paying the bridewealth or part of it. Other aspects of the marriage rites were ignored and by then were unnecessary.

Many relationships contracted during the war ended with the crisis, leaving some unlucky women to cope alone with the children that resulted from the liaisons. In some instances the soldiers did not survive the war, in which case their erstwhile female partners ended up as unofficial widows whose parents bristled with the embarrassment and associated ridicule of having illegitimate grandchildren at a time when such a development was considered odious.

A handful of women not known to have contracted a sexual relationship with soldiers acted as their pimps. Two notable women in this trade were Pauline, the Iyase-omu of Onicha-ugbo; and Gladys Obi, the ritual specialist and contractor from Obamkpa. Gladys presents a good example of women who took up more than one economic function during the war in order to cope with the emergency. The female pimps eased the strain of the fighting on the federal soldiers and lent support to the federal war effort, knowingly or unknowingly. Gladys explained that the women she sought for the soldiers were among those whose condition during the emergency was particularly pitiable. Obviously the level of privation such women suffered made them amenable to prostitution. Their situation was similar to the World War II experiences of Korean women, whose poverty was instrumental in their being forced into prostitution by Japanese soldiers.[47]

The pimps co-ordinated the meeting of two willing individuals. The soldiers hardly asked if a woman was married or at least prior to their meeting. The entire business was done discreetly and yielded great dividends for the organizers. Gladys Obi, for instance, was absorbed into the employ of the military unit in Asaba as the *magajiya*,[48]that is, the mother of the barracks, where she also was given accommodation. As *magajiya*, she became the superintendent of the female members of the barracks. Because of her knowledge of midwifery, she functioned as the barracks' obstetrician, attending to soldiers' wives during pregnancy and at childbirth. She was assigned two junior-ranked soldiers as her adjutants, indicating the degree of her influence. The range of her activities was widened, albeit informally, to include the provision of counseling services for married couples within the barracks. Her job as a contractor for the military unit in Asaba was one of the fringe benefits she derived from working as a pimp. Looking at it more closely, Gladys Obi in her office as *magajiya* would seem to be a caricature of the omu or the barracks' version of that office.

FEMALE LEADERSHIP ROLES

The war did not completely cripple female leadership skills. Women provided leadership for themselves during the emergency without relying on administrative procedures as they existed before the crisis, and this helped them immensely. Among Asaba women who fled the carnage in their town, taking refuge at Achalla Ibusa, a hideout on the outskirts of Ibusa, Gboliwe Nwoji emerged as their facilitator and leader. She not only rallied round the displaced women in that hideout but encouraged their collaboration for their joint survival. Under her, they formed a community of mutual helpers until the end of their displacement.[49]

Encumbered by laws and orders restricting movement and interrupting interpersonal contacts, the omu could not provide adequate leadership for the female members of their respective towns as in peacetime. Although they maintained contacts with their group members, the *otu-omu*, they were handicapped and unable to carry out to the fullest their normal administrative functions during the interim military control of their towns. Yet they remained conscious of their role and whenever possible provided leadership for women under their jurisdiction without challenging the orders of the battalion commanders of the Second Division in Anioma.

Efforts of the omu to guarantee the welfare of women in their towns occurred at different stages of the war in Asaba and Ibusa. In the former, Omu Mgbo-ushie advised the dispersal of men during the period of unrestrained killings in the town. Just before the end of the war, her leadership was terminated with her murder by federal soldiers who blamed their military losses on her spiritual prowess. At Ibusa the omu forestalled the old practice by which Ibusa women attended market sessions in other towns but particularly in Asaba. At the commencement of the military operations the diokpa of Ibusa, the town's local ruler, had wisely advised a suspension of that practice on the premise that it exposed the women to grave danger, particularly since they could not fathom the direction from which federal soldiers would enter Ibusa. The suggestion was meant to preclude a situation in which Ibusa women might be caught unawares in case the federal advance came from either Asaba or Onitsha in Biafra. As it was, the women of Ibusa did not all comply with this injunction, and trade outside Ibusa continued until the evacuation of the town in Easter 1968.

After the return of Ibusa refugees in 1969, the omu called the women together and placed a ban on commercial activities outside the town. Added to the menace from soldiers and stray bullets, cases of abduction of women were growing by the day, making movement unsafe for them. The omu put a tone of finality on her injunction by dropping her staff of office in front of her female subordinates. In spite of the general atmosphere of indiscipline and disregard for established authority prevalent during the emergency the women of Ibusa took the warning seriously and adhered to it till the end of the war. It is believed today that the subsequent growth of the market in Ibusa derives from this incident.[50]

This development in Ibusa in which the Omu took steps to provide guidance for Ibusa women is in striking contrast to that which occurred in Onicha-ugbo, where the Iyase-omu exploited the war situation and functioned as a pimp for the federal soldiers. In place of upholding the honor of womanhood as understood by the community and according to the stipulations of her office, she undermined it by covertly encouraging women into commercial sex. She ensured the troops' comfort by her activities but at the same time lived to be blamed for working against the institution she was chosen to uphold.

ANIOMA WOMEN IN "NIGERIA" DURING THE WAR

Anioma women were not all found in their geographical area during the civil war. Besides those in Biafra, some were scattered in the western part of the country, especially in Lagos and Ibadan, the two major western cities—but not in northern Nigeria. These women for various reasons remained outside their towns during the crisis. Those in Biafra felt they would be safe in the Igbo heartland, but others located in territory completely under the control of the federal government stayed back because of the demands of their job or that of their spouse. The women who found themselves in parts of Nigeria outside Igbo areas did not have an easy time. They experienced fear, insecurity, and constant threat to their lives, limitations on their freedom, denial of their rights, and emotional distress in varying degrees. Senior civil servants suffered less than those lower down the scale.[51] The tribulations of Anioma women outside Anioma and Biafra were exacerbated with Biafra's entry into the Midwest in 1967. When the news of that incursion reached Lagos, people of Igbo origin were sought, arrested, and detained at the Ikeja police station in Lagos. The timely intervention of Nigeria's head of state, who declared that he was not fighting the Igbo but Ojukwu, led to their eventual release.[52] His intervention forestalled what some postulated might have resulted in yet another massacre of the Igbo.

On 1 June 1967, two months before Biafra's incursion into the Midwest, the federal government promulgated the Armed Forces and Police (Special Powers) Decree of 1967. It "conferred special powers on every member of the Nigerian Armed Forces and the Nigerian Police Force to arrest, during the period of emergency, any person who in his presence commits any offence or whom he suspects upon reasonable grounds of having committed an offence." The decree further "empowered the Chief of Staff of the Armed Forces or the Inspector General of Police to order the detention in civil prison or a police station of trouble makers if they are satisfied that such persons are, or recently have been, concerned in acts prejudicial to public order."[53]

The Nigerian head of state would seem to have promulgated the above decree in the best interest of the nation at a time of trouble. But it provided adequate cover to unscrupulous soldiers and police officers to molest people of Igbo extraction. Hence, the presence of armed soldiers in all strategic places and at bus terminals became a constant feature of Lagos life during the war. Anioma women in the city of Lagos were forced to be cautious in their movements. Many wisely kept themselves indoors except when unavoidable. Artisans and other self-employed workers whose business billboards bore Igbo names removed them. It became very risky to be known or identified as an Igbo.

An official announcement through the media credited to the federal government and authorizing people of Igbo origin to be issued with identity cards heightened the tension in the city and the insecurity felt by the Igbo. They were to carry their identity cards on their persons whenever they were outside their homes. The announcement led to a rumor that the Nigerian government, through that medium, intended to find out the exact population of the Igbo in Lagos, with the plan of eventually exterminating them. Every Igbo man and woman was issued with an identity card.

As instances of maltreatment and brutality against the Igbo continued to escalate in Lagos, Anioma women devised means of escaping victimization. They changed their dress styles, appearing only in the standard Yoruba attire of *buba* and *iro*, i.e., Yoruba-type wrapper and matching blouse, which is different from the customary attire of the Igbo or any other Nigerian ethnic group. They also stopped conversing in front of strangers in Igbo. While on one hand they were making efforts to escape trouble, on the other hand, Nigerian soldiers intensified their hunt for Igbo people. On a number of occasions, soldiers disrupted transportation in a bid to track them down. Public vehicles were stopped at various termini and passengers were ordered to disembark only to reboard the vehicles in a queue, but not until they had each given their names and ethnic origins. Men and women discovered to be Igbo were separated from the rest and were not allowed to reboard the vehicles or to continue their journey. To escape such traps, Igbo men and women able to speak other languages claimed to belong to other ethnic groups. The unfortunate ones who gave out their names and correct particulars and others whose disguises were punctured were taken away. Some disappeared and were never seen again.[54]

In June 1968, at Tinubu Square, Lagos, both public and private vehicles were stopped, and many people suspected to be Igbo were publicly executed. One basic issue in these occurrences was the nondistinction made between the Igbo of the former Eastern Region and those of Anioma. The peoples of Nigeria treated both alike. As it were, very few Igbo from the Eastern Region remained in Lagos or in other parts of Nigeria after the declaration of secession, so that the majority of the Igbo found outside Biafra and Anioma at this time were from Anioma.

Organized hunts for the Igbo and other forms of harassment meted out to them by non-Igbo in Lagos induced many to walk to their places of work, no matter the distance, and to shun the use of public transportantion. Midway through the crisis a good number left Lagos for their towns in Anioma or for less politicized towns in obscure parts of the former Western Region. This latter alternative was preferred because of the tension in Midwest State and the tight security there.

Some Anioma who remained in Lagos during the war recalled that their greatest discomfort came from people of Yoruba origin who taunted them and often told them to leave their city and return to Igboland. It was also common to hear a Yoruba addressing an Igbo acquaintance in public, within the hearing range of a police or military officer, with the uncomplimentary term of *Okoro*, an Igbo word meaning "young man," a term other peoples of Nigeria then used in referring to the Igbo. Such mischievous acts in most cases resulted in the rough handling of the hapless Igbo. Mr. Nzeribe, the late Flora Nwapa's husband, was a victim of such unjust brutality towards the Igbo in Nigeria during the war. He was not only beaten up for being an Igbo but was also incarcerated after the attack.[55]

The general feeling of other peoples of Nigeria towards the Igbo during the emergency could best be described as one of antipathy. They were seen and treated like the black sheep of the nation. Not many people wanted to be associated with them or to be recognized as a friend of an Igbo. Their situation was made worse by instances of real and suspected cases of Biafran attacks on Lagos and insurgence against the Nigeria's federal government. Incidents such as the bombing of Lagos by a Biafran plane and several other explosions helped to make the Igbo an unwanted group in the country's capital. Of all groups, female traders of Igbo extraction mostly regretted their stay in the capital city. They were often on the receiving end of an unprovoked barrage of insults and other acts of intimidation from the non-Igbo peoples of Nigeria. The maltreatment of the Igbo increased anytime the war was going badly for Nigeria.[56] The soldiers, the police, and the civilians all together tormented those Igbo found in Nigeria during the crisis, although the government usually used them as showcases to prove that the Igbo were welcomed in Nigeria. These unpalatable experiences added new but negative dimensions to the women's overall concept of intergroup relations in the country.

Chapter 6

HANDLING POSTWAR CHALLENGES

The sufferings of women in Anioma during the Nigerian civil war terminated in part with the capitulation of Biafra on 12 January 1970. With the flight of Odumegwu Ojukwu – the Biafran head of state – to Ivory Coast on the eve of capitulation, Major General Philip Effiong, his assistant, took charge of affairs in Biafra. In an official ceremony held at the Dodan Barracks, Lagos, on 15 January 1970 to mark the end of hostilities, Major General Effiong surrendered to Major General Yakubu Gowon, the Nigerian head of state. He renounced secession on behalf of the Republic of Biafra and accepted the authority of the federal military government of Nigeria.[365] Julian Crutchley and A. J. Parrington[366] likened this defeat of Biafra by the federal government to the defeat of the south by the north in the American civil war. Ironically, the formal surrender of Biafra went unnoticed by the bulk of the rural women in Anioma, many of whom least anticipated such a sudden and undramatic end to the national crisis. Few women in Anioma reported hearing the media broadcasts of Phillip Effiong or of Yakubu Gowon in which the latter announced that "the so-called rising sun of 'Biafra' is set forever."[367]

AFTER THE WAR

In a matter of days many more people in Anioma learnt of the termination of hostilities. The news spread widely in many towns through the efforts of federal soldiers. The initial response of the women varied from place to place. While some were excited and happy, some out rightly disbelieved the information. One set of women, comprising those who had taken refuge in the bush and others in the towns in Aniocha that presently constitute the Oshimili local government area,[368] suspected a ruse from which the federal troops hoped to benefit. As a result, the displaced Ibusa women refused to leave their temporary places of refuge until federal soldiers forced them out of their hideouts.[369]

The general unwillingness of many displaced individuals to return to their homes was acknowledged by James Oluleye, the commander of the Second Division in the Midwest, and also by the Midwest military governor. A military helicopter was dispatched to fly over the bush and the various hideouts in Anioma to inform the people of the end of the war and to encourage them to return to their homes. Lydia Akazue and Augustina Okogo, both from Isheagu, were among the women who accepted the encouragement and eventually decided to leave their hiding places for their homes by this means.[370] Anioma women who dismissed the report about the end of the war had good reasons for their reaction. In some of the towns, including Okpanam and Asaba, nothing immediately changed in the attitude of the federal soldiers towards the people. The women contended that the soldiers still went about with their rifles, which to them were symbols of intimidation, death, and sorrow. It was not totally illogical for them to have hoped that the end of the crisis would initiate a complete change in the combatants' attitude towards them and also compell the soldiers to lay down their arms. Since their observations ran contrary to their expectations, they surmised that the war could not possibly be over.

The federal soldiers in Anioma remained as high handed as ever, intimidating and beating up the people at will. In one instance, a couple making their way back from Biafra to Anioma after the crisis was shot dead by a federal soldier because of the husband's refusal to relinquish his wife to the soldier.[371] Nobody reported the case, and the soldier got away with the murder. In another instance, two Nigerian soldiers – Festus Oko and James Alizor – beat a bicycle mechanic to death at the Ute-Erumu ward in the Ika area and dumped his body inside a well. This time, the soldiers did not get away with their crime.[372] There were other similar cases of persons shot for flimsy reasons at about the time the news of the end of the war was making waves in many towns in Anioma.

The harassment and molestation women suffered at the hands of federal soldiers in the course of the war did not automatically end with the cessation of hostilities. Frequent rough handling of civilians by soldiers remained a feature of life in a number of towns, months after the war. Some beautiful young women were within this period abducted and forced into "marriage" by federal soldiers.[373] By this time the purpose of the abduction was to celebrate the defeat of the Igbo and the victory of the federal troops. The women thus abducted became the war booties of the victorious soldiers. In response to the postwar abduction of women, adolescent girls in Okpanam were reluctant to stop disguising themselves as old women after the announcement of the cessation of hostilities.

Looking at the civilian–soldier relationship immediately after the war, the picture that emerges suggest that a good number of federal combatants utilized that period or the occasion of their victory to accomplish what they could not do during the war. The commander of the Second Division in Midwest State admitted his difficulty in controlling the army in peacetime. It was not easy, he noted, for the soldiers to adjust from a war mode to a peace mode.[374] What happened in the Midwest immediately after the war also took place in the former Biafran enclave, with the situation worse in the latter than in the former. In effect, federal soldiers continued to harass and attack civilians weeks after the announcement of the cessation of hostilities.

What helped to convince most people in Anioma of the end of the war was the gradual return of whole families and individuals from Biafra and from other parts of western Nigeria to Anioma.

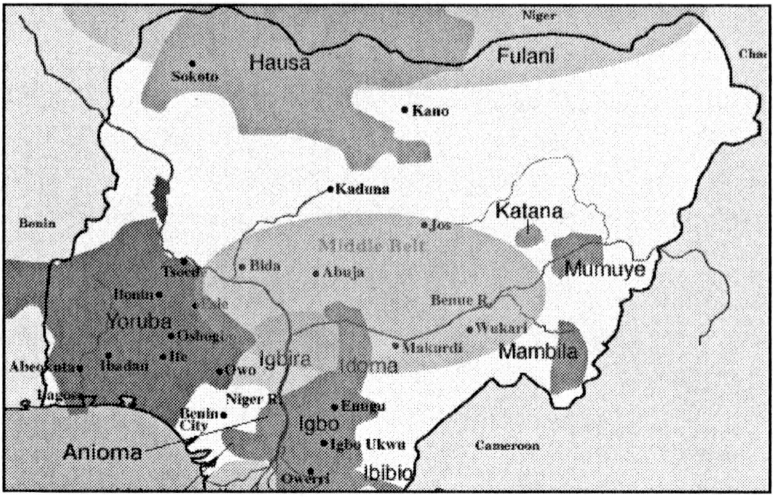

Middle Belt

Some who made their way home from Biafra were ferried across the Niger River but completed the journey on foot. Those who owned vehicles took the longer route through the Middle Belt to Anioma because of the destruction of the Niger Bridge separating Biafra from Anioma. The sight of these returnees persuaded those female folks who feared that the military contest would never end of its termination. Some gave vent to their feelings of relief and gratitude for the long desired, or in some circles, unexpected happenstance. People rejoiced as they received friends and relations who had spent the war years in Biafra. Agnes Odagwe, in Utagba-uno in the Ukwuani area, and Catherine Agbon, in Otolokpo in the Ika section, had at different times during the crisis individually promised themselves a good public dance any day the war ended. Each was true to her word and entertained her neighbors to an open dance in commemoration of the return of peace in the country and in their communities specifically. Coincidentally, both women made the same pledge, each without being aware of the other, and survived to fulfill their vows when conditions for them materialized for the better.

People in Anioma celebrated the end of the war in a variety of ways. There were thanksgiving services in many Christian churches in different towns even after the three-day national prayer session decreed by Lieutenant Colonel Gowon.[375] Not to be outdone, those who subscribed to the indigenous religion performed rituals and made sacrifices, according honor to their deities for seeing them through that trying period. They felt honored that the confidence they reposed on their gods was not misplaced. It was observed in chapter 3 in many towns people believed and declared that one or more of the following were responsible for averting the rage of the federal army on their towns or for warding them off completely at the commencement of the 1967 military campaigns in Anioma: the guardian spirits of their towns, a renowned ritual specialist, and the omu. Also, in the previous chapter, it was equally observed that one of the ways individuals of both sexes sought to safeguard their lives and to survive the period of emergency was to recourse to traditional mysticism.[376] Hence, when the war ended individuals and whole communities demonstrated their appreciation to the spirit beings that they felt were responsible for their survival. Female adolescents in Okpanam used the tragic experience of the war to compose songs in commemoration of that event and also to form groups that danced to those songs to entertain their town.[377]

The celebratory mood did not affect Anioma's entire population. As some women danced and embraced each other at the restoration of peace in the nation, others were pensive over the wasted years and wasted opportunities that resulted from the war but especially their condition by the end of the crisis. The civil war, no doubt, aborted the dreams of many. Tina Okwuashi from Onicha-ugbo lamented having ever again to claim Nigeria as her nationality. She had anticipated a new life in a new republic, where all things would become new and the Igbo on both sides of the Niger would be free to be themselves.[378] She did not hide her disappointment about the eventual outcome of the military contest between the Republic of Biafra and the Nigerian government. Similarly, a good number of people in Issele-ukwu had looked forward to Biafra's victory with nostalgia. The Biafran propaganda during the war was so effective and convincing that these individuals never doubted the Biafran government's claim of the invincibility of its army. It came as a surprise to them that the Biafran army came off badly in the conflict and ended up surrendering to the Nigerian head of state.[379]

The relief most women felt over the end of the war did not imply that the return of peace to the nation meant the dawning of a new era; neither were they convinced that all had become automatically all right for them. It was only natural that they would feel eleviated by the expiration of the emergency situation under which they lived for so many months and for which they grappled with a number of privations. According to the testimony of one of the women "the end of the war meant that our freedom was restored and all the restrictions put on us were removed."[380] J. O. G Achuzia, a former Biafran military officer from Anioma, wrote: "To some, the end of the war was the end of a tragedy and the hope for a better tomorrow. To others, it was the end of hunger and starvation."[381] He was careful not to speculate on what the future had in store for the surviving victims of the crisis.

BEGINNING ANEW

Damages in Anioma were considerable if taken in isolation or if compared with the rest of the federation and with the rest of the Midwest State, which was not exposed to any form of military brutality. Yet Anioma's damages were minimal when compared with the situation in East Central State, the main theater of war. To appreciate the situation in Anioma, the Midwest military governor reported that his state was the most unfortunate victim of the Nigerian crisis besides the Republic of Biafra.[382] Towns that sustained considerable damages in Anioma are found in Aniocha, where the federal soldiers combated direct challenges from Biafran troops throughout the duration of the crisis. Although federal soldiers faced much provocation from Biafran infiltrators in towns in the riverine section of Ukwuani, infrastructural damages were insignificant because the topography of the area did not encourage much physical development before the war.

The majority of the displaced persons of Anioma, most of them from Aniocha, met desolation on their return home after the crisis. The returnees to Isheagu met a giant forest where previously their town stood. It was difficult locating the charred remains of their former homes. Many people in Aniocha met buildings that were burnt or laid waste by bullets and bombs with properties lost to looters. Compounds as well as whole communities were pictures of neglect with weeds growing everywhere. The grim realities of the war dawned on many after the cessation of hostilities. The extent of the losses sustained had a sobering and demoralizing effect on the people. For those who were in Biafra during the emergency, similar sights of ruin and neglect in the extinct republic appear not to have mentally prepared them for what they saw in their communities in Anioma. The women in particular expressed their surprise, disappointment, and grief at the horrifying pictures of their burnt down, damaged, or dilapidated residences, and at the realization of other losses sustained as a result of the war. Obviously, with the Midwest officially part of federal Nigeria during the crisis, those from Anioma who lived in Biafra throughout the emergency least expected the fate that befell Biafra to be the lot of Anioma. Quite a good number of returnees had little or nothing with which to commence their individual rehabilitation.

The situation in Aniocha after the war differed from that in most parts of the Ika and Ukwuani areas. In the Ika area, Otolopko and Ute-okpu, for instance, were not occupied by federal troops during the war and therefore did not feel much of the impact of the crisis. Similarly, the nonriverine areas of Ukwuani did not sustain infrastructural damages to the level witnessed in Aniocha, which in addition to serious infrastructural losses claimed about 60 percent of the entire victim count of the war in the Midwest.

The people of Anioma who did not abandon their homes and who were not displaced by the crisis were not all threatened with prospects of a bleak future at the end of the ordeal. Some who remained in their communities were able to safeguard much of their properties from vandals and thieves. In contrast, their colleagues who deserted their homes and took shelter elsewhere left virtually all they had acquired over the years to the mercy of unscrupulous people. Part of what the displaced took from their homes, hoping to safeguard them, were subsequently lost in the course of their wanderings.[383] In Isheagu, Asaba, Ibusa, all in Aniocha, and the riverine communities of Ukwuani that bordered Biafra, but separated from it by the River Niger, some who remained in their towns for the greater part of the war still lost their homes and properties.[384] In Isheagu, for instance, the entire town was razed in May 1968 and was unoccupied until 1970. The consensus has been that families that lost most in terms of material wealth had vacated their homes for other locations.

The economic hardship induced by the war engendered different degrees of starvation and hunger, depending on the individual's location during the emergency. Most women emerged from the crisis terribly emaciated and looking like ghosts of their former selves, unconsciously eliciting pity from their neighbors.[385] The wretched state of the people was evident in their threadbare clothes. War victims of all ages were obviously sick or unhealthy. The worst hit were the children. There were widespread cases of yaws among erstwhile bush dwellers in Anioma. Also, a number of children returnees from Biafra were suffering from kwashiokor (extreme protein deficiency), a health problem observed with Belgian children during World War I.[386] Widespread starvation leading to various health complications was a recurrent feature of wars in the last century. Lydia Akazue, who spent the war years with her family in a bush on the outskirts of Isheagu, recalled that her children were so malnourished and

Nigeria in 1970

sick that their natural color gave way to a reddish and orange hue. From her description, the children obviously suffered from marasmus, which results from insufficient intake of food, causing the body to waste away and in the process produce a terrifying appearance.[387]

The pressing needs of the civil war survivors in Anioma, including the returnees and their dependents, were for food, medication, and resettlement. The immediate challenge facing the people was how to get out of their predicament. The military governor of the Midwest informed his "subjects" after the cessation of hostilities that the state's need for rehabilitation was more than its financial capacity. He encouraged communities that were battered by the war to take steps to rehabilitate themselves as a means of motivating the government to come to their assistance.[388] He insisted that the state government could not provide maximum social and economic services unless the people were willing to perform their civic duties. With these pronouncements, the governor made it clear to the Anioma that the work of rehabilitation would be undertaken jointly by the government and the people. In effect, rehabilitation in Anioma was to a considerable extent a personal and communal affair, but the efforts of the people were to be complemented by the input of the state government, with assistance from the federal government.

GOVERNMENT AND REHABILITATION

Anioma returnees who could manage their partly destroyed homes resettled themselves in their houses not minding the missing shutters and roofs. Others who lost their residences or had them damaged and uninhabitable moved in with relatives and friends whose houses were in better condition, and who were willing to share their accommodation. In Asaba, Ibusa, Oko, and Okwe, all in Aniocha, houses that were in relatively good condition were overcrowded, but this did not bother the inmates, who were greatly relieved to have found shelter. Those unable to find accommodation with relatives and friends moved into available houses whose rightful owners were yet to return to the town or had settled down in towns and cities outside Anioma.

The people of Anioma exhibited much tolerance for each other during the process of re-adjustment after the war. Those who provided lodging for others did so irrespective of the discomfort to themselves and to their families. Generally, the loss of houses, property, and the scarcity of money forced many to live for some months after the war as though they were still under an emergency. The obvious difference was the reduced spate of killings and the freedom with which the people moved about in their towns.

With the need for shelter temporarily addressed by the people themselves, they turned their attention to other aspects of their rehabilitation. The federal and state governments were not unsympathetic to the plight of the war victims and therefore did not leave them to grapple alone with rehabilitation after the war. Lt. Col. Yakubu Gowon who championed the cause of "One Nigeria" during the war anticipated the eventual victory of the federal forces from the standpoint of their military superiority over the Biafran army. In 1968 he promulgated Decree 41, which provided for a National Rehabilitation Commission for Emergency Relief Operation and Post-War Rehabilitation, Reconstruction, and Reconciliation (the three Rs). The responsibility of the National Rehabilitation Commission was to collect and distribute medication and other gifts from foreign governments and from international and nongovernmental agencies to the three eastern states, namely, East Central State, Rivers State, and Southeastern State.[389] These were collectively known as the Eastern Region until the eve of the civil war. Splitting the country into twelve states resulted in the excision of Rivers and the Southeastern states from the former Eastern Region. Midwest State was excluded from among the states to benefit from the assignment of the National Rehabilitation Commission because of its being officially in the territory controlled by the federal government of Nigeria during the war, an area that was supposedly not to have been militarized.[390]

To guide the nation in postwar rehabilitation and reconstruction, the Federal Ministry of Information in October 1968 published an official pamphlet prepared by the commissioner for finance titled *Blue Print for Post-War Reconstruction*.[391] The document stated as follows:

- The surviving victims of past disturbances and of the present military operations shall be cared for with the utmost compassion.
- The surviving Federal troops shall be amply rewarded for their gallant and devoted services to the nation.
- All soldiers, no matter on which side they had fought, shall be rehabilitated and faithfully employed at the end of the military operations. It must be noted that one good thing

about the present emergency is that it has helped to reduce unemployment throughout the country. It would be a mistaken policy of the worst kind to allow the Federal troops and the rebel soldiers to go unemployed.

- Those whose property have been destroyed or damaged, as a result of civil disturbances, shall be reasonably compensated.
- All those who had fled from their normal places of residence or business shall be resettled, and if possible, helped to make a new start.
- All roads, bridges and public buildings destroyed shall be reconstructed.
- With immediate effect, a special fund into which an amount of 1 million pounds will be contributed annually, starting this year, has been created.

Since Midwest State was not one of the beneficiaries of the national rehabilitation program, its military governor in July 1969 revived an existing Rehabilitation Committee in the state and rechristened it the Reconstruction and Rehabilitation Committee. The Midwest Rehabilitation Committee was first set up in 1963, following the disengagement of Midwest citizens in the Western Region after the excision of the Midwest from the old Western Region. The committee's first assignment was to find office spaces for the new region and to resettle civil servants and other workers who were unceremoniously and hastily disengaged from the Western Region. The second task it tackled hinged on the displacement of persons in Nigeria as a result of the 1966 national disturbances that left as many as 50,000 people of Midwest origin displaced, according to the official record of the state.[392]

The military campaigns in Midwest State during the civil war necessitated the widening of the terms of reference of the State Rehabilitation Committee to include the reconstruction of destroyed infrastructures. This, also, agreed with the sixth provision of the federal document on reconstruction. The Ministry of Community Development and Rehabilitation was created by the state government to enable it tackle the postwar problems of rehabilitation, reconstruction, and reconciliation and to co-ordinate the program. Under the ministry were grassroots' rehabilitation committees, set up in many towns and districts in Anioma, and placed under the supervision of local rulers.[393] The grass roots committees were formed according to the needs of the various towns and to guarantee an efficient execution of the program.

The aims of the state rehabilitation exercise were to heal the wounds inflicted by the war and to restore normalcy, mutual understanding, and better relations among the various ethnic groups in Midwest State.[394] The emphases of the program, however, included the reconstruction of roads, bridges, schools, and public buildings damaged in the course of the war. To support the exercise, money was raised internally for the committee. According to the arrangement, state commissioners were made to donate 15 percent of their salaries to the coffers of the committee for a period of three months while other civil servants parted with 5 percent of theirs within the same duration.

The state rehabilitation program was encapsulated in the theme "Winning the Peace." The military governor of the Midwest was so optimistic that the reconciliation of all Nigerians, both within and outside the Midwest, would be easy to achieve in the course of the rehabilitation exercise and predicted that it would be accomplished within six months after the termination of the war.[395] He was not alone in making such presumptions. In 1968, the head of state announced in a national broadcast that the Nigerian government shall "take all measures to enhance reconciliation and national unity."[396] The promulgators of the state rehabilitation program did not pretend to take on more than they were prepared to tackle. Theirs was a trim program of reconstruction and rehabilitation, but they were sincere about what they intended to accomplish unlike the ambitious federal government's Blue Print for Post-War Reconstruction.

In spite of the focus on infrastructural restoration, the State Rehabilitation Committee began its work by addressing the urgent needs of Anioma war victims for relief and medical attention. The peoples of the state had been encouraged to increase their agricultural output as the foremost and quickest means of ensuring the success of rehabilitation. But before the impact of that could be felt, food and medication were distributed in the affected communities through the joint efforts of the Rehabilitation Committee and the local Red Cross team. The local rulers who were put in charge of their towns' rehabilitation committees assisted in this responsibility. The incorporation of the local rulers was to guarantee that supplies reached the target group – the returnees, the displaced, and other war destitute. Corn meal, oatmeal, corned beef, Norwegian stockfish, and a brand of rice, locally called *alikama*, were distributed to the people as relief materials.

The distribution of relief materials in Anioma preceded the end of the war and was previously coordinated by the various military units in the area. Women from Asaba, Ibusa, Oko, and other towns who had spent some time in the refugee camps in Asaba received these items through the federal unit in Asaba. Intermittently during the crisis, as dictated by the fortunes of the war, the people of Ogwashi-ukwu also received food aid from soldiers of the Second Division stationed in their town. Some of the food items were donations from Misericordia and Caritas International. When, in 1969, the indigenes of Ibusa left the refugee camp in Asaba for their town under the auspices of Father Osia they were not allowed to move into their homes but were resettled on school premises until the war ended. During this instance of confinement, the Rehabilitation Committee was responsible for their food needs. The sick among them received medical attention from the Red Cross team that ran a cottage hospital in the camp for refugees. The Rehabilitation Committee recorded a greater degree of success with Ibusa war victims than in towns where the people were not similarly confined.

The uncertainty of military operations and the resultant instability in Anioma during the fighting complicated the work of the committee in many towns at this initial time. In their postwar operations, not all those who had access to the relief materials were in dire need of them; similarly, some individuals who needed them did not receive. Those who received food items used them as they wished. Women, in particular, exchanged what they were given but did not want for what they preferred but did not receive. The thrifty ones hoarded their rations, not knowing for how long they would enjoy government assistance.[397]

The work of the Rehabilitation Committee in dispensing food items and drugs to Anioma war victims continued for three months after the end of the crisis before it was suspended,[398] partly because the federal government felt that the people had reasonably adjusted and were no longer in need of food aid.[399] Midwest State's relief operation in Anioma was terminated at about the same time the operation in East Central State was halted. The Nigerian government, piqued by the interference of various international organizations during the war, was reacting to their meddling by halting the relief operations when it did. Both foreign nations and humanitarian groups' offer of assistance in this regard as well as that of church groups were rejected, one accusation against the churches being that they went far beyond their humanitarian duty and made a bad situation worse by becoming active Biafran propagandists. There was no doubt that the accusation was true of such Catholic groups as Caritas, African Concern, and the Irish Order of the Holy Ghost, stationed in Biafra where they had over a hundred priests who were in the enclave during the hostilities.[400] But such blatant priestly involvement in favor of Biafra was not reported in Anioma. Nevertheless, the Nigerian government regarded the churches and their expatriate clergy as "political priests" and expelled the majority of them after the war with the result that there has been a noticeably high reduction in the number of expatriate missionaries in Nigeria since after the war.[401]

In spite of the suspension of relief activity three months after the war, in August 1970 the Midwest Rehabilitation Committee embarked on an emergency assignment when some 150 fishermen and their families living on the bank of the Niger River became homeless due to an unusual rainfall that destroyed property estimated at hundreds of pounds.[402]

More dedication was observed in Anioma in the distribution of food items than of drugs. The unavailability of drugs after the war compelled most women to rely on indigenous products and remedies for their health problems and those of their wards. The menace of yaws, common during the hostilities, was combated by applying the infected areas of the body with an indigenously manufactured herbal cream that was mixed with the ointment *udeaku*.[403]Alongside the relief operation was the distribution of building materials to surviving war victims in the Ika and Aniocha subsections of Anioma. The Ukwuani area did not receive building materials since it did not suffer infrastructural damages as did the Aniocha and Ika areas. Bags of cement and bundles of zinc were handed over to local rulers, the respective chairmen of the grassroots' rehabilitation committees, in trust for those who either lost their homes in the war or had them destroyed. In reality few of the affected people obtained their allotment of zinc or cement. In many towns the government's supplies fell far short of what was needed to go round, and what majority of the people received was inadequate for the repair of their damaged houses. The trust reposed on the chairmen of the grassroots' rehabilitation committees was unduly abused. Their aides reserved for themselves more than their fair share of the materials and distributed the remaining to the people. Consequently, not many rebuilt their houses with what was provided by the government. As an alternative, some made use of locally available materials in fixing their homes, pending when their circumstances would improve to sustain the construction of better houses. Those who preferred better structures in place of the old ones waited until they were able to supplement what they received before embarking on a thorough restoration of their residences. Generally, better structures than what previously existed were erected in Anioma after the war.

Women were marginalized in the distribution of the building materials provided by the state government. All categories of women, including widows, were neither given zinc nor cement on the argument that they did not own houses and were not heads of households. No consideration was extended to those who lived through the hostilities but lost their husbands in the crisis and emerged as family heads. This mistreatment of women was the result of the age-old custom of the Igbo, which did not make provision for females to own property or for married women to inherit from their husbands. The marginalized women had to rely on their siblings and generous relatives for the restoration of their damaged houses. Where no assistance was forthcoming, they ended up as long-term tenants in other people's homes. As late as 2000, thirty years after the war, some are still awaiting the reconstruction of their homes.[404]

The achievements of the Midwest government in rehabilitation and reconstruction in Anioma were clearly evident in school repairs, and to a lesser degree, in the provision of medical facilities, and the restoration of destroyed and previously uncompleted roads. The State Rehabilitation Committee received commendable assistance in the execution of some projects from two American agencies—the United States Agency for International Development (USAID) and the American Friends Service Committee, the standing committee responsible for the overseas work of the Religious Society of Friends (the Quakers). USAID and the Quakers' Service Committee entered into agreements with the State Rehabilitation Committee on behalf of the state military governor. The two American agencies' generous financial aid and commitment to reconstruction in Anioma made possible the rapid but gradual return of life to its prewar state in the battered towns.

Towns in the environs of Asaba and Ibusa, which were later reconstituted as Oshimili local government area,[405] benefited from the accord between the USAID, the Quaker Service Committee, and the State Reconstruction Committee. The inputs of the two foreign agencies were complemented by the collaboration of the local people in the affected towns. By the terms of the agreement, the State Ministry of Education determined the areas of need, directed the distribution of furniture on the basis of need, and paid the wages for all skilled labor. The receiving towns supplied the unskilled labor, provided storage facilities, and ensured the security of the materials received from the Quaker Service Committee. The Quaker Service, on its part, supplied the materials, coordinated, and supervised the workers.

Damaged schools in the selected towns were restored fully or in part through the above arrangement and subsequently furnished. In Asaba six schools each with six classrooms, the headmasters' office, and a store were restored. Ibusa, Achalla, and Asaba each had one school fully restored. In Achalla, Okwe, and Ibusa, intense community efforts were expended for school rehabilitation. With the progress made in the selected towns, idle school pupils were able to resume classes by December 1970.[406] For indigenes of Ibusa, who were confined to the school premises in their town since the beginning of 1969, classes commenced in the camps before the end of 1969. They were organized by trained teachers among the refugees. The £260,000 released for school repairs in the 1970/1971 fiscal year facilitated the restoration of educational institutions in Anioma until 1971.[407] Funds provided during the course of the war by the Irish Catholic Order and Misericordia (of German origin) for the Catholic church in Anioma supported the building of mission schools in Ubulu-ukwu, Asaba, Agbor, and Okpanam.[408]

The Midwest governor extended a special consideration to war orphans during the rehabilitation exercise. These were postprimary school children whose fathers or sponsors died in the war. Scholarships received from the federal government in the course of the crisis were awarded the students. To qualify, mothers of affected students or any other close adult relative provided evidence to the school principal that the child's original sponsor died in the war.[409] Names of qualified orphaned students were compiled by school principals and forwarded to the Scholarship Board of the Midwest Ministry of Education, whose responsibility it was to remit the fees that would originally have been paid by the students' parents to their respective schools until the completion of their secondary school education. There was no discrimination of affected students on the basis of sex. Boys as well as girls gained from the program. Incidentally, one of the recipients was from the former Eastern Region[410] but lost his father during the uprising, at the hands of other ethnic groups in the Midwest, against the Anioma in wake of the federal troops' arrival in the state. The scholarships encouraged the education of girls and prevented their withdrawal from school because of the death of their fathers, the inability of their mothers to cope with the task of putting them through school unaided, and the cultural bias against the education of female children in Anioma at the time. As a rule, the scheme arrested the spate of dropouts from secondary school education in Anioma, which produced the highest number of war orphans in Midwest State. The scholarships were not extended to primary school pupils since Midwest State operated a Free Primary Education Scheme whereby elementary education was free for all its citizens.

In spite of the benefits of the scholarship exercise, not very many students profited from it. Certain widowed mothers prevented their eligible daughters from utilizing the fund so that the girls could assist them at home with one trade or another. These women preferred their daughters joining the labor market and bringing in some much-needed currency rather than continuing with their schooling, a venture that did not promise any immediate financial return.[411]

On the other hand, certain girls of secondary school age whose parents survived the war were unable to continue with school. Their major impediment was the postwar currency crisis, which will be discussed later, that affected the Igbo on both sides of the Niger. Parents in Anioma who felt the brunt of the currency crisis were mostly farmers, artisans, and other self-employed indivuals whose income shortly after the war was too poor to sustain the cost of their children's education, especially the females.[412] In this group were also the returnees from Biafra who came home with mostly Biafran currency that became useless for transactions after the war. Given the challenges faced by the Anioma at the end of the war, the benefits of the scholarship scheme would have been felt more fully if scholarships were awarded for one full academic year to all postprimary students in Anioma or to those in Aniocha who felt the impact of the war more than others.

The overall development of Midwest State was the anticipated end of the rehabilitation exercise.[413] In line with this, the period after the civil war saw an increase in the number of hospitals in Anioma. Until 1970, only three government hospitals and very few dispensaries and maternity centers[414] existed in all of Anioma, reflecting the poor health condition of the state. The situation improved during the Rehabilitation exercise with the construction by the government of five new hospitals and four rural health centers in the Midwest. Out of this number, two hospitals and two health centers were sited in the following towns in Anioma[415]: Ibusa, Isheagu, Obiaruku, and Akwukwu. Indigenes of these towns presumed that the gesture was official compensation for their ordeal during the war. They were unaware that the federal government encouraged the expansion of healthcare services throughout the country and made available the sum of £35.5 million in October 1970 as grants-in-aid to the twelve states of the federation for that purpose.[416]

The poor postwar health standard of Midwest State was further compounded by the shortage of medical staff. This deficiency was also observed in other parts of the nation after the war. In order to solve the problem, the Midwest State government awarded repayable scholarships to medical students both to enable them complete their studies and as an incentive to postprimary school students to aspire to that field of study.[417] The state and federal governments were not the sole sponsors of health centers in Anioma after the war. Misericordia—through funds provided during the hostilities—also funded two rehabilitation hospitals for war refugees, one each in Ibusa and Ebu.[418]

Road rehabilitation in Anioma and in the rest of Midwest State was undertaken from October 1970 until the end of 1971.[419] All the roads in Anioma were in very bad condition partly as a result of the war and also from neglect. The delay in rehabilitating them immediately after the war affected among other things the transportation of locally produced food items, making distribution difficult and slow; and sometimes creating artificial scarcity of needed commodities. The resultant increase in the prices of goods in the state necessitated the setting up of a Price Control Committee in July 1970 with seventeen price inspectors. The committee fixed commodity prices and intermittently carried out raids on retailers to ensure compliance with official prices of goods and to forestall undue profiteering. The price hike was more frequently indulged in in Anioma, where many people desperately needed to recoup from the war.[420]

Similar to the delay in road reconstruction, the electricity supply to Aniocha, disconnected in 1968, was not promptly reconnected after the war. Rather, the state government attempted to improve living conditions in the war ravaged areas by other means. The state government accomplished two things: the reconstruction of destroyed markets and the initiation of projects aimed at enhancing the circumstances of the local population. One of the markets rebuilt at the end of the war was Ogbe-ogonogo, situated in the center of Asaba town. The state government and the Asaba Urban District Council jointly executed the project by the end of 1970. The Asaba Urban District Council hired and paid for the skilled labor, and the government supplied the building materials. Some structural work was also undertaken at the Cable Point market, often called Ogbe-olie, and also in Asaba town. Damaged modern conveniences were restored with new ones constructed in Ogbe-ogonogo market.

The reconstruction of the markets in Asaba was a boost to the economy of Anioma towns bordering the Niger but particularly to Asaba. Before the outbreak of the war, the two markets were pivotal to the economic activity in the town. Traders from towns across the Niger and from the Asaba hinterland visited these markets until their destruction in October 1967. Following their restoration, farm produce and trade goods were again shipped into Asaba in increasing quantities from such places in East Central State as Nsukka and Abakiliki and also from other sections of Anioma. The restored markets gave women easy access to the goods they needed. Besides, their proximity reduced the difficulty in going to distant places to trade.

The Ministry of Social Welfare provided machines to facilitate the processing of cassava into garri in 1970. The machines were made available to women in Isheagu and in Achalla. American Friends Service Committee of the Quakers donated communally owned and operated fishing boats to Oko-ogbele, Oko-anala, Oko-amakom, and Isheagu. Their availability encouraged an increase in the number of fishermen in these communities and led to a surplus yield from fishing. Thus, by March 1971, these towns had enough fish to eat and extra to sell.[421] The Quaker Service Committee also provided some block-making moulds for the people of Oko and set up a carpentry workshop in Ibusa where doors, window frames, and shutters were made. The State Government's subsidized stores in Ogwashi-ukwu and in Asaba patronized the workshop, purchasing its goods.

Another attempt made by the state government to provide employment was in reconstructing the badly destroyed Midwest Textile Mills located at Asaba. Repairs were estimated to cost over £2,000,000, about half of what was invested to set it up originally. The dearth of employment opportunities after the war led to a feverish rush for jobs at the revamped textile company and in a few other industries. After its reconstruction the mill reabsorbed its displaced workers and filled existing vacancies with new staff.

The direct input of the federal government in the rehabilitation exercise came in the form of the Federal Ministry of Defense opting to pay rents on civilian buildings used by the federal army during the war. The compensation was paid to civilian property owners in Midwest State and also in the three eastern states. For Anioma, the Nigerian military headquarters calculated the rent for recipients at the rate of £2 per room per month as suggested by the Midwest military governor.[422] The paltry sum paid as rent was nonetheless useful in alleviating the plight of war victims and was all the external financial aid some of the women received after the crisis. As is often the case with such government programs, all civilians whose houses had been used by the federal troops did not receive any payment for the use of their homes. Some of the claims put up were discountenanced by the Nigerian army headquarters, which claimed that the petitioners had no cogent basis from which to ask for compensation.[423]

Some aspects of the rehabilitation exercise generated various degrees of emotional trauma for the Anioma. One of the vexing issues hinged on the reintegration of displaced civil servants of Anioma origin into the Midwest civil service. In the Winning the Peace program, provision was made for the reduction of the level of unemployment in the state, and, as noted, the aims of the state rehabilitation program was to heal the wounds inflicted by the war and to restore normalcy to that multiethnic state. Based on these targets, many people in Anioma considered the rehabilitation process incomplete without the reabsorption of displaced Midwest Igbo civil servants in the state's Civil Service Commission. As it turned out their expectation amounted to forlorn speculation.

Displaced Anioma civil servants who went back to their jobs after the war were not readily reintegrated. Their applications for reabsorption were either turned down or ignored. Eventually, some of the civil servants were either dismissed or compulsorily retired.[424] Months elapsed before others were recalled. This delay in reabsorbing former Anioma employees of the state generated fear and anxiety in those affected especially after a Board of Inquiry was set up by the state military governor to screen candidates seeking reabsorption. Many anticipated the worst, and the fearful ones looked forward with trepidation to letters summoning them before the board.[425] In the screening, attention was focused on the part each person played during the Biafran occupation of the state. Those considered "the most guilty" were summarily dismissed from service, but those classified as "the less guilty" were reabsorbed but demoted.[426]

Of all the displaced civil servants of Anioma origin, teachers received best treatment. The majority returned to work without much fuss. This was done partly for propaganda purposes and also to bolster the school system, which in some towns became moribund during the war. It would have been ridiculous if after the heavy investments in school rehabilitation in Anioma that teachers were not engaged to revitalize the education system in the affected towns or that teachers were employed from among other ethnic groups in the state to teach in Anioma schools while teachers of Anioma origin were disengaged.

Excluding the displaced civil servants, certain other individuals in Anioma lost their positions in the state after the war. One such victim was Obi Oyetenu, the asagba of Asaba, the local ruler. From the post as vice-chairman of the state's traditional rulers, to which he was appointed before the war, he was demoted to an ordinary third-class chief. The asagba left Asaba at the arrival of federal troops in the town and took refuge in Biafra. His absence from Midwest State necessitated another local ruler filling his position, but there was no justification, except on punitive grounds, for his demotion after the war to a third-class chief even without his being restored to his former position as vice-chairman.

The Midwest military governor did not act wholly on his own initiative in his treatment of displaced Anioma civil servants but in compliance with the attitude of the federal government towards the Igbo after the war. In 1968 and again in 1970, Lieutenant Colonel Gowon promised the restoration of the Igbo (in the secessionist territory) to their previous posts as they reappeared from their hiding places. Yet, in 1970 he promulgated Decree 46, which was not restricted to any state or group of people, but by its content was applied to the three eastern states and to the Midwest, sections of the country where there was military action between September 1967 and January 1970. Decree 46 clearly stated that where the appropriate authorities were satisfied that between 15 January 1966 and 15 January 1970, a public officer was involved in any hostile or subversive act or rebellion against any of the governments in the federation, such an officer would be dismissed, removed, or compulsorily retired from service.[427] It further stipulated that any public officer found to have engaged in counseling, aiding, or abetting any other person involved in any hostile or subversive act or rebellion against any government in the federation would receive similar punishment. The document also provided that where the conduct of a public officer was such that his continued employment in the relevant service would not be in the interest of the public, such an officer would be dismissed, removed, or retired compulsorily. The decree was promulgated for the following reasons:

> To prevent Igbo civil servants and corporation officials from being reintegrated in the public service of the federation; the public service of any state of the federation; the service of a body corporate or incorporate established under a federal or state law; and in a company in which any of the governments in the federation had controlling or substantial interest.[428]

There was no room in the document for civil proceedings to be entertained by any court of law in the country in respect of any decision taken in conjunction with the stipulations of Decree 46 of 1970.

The attitude of the Midwest military governor to displaced civil servants of Anioma origin cannot be divorced from a combination of two factors:

1. The federal government's stance against the Igbo and the ghost of Biafra, and
2. The internal animosity towards indigenes of Anioma as a result of the ambiguous relationship between the ethnic groups in Midwest State, which was exacerbated by the incidents surrounding the incursion of Biafra into the state in August 1967.

The second point is supported by a classified report of an administrative meeting of the state's permanent secretaries held in October 1967, more than two years before Gowon's Decree 46. Based on Biafra's six-week occupation of Midwest State the report stated as follows:

> There was no longer any basis for mutual trust, confidence, and peaceful co-existence between the Midwestern [Igbo] and the rest of the Edo-speaking Midwest ...the general feeling was that they no more wanted to have anything to do again with them; if they were brought back His Excellency might have a terrible crisis on his hands.[429]

Some of the suggestions of the permanent secretaries towards solving the problem generated by the presence of an Igbo group in the state were:

- merge them with East Central State;
- constitute them as a separate state;
- declare their geographical area a Special Area like the Union State in India.[430]

Both the provisions of Decree 46 and the internal animosity in Midwest State towards the Igbo were responsible for the state government's treatment of displaced Anioma workers and the punitive measures meted out to them.

Another group of Anioma indigenes affected by Decree 46 were the military officers of the Fourth (Midwest) Area Command, accused by the federal government of complicity in Biafra's incursion into the Midwest in August 1967. These officers accompanied the invading army to Biafra when their scheme of taking Lagos was foiled. The military officers from Anioma and the participants in the January 1966 coup that precipitated the civil war were arrested and detained together immediately after the war. The head of state set up a commission of inquiry, headed by Brigadier Adeyinka Adebayo, to investigate their pre- and wartime activities.[431] The coup plotters escaped execution through the intervention of some Nigerians and international human rights' organizations, but the treatment meted out to and the judgment passed on the Anioma military officers were based on the bias of the authority towards particular individuals. As a result, those who had friends in the federal army were lightly punished with retirement but with benefits. Some of the junior officers were accepted back in the army while the rest were dismissed without any entitlement. The Supreme Military Council explained that the senior-ranked officers were dismissed because of their failure to influence decisions in the defunct Republic of Biafra in favor of "One Nigeria." The fear was also expressed that their reabsorption would undermine discipline in the Nigerian army.[432]

Under Gowon's military regime, the detainees were subjected to strict prison terms in addition to continual relocation, from one prison to another, throughout their years of incarceration. For the first three years of their confinement the accused military officers were remanded in total isolation. When in 1973 they were dispersed to different prisons, the unmarried ones were not permitted to receive visitors; their married counterparts were allowed visits from their spouses once every three months, a situation that undermined the marriages of some of the officers. The wives of the incarcerated officers were put at a disadvantage by their husbands' imprisonment, but what many of them considered unbearable was the stigma associated with the immurement. The weight of that unanticipated social reaction bred a sense of incapacitation and insecurity in the women, leading to different reactions. One of the women affected confessed giving up her job as a result.[433] However, they were all excluded from some of the benefits of the Rehabilitation exercise.

Women whose husbands were retired or dismissed from the civil service and from the military both shared in their husbands' humiliation and inherited in part or completely the burden of running their homes as most women did during the war. It is not always possible to extricate women from the experiences of their husbands; rather, from some of the ordeals of the men, the challenges faced by the women can be better appreciated.

This handling of war victims in a crisis where there was "No victor, no vanquished," as Gowon asserted after the capitulation of Biafra, was described as "a good show of magnanimity after victory" by the commander of the Second Division of the Nigerian Army in Midwest State.[434] It pleased some Nigerians outside Anioma and East Central State that the Igbo were not allowed to go unpunished for the events that took place in the country between January 1966 and January 1970, although the Igbo were in the main the aggrieved party. From much of the official federal policy during the rehabilitation exercise, the head of state failed to actualize his promise that there would be no second-class citizens in the country. The *Daily Times* editorial of 19 August 1970 reported that the general amnesty announced by General Gowon at the end of the civil war was misleading and should not be construed to mean that enthusiastic proponents of the Biafran secession should go free or enjoy similar privileges along with the unwilling participants in that treasonable act.[435] Also, Adeyinka Adebayo, the highest ranking authority under Gowon, declared shortly after the war; "The Igbo, having lost the war, would not be permitted to win the peace."[436] From these indications, the Midwest military governor's prediction that it would not take the nation more than six months to reconcile the various ethnic groups was at best a personal wish with little hope of actualization by those in power. Not even Lieutenant Colonel Gowon appeared to have taken his promise to the nation very seriously; that he would take all measures to enhance reconciliation and national unity unless one concludes that most of his actions were again the product of external influence.[437]

The handling of Anioma workers displaced by the war followed the pattern often replayed in the country when matters concerning people of Igbo origin are contested. Anioma civil servants were disciplined with dismissals, demotions, and retirements for their role during the Biafran occupation of their state; but their Edo-speaking neighbors were not punished for their atrocious and malicious murder of the Anioma in the wake of the encroachment of federal troops into the same state. Similarly, the champions of the July 1966 countercoup who decimated military officers of Igbo extraction, including the then head of State as well as Igbo civilians in the northern and western parts of the country, were neither arrested nor questioned for their actions.

Another destabilizing act of the federal government during the rehabilitation exercise was its postwar currency exchange. It destabilized the Anioma as well as war victims in East Central State. In the bid to deny Biafra foreign exchange during the war, the Nigerian government changed its currency in 1968 but left the coins unaltered. Thus, all through the war the Nigerian coins and the Biafran money were in circulation in Biafra and in Anioma where they were used extensively for the transborder trade. At the end of the war a good number of Nigerians, particularly those in the war areas and border towns where the transborder trade had thrived, had both the old Nigerian coins and the Biafran currency. Currency soon became the key issue of immediate resettlement during the rehabilitation process. Only the new federal coinage was the acceptable legal tender everywhere, but it was in very short supply.[438]

Shortly after the war, the federal government directed all citizens in possession of both the banned Biafran currency and the old Nigerian coins to deposit them with the Central Bank. The majority of the citizens in question were, of course, in the eastern states and in Anioma. In compliance with the directive, people trooped to the bank for that purpose. The majority dumped all their illegal notes at one go on the assumption that they would receive an equivalent amount in return. The official decision on the next course of action was deferred for five months, largely because of the delay in opening up most of the commercial banks.[439] The federal government first described the Biafran currency as "worthless" and "useless" and concluded that depositors would get nothing in return for them. Within a couple of weeks, there was a change of policy, and perhaps of opinion, and the head of state offered in return for all the illegal currencies the sum of £20 to each depositor irrespective of the amount lodged in the banks. The federal government justified its action with the claim that the Biafran government looted the vaults of the Central Bank branches in Benin City and in the former Eastern Region, implying that the £20 reward was a magnanimous move on the part of the administration. The process of redeeming the banned currencies was complicated by the undoubted involvement in currency dealing both by military personnel and civilians.[440]

Many in Anioma were disappointed and devastated over their loss as a result of the twenty-pound compensation. Some, out of frustration and despair, decided to forgo the reward. They considered it unnecessary to take all the trouble queuing in front of bank premises for hours or for days on end, under the sun and in the rain, for such a paltry sum.[441] The after effects of the currency exchange were far-reaching. It gave rise to mistrust among relatives and friends. Individuals who did not personally change their own old currency were unable to appreciate that they were not being cheated when their emissaries failed to bring back something close to what they gave to be deposited for them, especially when they had to split the £20 with their emissaries. This feeling of mistrust was mostly expressed by the uneducated.

A female teacher from Asaba who traded extensively during the war recalled that, out of caution, she did not deposit all her illegal currency at once when the announcement for it was made. She waited until she heard the federal government's verdict on the exchange rate and then embarked on an installmental exchange using banks in East Central State instead of in Midwest. As a result, she succeeded in receiving more than the fixed amount of £20 per person.[442] With the exception of a success story like hers, the £20 compensation complicated the already circumscribed situation of many people after the hostilities. Those who were already battered by the crisis were further impoverished by the devaluation, which has been referred to as a subtle way of exacting war indemnity.[443]

The people of Anioma, along with the Igbo of East Central State, suffered from the punitive measures of the federal government towards the vanquished. Two official acts that impacted most negatively on the Anioma were the provisions of Decree 46 of 1970 and the currency exchange. Nevertheless, their kith and kin in the former Eastern Region suffered more under the federal government's punitive measures.

A year after the end of the war the federal government announced some increases in the wages and salaries for the public and private sector workers in the country. These took effect from January 1971. Four years later another increase—known as the Jerome Udoji award—was also announced, beginning from January 1975. These were widely welcomed by Nigerians just emerging from the war and its privations. The 1971 financial bonuses were not enjoyed by many of the displaced civil servants in Anioma whose fate was hanging in a balance when the payments began, and also by the disgraced and incarcerated Anioma military officers who were eventually dismissed from the Nigerian army, some of them without benefits. The federal government's salary increments were aimed at alleviating hardship in the nation. Instead of achieving that for all the citizens of the country, they compounded the situation of Anioma war victims excluded from the windfalls, as they were ultimately unprepared for the breathtaking inflation the payments generated.[444]

In 1975, after years of distressing experiences, people in the environs of Asaba and Ibusa in Aniocha had reason to reassess their perception of the Midwest and federal governments. What was responsible for the reassessment was the creation of the Oshimili local government area comprising towns in the Asaba-Ibusa environ, with Asaba as the headquarters. The towns that made up the new local government area were among the most battered by the war. This most welcome feat was accomplished by the Brigadier Murtala Mohammed administration after the removal of Yakubu Gowon from office through a *coup d'état* in 1975. The people of these towns saw the creation of the local government area as an official gesture intended to bring development to the devastated environ. In Asaba especially, the politically conscious class believed that the government's intention in creating the local government area and in making Asaba its headquarters was to pacify and compensate them for their grueling experiences in the war.[445] But the creation of more states and local government areas in the country in 1975 was simply one of the nine-point program enunciated by Yakubu Gowon as prerequisites for the return to civil rule after more than eight years of military rule in the country.[446] The interpretation given to the fulfillment of that promise in Asaba was exaggerated. It, nonetheless, exposed the gullibility of the people at the time. Notwithstanding, constituting them into a separate local government area helped to infuse hope in many individuals after their trauma from both the war and from the process of rehabilitation. It achieved more for the people psychologically than the Winning the Peace Program and the National Rehabilitation Plan.

The foregoing discussion has disclosed the attempts of the Midwest and federal governments at rehabilitating the people of Anioma after the Nigerian civil war. Their input and financial expenditure notwithstanding, the populist opinion in Anioma has been that nothing was done for them by the two administrations. Part of this assessment stemmed from some incidents that occurred during the rehabilitation period. Towns in Aniocha had variously appealed to the federal government for assistance with projects beyond their capacity to execute and with the arduous task of reconstruction and rehabilitation. In August 1970, Ibusa requested the reopening of the general post office in the town that served the entire Aniocha area. The post office had been destroyed during the war and remained nonfunctional for many months after the crisis.[447] The federal government did not directly respond to the appeal, but in March 1971 it provided the sum of £5,000 for the wiring of telephone lines damaged during the military operations in Asaba and its environs.[448] Two months later, in May 1971, residents of Asaba, unsatisfied at the extent of reconstruction in their town, wrote to Shehu Shagari, the federal commissioner for economic development, rehabilitation, and reconstruction, asking him to inquire into the plight of the people and to assist them with rehabilitation. The commissioner wrote back, saying, "the Federal Military Government is unable to approve your war damages claim."[449]

The overall efforts of the federal and state governments fell short of what the people anticipated. Hence, the topic of postcivil war rehabilitation was dismissed by the majority of the people in Anioma as mere official jargon.[450] Obviously that cannot be a balanced or an objective assessment of the situation. Yet it points to the basic truth that many war victims did not feel the impact of the National Reconstruction Plan or the State's Winning the Peace Program and therefore concluded that they were neglected by the state and federal governments after the war. In towns where relief and building materials were distributed, what was provided by the state government was insufficient for individuals who needed them, although the state's Rehabilitation and Reconstruction Committee acknowledged the federal government for its substantial help in their work, especially for "the ready financial and material assistance and encouragement...."[451]

The implementation of the rehabilitation programs did not realize Yakubu Gowon's goal for fighting the war, which he stated in July 1968 as guaranteeing "equal status and opportunity for all ethnic groups" that would lay a "sounder foundation for political stability and more rapid and even development." Moreover, it was also deficient in bringing to pass Gowon's promise that: "There will be no second class citizens in [the] country."[452] Similarly, the flaw in the state government's scheme was its focus. It was not people-oriented but concentrated on damaged infrastructure. While that on its own improved the circumstances of the people, the greater attention given to infrastructures precluded the government from investing directly and adequately in the victims' welfare. In addition to that, most official measures were punitive and consequently muddled the positive steps taken by the state administration towards the people's rehabilitation.

INDIVIDUAL EFFORTS AT REHABILITATION

As already stated, the military governor of the Midwest informed the people there that the state's need for rehabilitation was more than its financial capacity could meet. Nine months later, the same points were restated by the state's commissioner for health on behalf of the governor.[453] The people of Anioma did not wait for the state governor before commencing with their rehabilitation projects. In the euphoria that attended news of the end of the war, individuals visited each other, empathizing with one another over their plight and rejoicing mutually on their survival. Those who were not displaced welcomed home the returnees who had taken shelter outside their towns. It was in the course of the visits that women apprised themselves of each other's needs. Those who had reserves of clothes made donations from their reserves to the unlucky ones who were in dire need of decent body coverings. The mutual encouragement given and received during these meetings was therapeutic and soothing to those who felt themselves terribly battered by the war.

Women did not rely solely on the food items given out by the State Rehabilitation Committee or by the federal military units. In addition to the individual efforts at securing needed relief materials, aid was communally organized in many towns. Groups of people who were outside Anioma during the crisis or in sections of Anioma little affected by the emergency rushed in second-hand clothes, drugs, and food to their respective communities for distribution to the needy. Food also came through farmers in the less brutalized towns who were able to farm but unable to move beyond the confines of their communities before the termination of the military operations. They channeled their farm proceeds to the poorer towns. The major problem was the long distances to be covered on foot. The intention of the farmers was primarily to make money, but their effort helped to improve the food situation in the places visited.

Between 1968 and 1969, the number of Anioma indigenes in different parts of the Western Region had increased beyond what it was in 1967. Thus, by 1970, many of those outside the militarized areas of the country had considerably resettled themselves and were in a position through their various town unions to give aid to others who were less privileged. Igbo migrants formed town unions in different parts of the country where they sojourned. These unions, later called associations in compliance with government statement that unions were fostering political ideas,[454] provided security and collective insurance against natural and other disasters to individuals from a given locality. The unions encouraged unity and cooperative efforts and in various ways offered assistance to their hometowns through the parent body.[455] They were known to operate efficiently in cases of emergency. Anioma indigenes residing in the western part of the country and those outside the country supported their towns after the war. There was no town in Aniocha that did not benefit from external help or was at pains to point to individuals who also benefited from comparable assistance. It was such organized help that partly enabled many families to recoup after the war. The majority in Anioma who had access to external aid was not as indigent as war survivors in East Central State, the former Biafran enclave.[456]

With the war over, town leaders took steps towards the spiritual rehabilitation of both the people and their towns. This was accomplished through general ritual cleansing and was done all over Anioma for the population and for the land to avert any impending catastrophe that might result from the anger of the venerated gods of the land. The civil war had encouraged a disregard of the moral code of the people. Part of what the spiritual leaders did was to carry out ritual purification for those women whom they felt transgressed the laws of the land in the course of the crisis by conducting themselves in manners considered inappropriate by the norms of the people.

Some of these women did not need much prodding before taking steps to rid themselves, albeit temporarily, of the stigma of their behavior. Women in Aniocha and Ukwuani sections of Anioma confessed their actions to their various female leaders – the umuada, ada, or the omu. Their counterparts in the Ika area took similar steps with the nwunye wives mentioned in chapter 1. The female leaders supervised the purification rites and counseled the affected women appropriately. In spite of these efforts many injured husbands were most reluctant to take back their wives because of the belief in Igboland that doing so would lead to their death or to some other disaster. The women's repentant acts, vigorous cleansing ceremonies, and obvious willingness to return to their matrimonial homes did not impress such husbands.[457]

Women supervised the ritual purification of other women but local rulers in conjunction with ritual specialists saw to the cleansing of the land and the rehabilitation of the sacred buildings that were destroyed during the war or left dilapidated because of military operations. With these ceremonies and reconstruction work, the various community leaders felt convinced that they had precluded any retribution that might be visited on the land and its occupants as an aftermath to the people's activities and those of the soldiers during the civil war.

The federal government had promised in its *Blue Print for Post-War Reconstruction* that those who fled their normal places of residence or business would be resettled and, if possible, helped to make a new start. In July 1968, Yakubu Gowon announced in a national broadcast that the federal government "shall make all necessary arrangements to ensure the security of all Nigerians wherever they choose to reside and take all measures to enhance reconciliation and national unity."[458] Many indigenes of Anioma who fled northern Nigeria as a result of the national disturbances that preceded the war were most reluctant to return to their former places of abode. Their refusal was an indication that they doubted the veracity of these official statements, and the federal government actually made little effort beyond the ordinary to encourage their return. Their prewar experiences in these places culminated in a phobia and have remained one of the lasting consequences of the political turmoil that rocked the Nigerian nation from 1966 to 1970.

Those who were determined not to venture outside Igboland for fear of a recurrence of what forced their exodus from other regions of the country looked to their kith and kin for assistance in resettling themselves and their families. Some opted to farm while others decided on one trade or another. The prospective farmers waited for a couple of months for the farming season to commence. Friendly and sympathetic relations, friends, and neighbors made land grants as well as donations of seed-yams and other seedlings to them.[459] The artisans among them acquired the basic implements they needed for their trade and continued as before.

On the part of the women, many went back to their prewar vocations. In the course of readjustment some switched to better alternatives, but not immediately. The bulk of them, however, took to trading. Trade was the avenue opened to the majority of the people. For one reason, the termination of the war in January, in the middle of the dry season, meant a delay in the commencement of farming activities. In the meantime, women continued with trade as an emergency postwar occupation but went about it in a better atmosphere than during the hostilities. Female traders did not wait for the markets to be reconstructed before taking off with the business of buying and selling. In such places as Okpanam, Isheagu, Ibusa, Asaba, and Okwe, trade was sometimes by barter because of the relative scarcity of money. Indeed, the centuries' old system has proved handy during emergencies. It greatly helped individuals without ready cash to partake in trade.

While some women made use of the old market sites for exchanges, others converted sections of their houses into minisupermarkets, using tables to display their goods. Nearly all the adult women became traders of sorts after the war. Unimaginable odds and ends were sold and bought by women in their bid for self-rehabilitation. The redistributive trade spanned a wider geographical reach than was possible during the war, and different communities again hosted traders from as far afield as Abakiliki and Nsukka in East Central State. Market activities were profitable and female traders were able, from their market proceeds, to improve their circumstances. But this was not automatic. Interviewees reported that for the first six months after the war there was no extraordinary change in the situation of many rural women in Anioma.[460] Consequently, within that period, unemployed women accepted all manner of menial jobs as a temporary measure pending the opportunity for more enduring and rewarding activities.

The need for quick rehabilitation led to a multiplication of economic engagements, and most women took up as many as three different occupations concurrently. For instance, most school teachers were also shop keepers. When the farming season eventually commenced those who could combine agriculture with trade and with any other professional activity did so, and indeed many resorted to such an arrangement. Interestingly enough the women did not see their efforts as peculiar or as an undue rush for either money or wealth but as the normal response to their situation. Also, farming to the Igbo is a generalized activity, almost a way of life, and women were not recognized as professional farmers even though they were the major contributors to farm labor. With such a traditional concept of farming, any woman who combined any other engagement with farming rarely interpreted it as being involved in more than one occupation.

In Agbor and Asaba, a plethora of small-scale restaurants and drinking parlors sprang up unlike what existed before or during the emergency. Women were the proprietors of the majority of these drinking parlors. While formal jobs were hard to come by, these small-scale restaurants and drinking parlors provided employment for female adolescents and young adults who were out of school or unable to continue with their education. They also joined the labor force as shopkeepers. The jobs were temporary and the conditions of service were very fluid. Job security was hinged on the income generated by the employee for her employer. As long as the former was making reasonable profit, there was a chance of remaining on the job; otherwise she was replaced by another job seeker. The new businesses springing up in the war-devastated towns both provided employment and reawakened industrial activity, helping to bring about economic improvement to those places.

The end of the war saw a gradual influx of non-Igbo, mainly Yoruba and Edo traders in Anioma towns. It was one advantage the towns had over the more rural areas. The presence of free-spending federal soldiers in these places attracted non-Igbo traders, some of whom provided minor tasks for local youths. With time, the number of youthful girls and women in the rural areas decreased as they moved to the bigger towns and cities outside Anioma. The outside world seemed to promise better prospects but it did not turn out that way for all the semiliterate young women. These still had to contend with competitors from other parts of the nation for the few jobs available.[461]

The desire to resettle and to recover from the trauma of the war led women into some ingenious activities. One interesting response to postwar survival was observed in the effort of Rhoda Chenimuya from Isheagu. Rhoda emerged from the war with nothing except the clothes she had on her back and some quantities of Beans, received while at St. Patrick's refugee camp in Asaba. She carefully reserved part of her bean ration since she was not certain at the time how much longer the refugees would have access to free food items. Fortunately, her stock was not exhausted by the time the war ended. As her husband was waiting to return to his job as a laborer at the School of Agriculture, Anwai-Asaba, Rhoda supported her family by frying beancakes from the grains she saved while in the camp. To fry the cakes, she needed a frying pan. She had neither a pan nor the money with which to buy one. Undaunted, she picked a small battered and bottomless basin from a refuse dump, had the missing base fixed by a welder and converted it into a frying pan. People patronized her, but sometimes she bartered her cakes for items her family needed but had no money with which to pay.[462]

A good aspect of the reconstruction program was the motivation it gave to towns in Anioma to embark on development projects in response to the state government's challenge and promise to meet them midway through the process. Many town unions were revitalized for that purpose. Issele-mkpitime took up the challenge of building a maternity home and received an award of fifty pounds as government aid towards their self-help project. The Umu-ekeke section of Akwukwu-Igbo also received the same amount to facilitate the completion of their fishing pond.[463] The Asaba Development Association (ADA) recorded some important achievements worth mentioning in this study. These included the construction of a stadium in the town through communal efforts and without any government aid. Before the state governor could make good his promise of financial assistance, Gowon's regime was toppled and he was removed. Nevertheless, the stadium built solely by communal efforts stands today as the official stadium of the present Delta

State. Other achievements of the association were: rebuilding the palace of their asagba destroyed during the war, building a coed secondary school, and aiding local transportation by providing two minivans to ply the town. These tasks were undertaken piecemeal between 1972 and 1979.

The efforts of Asaba men provoked Asaba women who formed the Asaba Ladies League (ALL) in 1977 as part of their own initiative in the development of their town. Resourcefulness, as they put it, was the basis of eligibility for interested members. ALL embraced the educated and noneducated women, the old and also the young. The group was organized as a cooperative with the ultimate aim of enhancing the economic status of Asaba women. They raised money through regular contributions, levies, and open appeals for funds. What they received was invested in the construction of a building, which, on completion, they intended to rent out to persons needing office spaces and business centers. It was agreed that members of the league needing financial assistance for private businesses would borrow from what the group realized from rents on the building and pay the group back after a given period. Understandably, financial constraints prevented ALL from completing the structure as intended, but the ground floor of the building was properly finished. Money generated from the completed part swelled the league's coffers but not as much as would have been realized if the entire structure had been completed.[464] The importance of the building was not fully felt until 1992 when Delta State was carved out of the old Bendel State and the new state found itself in dire need of office space. One of the few available structures that could serve that purpose was ALL's partly completed building. The first military governor of Delta State had the building renovated and converted into state government offices. It served as the state's secretariat for over five years until the state's permanent secretariat was completed.

Many war victims were disillusioned with the rehabilitation efforts of the state and federal governments. They looked inward rather than outward for their total recovery. The tempo of individual rehabilitation was not sustained throughout the decade of the 1970s. Although the process continued beyond the Gowon administration, it slacked off in the mid-1970s. By this time a lot of changes and readjustments had taken place; many rural women in Anioma were beginning to forget most of their wartime experiences or had put them behind them, and the former rhythm of life had been considerably reestablished.[465] Yet, on a personal level, women in Anioma continued to improve their situation till the end of the military regime in 1979.

For their parts, the federal and Midwest governments' rehabilitation programs had no specific dates proffered by their various architects for their completion. The federal government incorporated its rehabilitation scheme in the National Development Plan of 1970–1974. In the same manner, the Winning the Peace Program was formulated as part of the overall development goal of Midwest State.[466] The commander of the Second Division in Midwest noted that official commitment to rehabilitation was pursued till 1972.[467] It is not far from the truth to say that these official programs ended with the Gowon administration in 1975. With the change of government then, the first priority of Brigadier Murtala Mohammed as Nigeria's head of state was what can be called "de-Gowonization." This involved the dismantling of the governing apparatus of Yakubu Gowon and the reversal of most of his programs.

In summary, irrespective of the attempts of Midwest and the Federal governments at reconstruction and rehabilitation, Anioma war victims were chiefly responsible for their recovery. This is attested to by Gowon's biographer; who wrote that one of the factors that helped the nation to recover faster than could have been expected was "the efforts of the peoples of the war affected areas in self-help."[468] Another tribute to the war victims' advance towards their rehabilitation came from Shehu Shagari, the federal commissioner for economic development, rehabilitation, and reconstruction in the postwar Gowon regime. After touring the war theaters, he confessed that he "was greatly impressed by the industry and vigour of the people themselves who were ready to rehabilitate themselves, their towns, and villages irrespective of the assistance from government and aid agencies."[469]

An aspect of the three Rs that received little attention from the two governments was reconciliation. In spite of verbal assurances to that effect by Yakubu Gowon, the head of state, and Major Ogbemudia's prediction that it would not take the nation more than six months to achieve, the Midwest and federal postwar rehabilitation programs went contrary to the spirit of reconciliation. As a result, the Igbo, on both sides of the Niger, still feel aggrieved and marginalized in the country.

CONCLUSION

An August 1968 editorial in *The Times*, London, stated "few wars in modern times have aroused such widespread anguish as that between the Federal Government of Nigeria and breakaway Biafra."[470] While this assertion at the time was indisputable, recent realities indicate that not all that should be known about that war and its impacts on the peoples of Nigeria have been made known. Attention is drawn in the present study to a significant segment of the Nigerian society whose experiences during the war have until now received little or no attention. Undeniably, different towns, smaller communities, and individuals in Anioma have different perceptions of the war and stories on the activities of both the federal and Biafran troops in their localities during the hostilities. Nevertheless, the crisis affected every aspect of the lives of women in Anioma, the Igbo section of Midwest State.

Anioma, located west of the river Niger, was part of the Western Region until 1963 when, with other minorities of that region, it formed Midwestern Region, renamed Midwestern State in 1967. Throughout its history Anioma's identity has been Igbo. Its solidarity with the Igbo heartland, east of the Niger, was never questioned and this was the reason for its strong support of Biafra during and after secession. Prevented by its location in Midwest State from forming a geographical and administrative unit during the civil war with the Igbo, east of the Niger, the Anioma contributed immensely to the success of the Biafran dream. Anioma men fought as Biafrans, and the women constituted the ROB unit of the Biafran militia, with an insignificant number participating in combat. The conviction that they would be safer in the Igbo heartland made a commendable number of Anioma people move into Biafra during the war, where they swelled Anioma population already resident there. But the majority, excepting those found in parts of western Nigeria, remained in Anioma until the end of hostilities.

The Nigerian civil war posed a multifaceted challenge to Anioma women. It was not an incident that swept only the region known as Biafra between May 1967 and January 1970, leaving an insignificant mark on other parts of the federation. Anioma felt the impact of the war. It was bombed and strafed during the first three months of the federal occupation of the area. And intermittently during the crisis, selected areas were subjected to military aggression. The military clashes occurred in the three sections of Anioma, with battles fought on the doorsteps of some families and leading to the displacement of many. The women had every reason to be petrified and terrorized by what went on around them. The predominantly hostile group of federal soldiers in their locality and the massacre of their men worsened the psychological torment they suffered from the actions of that group of soldiers.

Some obvious lessons have emerged from the present investigation. In the first instance, it is evident that wars and conflict situations do not always, or often, resolve the issues that lead to them. Pope Pius XII warned in 1932, some three decades before the 1966 disturbances in Nigeria, "Nothing is lost by peace, everything may be lost by war."[471] The wisdom in this simple statement was amply demonstrated during and after the Nigerian civil war. To begin with, the Igbo who felt mistreated and severely discriminated against in the federation[472] were, with the federal victory over the Biafran forces, forced to recant their secession. They were ultimately subjected to the lot of vanquished peoples through the punitive measures that were part of the national and Midwest postwar rehabilitation programs. Very little in these programs manifested "the generous and warm welcome awaiting all Ibos" or the promise to "forgive the errors" made by the head of state before the end of the hostilities.[473]

The soldiers and officers of the Nigerian army who were deployed for military operations in Anioma paid scant attention to Lieutenant Colonel Gowon's Code of Conduct for the operations and for the treatment of women and other civilians.[474] In assessing the performance of the federal troops in Anioma *vis-à-vis* the Code of Conduct it should not be forgotten that the military operations in Anioma during the emergency were inseparable from what was pursued by other divisions of the Nigerian army in Biafra. The Anioma, though outside Biafra, were subjected to nearly the same treatment as those in the seceding region. Deep-seated animosity was visible in the manner in which the soldiers of the Second Division carried out their assignment in Anioma. Their campaigns were not only to flush out Biafrans and reclaim the entire Midwest, they seem also to include shredding the numerical strength of Anioma as well as of the entire Igbo nation.

For logistic purposes, federal troops in the Midwest were concentrated in Anioma. Few towns, privileged by their inaccessible locations, escaped playing host to soldiers, yet a few of these towns, through their diplomatic maneuvers in addition to their location, were spared the agony associated with an occupation army. Federal soldiers pursued their assignment in Anioma with the understanding that the people were emotionally bound to their fellow Igbo in Biafra and therefore would sabotage by overt and covert means the federal government's stand on "One Nigeria." Disregarding the head of state's code, they clamped down on the people, and until the end of the war the Anioma were repressed and subdued, while the women in particular being exploited, abused, and violated.

There was also a correlation between the progress of the war in Biafra and the federal army's treatment of Anioma civilians. Gains made by the Biafran army at the expense of the federal troops led to intensification of the military's intimidation of

Anioma communities. The inclusion of the Midwest in the territory under the sovereign authority of the Nigerian government during the emergency did not guarantee the protection of the Anioma as it did the other sections of the state. The state military governor and the general officers who commanded the Second Division between September 1967 and January 1970, along with their brigade commanders, expended little effort in protecting women and other civilians during the hostilities as stipulated in the code. It was in 1969, barely a year before the end of the war, that the Second Division commander announced that civilians should report cases of molestation by federal troops. This notwithstanding, the menace posed by the soldiers did not cease until months after the war, thus showing the blatant disregard of the Nigerian military for the rights and privileges of civilians. From all indications, military security did not imply human security. Real security, according to Betty Reardon, lies in the well-being of the people, when they are protected against harm of any kind, when their basic needs are met, when they experience human dignity and human rights, when they are in a healthy, natural environment capable of sustaining life.[475] All these were lacking during the Nigerian civil war. But while it may be argued that the federal soldiers were unduly hard on the people, it should be borne in mind that the Anioma did not make their assignment an easy one. The Anioma made no pretence of their support for Biafra rather than for the federal government and they expended much energy in aiding Biafran war efforts even while officially and geographically in Nigeria.

The upheavals leading to the civil war and the military operations of the soldiers of the Second Division of the Nigerian army in the Midwest adversely affected intergroup relations in the country, particularly between the Anioma and other ethnic groups in Midwest State. The peaceful relationship between the Anioma on one hand and the Edo and the Urhobo/Isoko on the other was disrupted by the crisis. Anioma indigenes were grieved that many of their family members died at the hands of their non-Igbo neighbors when the federal troops arrived in the Midwest instead of from the soldiers' bullets. Ironically, most Anioma victims of the incursion were certain that their friendship with the Edo, Itshekiri, and the Urhobo/Isoko would ensure their safety in the non-Igbo sections of their state. They were proven wrong and were grossly mistaken, as demonstrated by their subsequent massacre in parts of the Midwest occupied by these groups.

What further aggravated the situation in Anioma and upset the peaceful coexistence of the ethnic groups in the state was the predominant number of soldiers of Edo and Urhobo/Isoko origin in the Second Division. All over Anioma, individuals recalled that the non-Igbo Midwest soldiers led most of the molestation and killings of the Anioma during the town-to-town reconquest of the area. John de St. Jorre confirms this with his statement that the massacre in Asaba was perpetrated at the instance of "an Ibo-hating major from Benin (a Bini) ...."[476] The attitude of the non-Igbo peoples of the Midwest towards the Anioma soured interethnic relations in the state. Until today the Anioma relate to the Urhobo/Isoko and the Edo with some distrust and are sometimes quick to recall the incidents of September 1967.[477] Despite the recent creation of Edo State, thus removing the Anioma from direct interaction with the core Edo-speaking group, the Anioma remain optimistic about a time in the future when they would constitute a state of their own. This, some feel, might help reduce the friction still subtly evident in their interactions with the Urhobo/Isoko, with whom they are lumped together along with the Itshekiri in Delta State. Excluding the strained relationship between the Anioma and other ethnic groups in the Midwest, the persecution Anioma indigenes in Lagos suffered at the hands of the Yoruba during the hostilities for a time equally strained good relations between persons of Anioma and Yoruba origins.

The soldiers of the Second Division of the Nigerian army presented themselves as an unprincipled and uncultured bunch. This is the apparent general conclusion, judging from their individual and collective actions in Anioma. Nevertheless, there were some disciplined soldiers in the rank and file and among the officer cadre, but their gentlemanly acts were shrouded by the scandalous acts of the majority of the combatants.

The federal troops' acts of brutality worked simultaneously in two ways. On the one hand they had the cumulative effect of strengthening the psychological attachment of some Anioma women to the core Igbo area, east of the Niger. On the other hand they had an entirely opposite impact, giving rise to an antipathy towards the Igbo on the east of the Niger. Some of the women who felt more attachment to the Igbo, east of the Niger, exemplified their conviction by joining the Biafran militia – the only unit of the Biafran army that accepted females among its membership, constituting the ROB women. They found in the militia the opportunity to avenge the deaths of family members and friends during the pogrom and in the raging crisis. A few joined in the fighting. Even though their efforts were not recognized, female combatants still claim a place for themselves among the men who have achieved the respect of their fellow citizens by their willingness to risk their lives for the sake of their ideals.[478] None of these women were known to have relatives in the Igbo heartland and the majority had never lived east of the Niger. Among the exceptions were Beatrice Nwandu, who completed her secondary education in Onitsha in 1966; and Tina Okwuashi, who also worked in Onitsha briefly before the eruption of the crisis. Other women from Anioma who felt an attachment with the Igbo, east of the Niger, took part in the transborder trade essentially on humanitarian grounds, to help fellow Igbo survive the war, and out of spite to frustrate the efforts and goal of the Nigerian army in Biafra. By their action the women publicly disclosed that in spite of their disadvantaged social standing they were not without an opinion of their own but, rather were capable of determining the eventual outcome of an intractable problem. Through the transborder trade female participants on both sides of the Niger prolonged the duration of the war for as long as was possible. Officers of the Second Division acknowledged that the trade strengthened Biafra's resistance. It undermined the federal attempt to force a quick surrender by starvation.[479] The federal officers never relented in crying out against the involvement of the Anioma in that trade relationship until the war ended. Efforts of the ROB women and the transborder traders reinforced the unity between the two Igbo groups during the hostilities.

Three factors contributed to the antipathy some of the Anioma felt towards the Igbo, east of the Niger, during and after the conflict: (i) an uncomplimentary remark by Biafran stragglers about Anioma women, (ii) the conclusion that the Biafran government did not protect the Anioma from the onslaught of the federal army, and (iii) the resentment against the war because of the losses that attended it. Women in Anioma fiercely maintained that Biafran soldiers were protective of them and treated them humanely, but some of the Biafran soldiers, out of frustration, perhaps, called some women "*Igbo Hausa*," which by implication meant that they were fake Igbo or double-dealing Igbo. The individuals thus addressed rarely tolerated this comment, especially in the face of their predicament for their support of Biafra's secession. Anioma's location outside the Igbo heartland could have played a part in this mistrust. Biafran soldiers, and perhaps other persons from the heartland, who were not in Anioma during the hostilities were at pains to appreciate the depth of support of the Anioma for Biafra and therefore doubted their sincerity, giving rise to some uncomplimentary comments and accusations.

The other reason for friction stems from the fact that many in Anioma were of the opinion that the Biafran government did little to protect them from the onslaught of the federal army after the Biafran withdrawal from Anioma.[480] Quite a good number of people in Anioma, including those born after the war, hold these grievances. As an after effect of the unassuaged hurt the Anioma feel towards their fellow Igbo, some among them deny any link with the Igbo homeland and would refer to themselves as people of the Delta rather than as Igbo, for indeed they are an offshoot of the Igbo ethnic group. In the Ika area, Igbo-akiri, a border town between Edo and Anioma, changed its name to Igbanke and relinquished its Igbo identity, claiming Edo origin but still retaining its use of the Igbo language.[481] The misunderstanding between the Anioma and the Igbo, east of the Niger, remains one of the negative effects of the civil war on the Igbo. By accusing the central Igbo of neglect and a lack of support and protection during the crisis, the Anioma failed to acknowledge the efforts of the Biafran army towards stopping the federal invasion of their towns at the onset of the war and midway through the crisis. The account of the Biafran attempts to relieve Anioma of federal troops is recounted in chapter 3. The attempt was initiated partly in the bid to do this and partly to lessen the threat on Biafran territory that further infiltration were made by the seceding army into Anioma from Easter 1968 until the end of the war.

The feeling of antipathy towards the people in the Igbo heartland was complicated by the sense of loss that attended the war. Loss of jobs, businesses, homes, houses, and other property added to the distress experienced by the Anioma during the war. For some people, it doused their support of the war, resulting in their blaming whatever and whoever caused the crisis. Such people could no longer see the link between Chukwuma Nzeogwu's coup of January 1966 and the hostilities that followed Biafra's declaration of secession in May 1967. Although Nzeogwu was from Okpanam in Anioma; to the Anioma, his coup d'état and the Biafran secession were distinct incidents, and they resented the latter, blaming it for their woes while the war lasted.[482] Notwithstanding, the majority in Anioma remained convinced of the justness of Biafra's secession and longingly anticipated the realization of the Igbo dream for independence. That they were disappointed in the end is doubtless. It was actually after the war that resentment towards the Igbo, east of the Niger, blaming them for the war, became very evident among the Anioma.

The sexual assault on women and the consequent uncontrolled spread of venereal diseases in the towns that played host to federal soldiers is not the first of its kind in accounts on war. Similar situations were noted with towns in Biafra[483] and in other war-torn areas in and outside Africa. It is undisputed that the number of female initiates into the commercial sex trade increases during war. This opinion is supported by a number of studies on different countries from Europe to Asia that have been affected by wars.[484] In the case of Anioma, the lifestyle of the federal soldiers gave a fillip to prostitution, aided the spread of venereal diseases, and provided a conducive atmosphere for the emergence of female pimps, an occupation that contravened the moral code of the people. Prostitution was not entirely the aftermath of women being forced to submit to the pleasure of the combatants but also a direct consequence of the privations they were subjected to because of the crisis. But the widespread raping of Igbo girls and abduction of women after the war contradicted the federal government's claim of "No victor, no vanquished."[485]

Wars and crisis situations provide the most appropriate time for assessing the extent of development in a given country or locality. Midwest State managed with extremely few medical resources until the war engulfed Anioma. The few available hospitals in that section of the state were grossly inadequate for the emergency situation the war created, showing that basic health and sanitation levels drop in militarized places.[486] The dearth of hospitals and health centers and the inability of existing ones to provide adequate services for those in Anioma were a reflection on the situation in the country as a whole. One positive effect of this deficiency was the federal government's postwar effort towards the expansion of the health sector in the country. The impressive sum of £35.5 million pounds (Nigerian pounds) was shared out to the twelve states of the federation to expedite the improvement of health services in their respective territories.[487] The allocation to the Midwest was used as reported in chapter 6 to construct, among others, two hospitals and two rural health centers in Anioma after the emergency.

The relative absence of expatriate missionaries in Nigeria was another aftereffect of the war. The involvement of various church groups and organizations in the politics of the war was resented by Nigerian officials, and as soon as the war ended, the government expelled many missionaries and severely cut down the number to be allowed in the country. It went further and handed over mission schools to the various state governments.

War impacts a people's economy as much as it does other aspects of a people's life. In addition to other changes it brought about, the Nigerian civil war reshuffled and reorganized female economic pursuits and activities in Anioma. The insecurity that prevailed during the emergency and restrictions on movements determined the economic engagements that flourished during the crisis. There was a general decline in the foremost economic activities of Anioma women, but the emergency and the food shortages it attracted brought about a multiplication of economic engagements and the display of some degree of ingenuity by women. Female entrepreneurs emerged from among those who made a living as food contractors and restaurant keepers during the war.

The declining status of ritual specialists was arrested by the war. The importance of these professionals was rediscovered and found useful by those in the militarized areas during the lingering insecurity. But unlike this group of professionals and their trade, the deathblow the war dealt the small-scale cloth-weaving industry has not been reversed these past three decades. Admittedly, the cloth-weaving industry in Anioma began its decline during the colonial era. Its demise, however, was speeded up by the war. In the first instance, many weavers lost their weaving equipment to the war. Second, the constant threat of death from military operations and the curtailed currency circulation made people least concerned with what to wear and with their overall appearance. The termination of the hostilities did not make female weavers return to their prewar engagement. The more urgent need for food and shelter forced professional weavers and other women into trade, thereby causing a diversion from their usual economic activities. Furthermore, the younger women were more intent on catching up on their education and on making quick money to facilitate both their personal rehabilitation and that of their families and not in learning weaving skills from either their mothers or grandmothers.

More importantly, many women in Anioma, from their observations during the war, realized how educationally and economically incapacitated they were. For some, the end of the war marked the end of a life of subsistence. A number of adult women courageously returned to school to be trained for a formal occupation at the end of which they switched to better-paying civil service jobs while others switched to better professions.[488] From this time on the education of women, which was not popularly supported before the war, received a boost in Anioma, with mothers spearheading the campaign at the family level.

The resilience of women in Anioma stands out clearly from this study. This was their greatest asset and was responsible for their self-recovery after their ordeal. In this regard, we can say that the war did have positive consequences. It inspired women to break out of their traditional roles to assume new ones. Their exertions during the period undermined the myth of incapability and fickle-mindedness often ascribed to women, at least to those in Anioma. The determination to live through the crisis made the feeble develop the measure of strength necessary for survival amidst great odds. Not all the men appreciated this change; hence some expressed the opinion that the war spoiled their women and made them less submissive. A number of them still look forward to the day when women are seen and not heard and when their leadership and managerial abilities become restricted and confined to their families as was the case in previous decades.[489]

The ordeal women passed through in Anioma was twofold: the first was the war, preceded by the pogrom; and the second was the process of resettlement afterwards. Many women emerged from the crisis sick, weak, malnourished, and mostly with nothing. The trauma of the war was not properly cushioned by the combined efforts of the Midwest and federal governments through their rehabilitation programs. The implementation of these plans ran contrary to their tenets. Instead of repairing the psychological and emotional damages sustained by women, they created further problems for the victims.

Commendable progress was made in infrastructural reconstruction but none in human rehabilitation or in national reconciliation. The punitive measures incorporated to the rehabilitation programs denied these exercises any therapeutic effect they might have had on the Anioma people. Some families are still languishing because of egregiously inadequate human rehabilitation. In addition, obvious cracks in national integration remain because the sections of the programs that should have taken care of reconciliation were badly handled. A proper rehabilitation program is positive and not negative. Punitive measures should have had no place in the postwar rehabilitation process particularly after the declaration of "No victor, no vanquished." In effect, the implementation of the programs was faulty and their positive aspects were vitiated by the punitive measures.

The short-term and long-term effects of war should make responsible governments steer clear of any course of action that can potentially result in military hostilities. Yet, where it is inevitable, governments should protect its civilian population, especially women and children, who constitute the most vulnerable in any society. It is imperative that Nigeria formulate concrete means of checking excesses by its soldiers. Some orientation is necessary to make professional combatants aware that civilians should be treated as friends and as individuals needing protection and not as enemies or combatants during crisis. Women must cease to be made objects of booty or weapons of war whereby molesting and abusing them become a means of displaying the superior strength of combatants. The Nigerian civil war has ended, and nothing of its kind is anticipated in the future. Nevertheless, these lessons will help inform and enrich the soldiers that the country produces and maintains.

Government must recognize that women suffer serious emotional and psychological torment during wars. The humiliation of being a victim of abduction or rape lives on in the minds of the victims and in the consciousness of their neighbors. The intensity of the pain many Anioma women felt over the brutality and abuse they suffered can only be imagined. The revelations of women in Anioma about the war should encourage the government to set up special counseling services that are female-focused to help the overall recovery of the war victims. Incidentally, many still have their experiences bottled up in memory, leading to occasional manifestations of varying degrees of schizophrenia. Such situations make postcrisis counseling services for women necessary and is an important aspect of the rehabilitation process.

The Nigerian government must make concerted efforts to bridge the gap between the various ethnic groups in the country. The scars of the war on intergroup relations are very obvious and if left to linger would continue to degenerate into further violent eruptions. To exact genuine reconciliation, a country and its people must face up to its past and learn the necessary lessons from that past. The recently established commission to investigate human rights violations in the country since independence might go a long way in effecting the much-needed reconciliation among the peoples of the country. Part of its activities includes conducting public hearings, researching and investigating cases, and dealing with reparation and rehabilitation matters. The commission is to determine underlying motives for abuses, identify the victims, and make appropriate recommendations for redress and reconciliation.[490] Already the Igbo from the two sides of the Niger have jointly testified to the atrocious treatment meted out to them since 1966.[491] It is hoped that the federal government would complement the efforts of the commission in redressing the wounds of the past.

Appendix A: Writings on the Nigerian Civil War

The civil war years constitute a challenging epoch in the history of Nigeria. Authors from within and outside Nigeria have written extensively on the subject with a focus on the region called Biafra from May 1967 until 15 January 1970. The first group of writings represents those of foreigners, most of them war correspondents. There are many works in this category and the themes treated are varied. Frederick Forsyth in *The Biafran Story* (1969) tried to justify Biafra's secession, while A. Waugh and S. Cronje in *Biafra: Britain's Shame* (1969) condemned Britain's support of the Nigerian government during the crisis. These and other foreign authors[492] in different ways canvassed for international recognition and support for the young Republic of Biafra in order to give it a chance for survival.

The second group of writings provides adequate information on the civil war. They are best described as introductory works, with writers providing brief or detailed accounts of the war and its effects. From these works readers are saturated with the causes, courses, and consequences of the war for the Igbo and other peoples of Nigeria. Taken as a whole, the contents of these books[493] reveal the divergent perceptions and convictions of their authors on the causes and consequences of the national crisis. A few examples include *Biafra: The Making of a Nation* by A. A. Nwankwo and S. U. Ifejika (1969); *Nigeria, Dilemma of Nationhood* edited by J. O. Okpaku (1972); and *The Struggle for Secession 1966–1970* by N. U. Akpan (1972). Other works also in this category that consider issues relating to the war, to the Nigerian nation, and to the Biafran Republic but whose subthemes cannot be given a specific heading include Bernard Odogwu's *No Place to Hide: Crises and Conflicts Inside Biafra* (1985), and Ken Saro-Wiwa's *On a Darkling Plain: An Account of the Nigerian Civil War* (1989).[494] Saro-Wiwa presented an unsentimental view of Biafra and Biafrans during their struggle for survival as a nation. His account provides insight into the feelings of the minority groups in the Eastern Region on the events unfolding around them. There was no pretense over his (and their) preference for a united Nigeria instead of being integrated into Biafra. Wole Soyinka, *The Man Died* (1972), and Elechi Amadi, *Sunset in Biafra* (1973), both narrated their mistreatment by the Nigerian and Biafran authorities during the war, showing the predilection for those in power to mistreat their presumed enemies.

Works by military personnel come third in this categorization. Writers in this group can be divided into two. One group writes about the 15 January 1966 purge. Among them are Adewale Ademoyega, who authored *Why We Struck: The Story of the First Nigerian Coup* (1975); and Ben Gbulie, who wrote *Nigeria's Five Majors* (1981). They presented their individual accounts of the *coup d'état* they were privy to, why it took place, how it was planned and executed, what goals and corrective measures the planners set out to achieve, and why the putsch failed. The other group of military writers is drawn from the Nigerian and Biafran armed forces. We have A. Madiebo's *The Nigerian Revolution and the Biafran War* (1980); Olusegun Obasanjo's *My Command* (1980); and J. O. G. Achuzia's *Requiem Biafra* (1986). These authors discuss their military careers and the execution of the war but, with the exception of Achuzia, also incorporate the January 1966 purge in their writings.[495]

Requiem Biafra includes an account of Biafra's Midwest operation, which marked the formal incorporation of Anioma into the theater of war. Although it does not discuss the input made by Anioma female members of the Biafran militia, a paramilitary group, it did acknowledge their presence in Biafra and pays a befitting tribute to them for the role they played. Achuzia, who is from Anioma and considered one of Biafra's well known military commanders, started his military career as a militia member. He gives extravagant details of his exploits in *Requiem Biafra*. His commitment to Biafra is suggestive of the close affinity between the Anioma and the Igbo, east of the Niger, and the preference of the Anioma to identify with Biafra instead of with Nigeria during the war. Alexander Madiebo, who also includes a brief treatise on the Biafran militia, in his book, was not specific on either the Biafran or the Anioma components of that organization. He treats both as one indivisible team. The militia was one of the avenues through which Anioma women contributed to the survival of the Biafran nation and the Biafran dream during the hostilities. The role of the Anioma female members of the Biafran militia is discussed in the present study.

Other works on the civil war that have direct bearing on this study include Emma Okocha's *Blood on the Niger: The Untold Story of the Nigerian Civil War* (1994), which considers the fate of Asaba, an Anioma border community and one of the closest towns to eastern Nigeria, during the conflict. Okocha discusses in some detail the execution of Asaba men by Nigerian soldiers under the command of Lt. Col. Murtala Mohammed and briefly noted similar killings in the environs of Asaba that fall within the Aniocha section of Anioma, but he completely excludes events in the Ika and Ukwuani sections. He relates to his readers how men met their death but does not inform them about what happened to women and how they survived the ordeal of the war and the challenges of rehabilitation.

In *A Social History of the Nigerian Civil War: Perspectives from Below*, written by A. Harneit-Sievers, J. O. Ahazuem, and S. Emezue (1997), Sydney Emezue made a worthwhile contribution with his chapter, "Women and the War," which he divides into two sections: "Women and Soldiers" and "Women and the War Effort". While the experiences of Anioma women can be discussed under these two subthemes, the prevailing conditions in Biafra and Anioma were not exactly the same during the hostilities. As a result, identical reactions to the soldiers and identical efforts towards the execution of the war cannot be expected from the two groups of Igbo women. It makes M. M. Green's warning on exercising caution in generalizations about the Igbo worth adhering to. Emezue's writing that focused on Biafra should not be extended without caution to Anioma in the Midwest. Meanwhile, a more detailed study on women in Biafra and the war is yet to be carried out.

Insight into the position of women during the Nigerian crisis may be gleaned from some fictional materials.[496] One of these is Flora Nwapa's *Never Again* (1975). Others are Buchi Emecheta's *Destination Biafra* (1982), and Anthonia Kalu's *Broken Lives and Other Stories* (2003). Nwapa used Anioma to form the background of her story. She constructed her narrative from accounts by women who lived through the war. Emecheta, on her part, focused on the dehumanization and victimization of women during the crisis. She recreated the evils of the war from the women's perspective but at the expense of the men, hence her male characters, in comparison to the females, were depicted as effeminate and insensitive. There are limitations in the use of fictional sources for historical analysis. Nevertheless, their contribution towards an appreciation of the subject is acknowledged.

Recently, pioneer work in most Anioma communities have been carried out by university students and presented as undergraduate research projects. A few graduate dissertations and theses also exist. The survey work is primarily on traditions of origin, the political organization of various clans, and some account of the trading activities of expatriate firms from the end of the nineteenth century until the early decades of the twentieth century. A handful of projects deal with the impact of the war on some Anioma communities. Two important works that fall within this category, though not directly on Anioma, are the doctoral thesis of Gloria Chuku (1995) and the undergraduate project of Ngozi

Ezeigwe (1996).[497] The latter's relevance borders on its mention of female combatants in Biafra while the vital aspect of Chuku's thesis is the discussion of the trading engagement of Biafran women, from east of the Niger, which took them to Anioma.

In general, very few works exist that concentrate on Anioma during the Nigerian civil war.

Appendix B: Stories by Anioma Women who Witnessed the War

These unedited personal accounts of women on the war are reproduced here to give a clearer picture of individual experiences during the war. The histories have been selected to reflect the experiences of the literate and illiterate women from the three subsections of Anioma, namely, Aniocha, Ika, and Ukwuani. The particulars of the informants are given in the Bibliography.

NGOZI OCHEI

Asaba, January 2000

Early in October 1967 I visited Asaba from Ogwashi-ukwu in the company of other civil servants. We were summoned to Asaba to collect our previous months' salaries. On arrival at Asaba we heard that federal soldiers had overrun the entire area, including Okpanam, our route to Onicha-olona. There was no way of going back. The alternative was for us to run to Biafra, and I did not like that option. My husband, my elder brother, and me tried to find our way through Ibusa to Onicha-olona, but the federal soldiers were not allowing people to cross the bridge separating Ibusa from Ogwashi-ukwu. They threatened that whoever crossed into Ogwashi-ukwu was a Biafran. They said that they heard that Biafrans were wearing white pants and asked the men in our company to show their pants. Some were questioned on why they were not wearing shoes. They nearly trapped my husband and brother.

When we arrived at the Anglican Mission in Ogwashi-ukwu, we saw that the town was deserted. We made a detour to Ubulu-ukwu and from there entered Onicha-olona, my husband's town, only to discover that everywhere in the town was calm. People in that town can only tell the side effects of the war but not the real trauma because they were spared the sordid aspects.

We were in Onicha-olona until 1968. Early that year there was an announcement that people should return to their homes and bases, that all had returned to normal. I went back to Ogwashi-ukwu, where I was teaching in one of the primary schools. My husband, a student at Adeyemi College of Education, Ife, was then on holiday. We were expecting our second son, and I was on maternity leave. Another of my friends was also on maternity leave. Almost every night people in our community would run about in a wild manner in reaction to a false alarm that Biafrans had come. This continued until the night the Biafrans came. The Biafrans were well prepared. They took the federal soldiers unawares, and easily discomfited them. We ran away from the town. I was in the same group with my friend, Mrs. Ofuasia. If we run into Nigerian soldiers we pretended to be in labor and shout all kinds of things until they allowed us to pass. But if we run into Biafran soldiers, they ridiculed us and called us names. Some of them said, "Hausa Igbo: see them! When they see white they turn white, when they see black, they become black. Nothing is happening to them!"

Before we arrived at Ubulu-uno we heard that soldiers threatened that any man wearing a white shirt would be shot. Sincerely, we had no way of knowing who gave the order. Some people said it was from Biafran soldiers while others claimed it was from Nigerian soldiers. We had no way of distinguishing who was who. Incidentally, my husband and Mr. Okpa, a fellow teacher, were putting on white shirts. Unknown to us somebody advised them to remove their shirts. Nothing happened to my husband, but Okpa was shot dead.

When I heard the news that Okpa was dead, I remembered that Okpa and my husband were together while I was in another group with my friend. I started crying, unable to believe that my husband was safe. We retraced our steps and went to search for them. We eventually ran into him, and he explained that the soldiers ran after them until they ran towards a house. In the confusion, they heard the sound of a gunshot, and one of the men in the group dropped. It later turned out to be Okpa. The owner of the house hid them but neighbors protested and threatened that if they did not leave the house they would throw a grenade into it irrespective of whether the new arrivals were enemies or friends. That same night my husband and those hiding in the house with him slipped away.

After rejoining ourselves, we decided to spend the night at Ubulu-uno. That same day the town crier made the following announcement: "If you are a stranger and you are not living in Ubulu-uno, please keep going, because if not, we will hand you over to the Nigerian soldiers. For your own interest, leave this night. Also, if anybody from Ubulu-uno hides any stranger, that person will be exposed." So we had to leave the town and continued with our journey with my bulging stomach and that of my friend.

We moved from Ubulu-uno to Ashama. We considered Ashama unsafe because we could feel the tension in the town. We left Ashama and went to Ubulu-ukwu, to the house of Reverend Ifeadi. He provided us with water, and we washed ourselves. He also gave us food. We rested a bit and decided to return to Onicha-olona. We were almost certain that the people of Onicha-olona were safe and enjoying some peace. Their only problem was scarcity of food and not this harassment of running up and down.

I spent three months at Onicha-olona. At the end of the period I went back to Ogwashi-ukwu and resumed work. At school we would run and eventually come back, usually the following day. In the night we would run again on the same false alarm that Biafran soldiers had come. It continued like this until the end of the war. We lived daily in a state of panic. Each hour we lived we thanked God, because we were so uncertain of staying alive the next moment. I resigned myself to fate. At the end of each month I would collect my salary and eat whatever I could. By this time I had given birth to my son. I would take him to school with me and keep him outside but beside my classroom, while I taught my pupils. There was a small boy in the same school in primary two. Daily he would come and stay with my baby. During recess, I would send him to buy groundnuts for our snack. Whenever I was in the classroom I had a rest of mind because this boy would have come out to stay with my baby. The little boy was living with the school's head teacher. One fateful day another alarm was raised about the presence of Biafran soldiers and in the stampede, the headmaster was shot dead. The little boy cried bitterly. I consoled him and promised him that he would live with me. That was how he moved into my house and lived with us until he completed his primary education.

We had no other plan during the war than to survive. We had no reason to plan for the future. Sometimes, just after preparing a meal or while eating, an alarm would be raised. We would simply abandon everything and run away. I would pick my child up, take a few items, and run away. To a woman the child was the most precious thing, and it might be that we would spend the night outside our home. Living under such a condition, I did not have any plans. How can I have plans? It was not very possible, particularly if your relations, brothers, and sisters were in Biafra and you are alone in the Midwest...

From my wartime experiences, the Nigerian soldiers were not all insensitive. I remember an encounter with them. The lady that assisted me when I was about to have my baby was able to do so because she was with some soldiers. Soldiers wherever they are like to have girls with them. Some women left their husbands and joined the soldiers during the war. Unmarried girls did the same. They felt that life was easier and the grasses were greener around the soldiers. This very girl and the soldiers were going to Agbor from Illah when they saw us by the roadside. At the time I was already in labor. The soldiers were very kind. They seemed kinder than the police did. They gave us a ride to Agbor. Actually, when the labor started I went to the maternity at Onicha-olona, but the midwife was not there. One of the casual workers tried to assist me but did not succeed. I, too, had no faith in her, so I decided to go to Agbor. The labor had progressed beyond the first stage, and with the pain I was standing by the maternity, which was along the road, when the soldiers drove up and gave me a lift to Agbor where I had my baby.

One thing with this war was that those towns that the soldiers did not settle in had fewer problems. I do not think that the people of Onicha-olona saw soldiers except those who ventured outside the town to Issele-ukwu. Their not seeing soldiers in the town did not mean that they lived in paradise throughout the war. The effects of the war were felt in the town. At the beginning of the crisis we heard that there was an embargo on onions. Many women were not worried about that since onions were not the main food ingredients, but later food became very scarce. Besides the food scarcity, the people lived in fear. They daily anticipated the arrival of soldiers in the town like in other towns, yet the soldiers never came. The uncertainty at the time led to the suspension of education. Schools then were centrally managed but in many communities people were not attending school.

I personally resent the utter destruction the war brought about. In my own town, Asaba, we lost so much. Moreover, it was after the war that we started having cases of different types of deadly diseases. Previously it was not so. I feel they were all the result of the war.

GLADYS OBI

Obamkpa, January 2000

Shortly before the arrival of federal soldiers to Agbor, I left the town and returned to Obamkpa. A month later I came to Asaba in search of my brother, who was kept under custody by federal soldiers. Years before then I had started practicing as a ritual specialist and a midwife. I learnt the skills from my mother. My father, until his death, was the leader of the *dibia* cult in Obamkpa. At a tender age I was informally apprenticed to my mother. The "gift" to operate in this field runs in families and was in mine.

The search for my brother brought me to Asaba and into contact with Nigerian soldiers. Shortly after making contact with them they approached me with the proposal to provide them with girls. The girls I linked them up with were those that were hard pressed and they came from Obamkpa, Ezi, and Onicha-ugbo. Some of the soldiers eventually married some of the girls. The soldiers made me the magajiya, and I became the mother of the barrack at Asaba and the superintendent of their women. I assisted the women during childbirth. As the magajiya, I lived in the barrack, had six assistants, and had my own set of military uniforms. Two junior soldiers were assigned to me. I settled quarrels and misunderstandings between the soldiers and their partners. Often the aggrieved partner would first report a case to me. Sometimes, they were the female partners, and the problem might be that their partners were not giving them enough money for food. The soldiers also brought cases to me, especially if they were displeased by the way their wives or partners treated them. I would first of all dispatch the soldiers under me to arrest and bring the offending woman to me. Usually, I rebuked them and taught them how to treat their men. Some of the girls were punished for their actions. My favorite punishment was to barb their hair and have them pay for it.

I did a lot of things during the war. I made charms for people. One of the charms was for those who wanted their lovers to love them very much or those who did not want their partners to separate from them. I gave luck to soldiers who wanted to progress in their career. I also treated women who had difficulty with conception. I washed their wombs and gave them herbal mixtures to drink. Some of them conceived that way. For the others I monitored their progress during pregnancy and assisted them during delivery.

Things were scarce and costly during the war. Because of this I traded in fish, salt, rice, and beans. I made bulk purchases for soldiers from Agbor and Obamkpa, sometimes with the use of military vehicles. I did not always insist on being paid when these goods were collected. My clients could defer payment for a time until they were able to pay. Although some soldiers paid me, some never did. Life was good for me during the war, but I had regrets throughout the period, and these were over the death of three of my relatives in Asaba.

GBOLIWE NWOJI

Asaba, June 2000

There were many Biafran soldiers in our midst before the arrival of the federal soldiers. The Biafran soldiers were all over the place and we felt safe. When they left, we did not know. One morning we saw federal soldiers everywhere. People going to the market and the stream saw a line of armed soldiers in combat uniform. Some wanted to run, but the soldiers halted them and told them to shout "One Nigeria." I was so afraid that I never came near the soldiers.

After the extermination exercise of Asaba men the soldiers went on a house-to-house hunt, picking up women. Most of them lost their husbands in the massacre. We were locked up at the charge office in Asaba. I told the soldiers that I left a child alone at home and asked for permission to go and bring him. I was allowed to do so but with an escort of soldiers. I entered my house through the main entrance but from the back exit, I ran out and straight into the bush. I did not stay too long before I left the bush for Ibusa with my children, intending to take shelter in my parents' home.

The day I arrived in Ibusa was the day federal soldiers shelled the town. We all trooped back to the bush. After some three months in the bush, I sneaked back into Asaba. I joined the women quartered as refugees in one of the camps. There, soldiers distributed food items to us. Towards the end of the war the Red Cross assisted them. In the camps soldiers continued to kill people. One day, we were packed into a military truck and driven to Issele-azagba. When the truck came to a halt, one of the soldiers with us told all of us to run away. From Issele-azagba, I ran to another bush called *Achalla Ibusa*.

There was much hardship in the bush. Federal soldiers were shelling us daily. We did not feel safe neither did we enjoy much peace. We would all be tensed up throughout the ordeal until the day's shelling was over. Women had a lot of bitter experiences in the bush. We made beds from sticks and wood. Those women that were separated from their husbands spent most of their days mourning them. Some women in our company gave birth in the bush under very hard conditions. We were always moving from place to place and running from bush to bush. We would leave our location and walk to Oko-ogbele or Oko-anala, towns farther from Asaba, all in search of a more conducive and unendangered place to settle.

Our primary occupation was bush combing. I picked palm fruits. Sometimes, I would find snails or tortoise and I would eat them. We depended on such things for our survival. Prior to the war, there were people, I suspect of Igbo origin from the east, who lived in these bushes or in their farms in the outskirts of some towns. In the course of bush combing, we sometimes came to their abandoned settlement. We would take advantage of the opportunity and pick those things they left behind that might be useful to us. Occasionally I attended the market in *Achalla Ibusa* and bought salt or soap. I exchanged part of what I bought for what I needed. Any woman with salt but in need of soap would give me part of her salt in exchange for part of my soap. When hunger became severe, we sold our wrappers or the extra pieces of clothing that we were able to bring with us for food. I entered the bush with some amount of money but before too long I exhausted my supply.

Besides bush combing and the occasional trade by barter, I sometimes made local spice using melon. My success at getting melon and the other necessary ingredients determined whether I would produce the spice and when. I sold them in bush markets and used the money to buy the food that kept my children and me alive.

While we suffered from food scarcity, we also encountered water shortages. We had no definite source of water and we lacked any meaningful receptacle with which to collect water. We felt the shortage of water keenly when any of the women in the bush with us gave birth. First of all, we would search for a man nearby who came out with his shaving kit so that we could borrow it. We used the blade to severe the umbilical cord. Next, we would frantically search for water with which to bath the baby. As it turned out, some of the babies survived but some died. We left everything to the mercy of God. We did the same for the sick among us. There were no medicines, so in cases of ill health or any health emergency, we depended on the local ointment, *udeaku*. We used it both for first aid and for treating all kinds of ailments. We were able to make the local ointment from the palm nuts that we constantly picked. Besides making *udeaku* with them, we ate them as snack and sometimes as food.

Late in 1968, we heard that life in Asaba was no longer traumatic. I sneaked back to the town. When we were leaving the bush, we did so with trepidation, not knowing what to expect. We actually were unwilling to leave the bush but for the announcement made by federal soldiers that whoever remained in the bush after the given deadline would be shot at sight even if they were little children. Moreover they claimed that those still in the bush were saboteurs. Our relations and friends already in the town pleaded with us to return. That was why many of us responded to the announcement. When I came back to the town, I had no house of my own to return to. My house was burnt down, perhaps by the soldiers I tricked when I ran away from the charge office. I had no house and I had no money with which to buy food or clothes while in the town. On the other hand the soldiers had food and in excess, but we had no access to them. The hardship was too much so I picked the refuse dumps where soldiers disposed of their spoilt food supplies. I searched for food items that had not decayed and took home whatever I found. Sometimes I picked decaying tubers of yam or a bag of spoilt rice. At home I would scrape off the bad exterior of the yams until I get to the portion that could still be eaten. For rice, I poured out the salvaged grains. I observed that rarely were the entire contents bad. Occasionally, it might be the middle section that was still good and eatable. Whatever I found that was still good I cooked and ate. I did the same with bags of garri and other items I was lucky enough to find. The interesting thing was that I picked dustbins with a pass. I did this until the war ended although very close to the end of the war I started to sell used clothes. I bought the second-hand clothes from a neighbor who was a dealer in second-hand materials. Armed with my pass, I went from house to house to sell them. Most traders and hawkers also went from house to house to market their products.

People were so hard pressed during the war. Women traded and hawked in order to survive. Some picked and sold snail, firewood, and all kinds of things. They engaged in these activities with their passes too. In Asaba, people were not allowed outside their homes without permission. To visit the farm, a woman must have a pass to avoid molestation. Those that attempted selling or hawking their wares without passes were apprehended and sometimes locked up. Federal soldiers visited the market from time to time without any obvious reason except to harass women. They looked out for those to give them money or those to befriend. Whenever they carry their guns about, even in the market place, we rarely felt safe. Markets were so affected by the war that some days we would spend just about an hour. It was just as if as soon as it convened the women would disperse because of fear or because of a false alarm.

Many of the buildings that were not destroyed were unoccupied. Soldiers had the habit of arbitrarily entering people's homes to interrogate them. Since not many of us could decipher what they were saying, we would simply keep quiet and not respond until they left. People were afraid to live alone by themselves because of the attitude of the federal soldiers in the town. Many individuals sought for acquaintances to share their homes with them. By this arrangement they kept each other company especially in case of any happenstance.

AGNES ODAGWE

Utagba-uno, June 2000

Biafran soldiers were the first to come to Kwale (Ukwuani). They made their first stop at Afia eze, the main market in the area and which was situated by the Ase creek. Before the war, Afia eze was a popular market for farm produce and food items. Traders from Ndosimili brought yams to sell at the market. Obiaruku and Ogume traders came with garri. The Ijaw came in canoes filled with fish and returned to their towns with yams and garri.

By this time, I was a trader. Before the war reached my town, I could travel freely to Abavo and Ute in the Ika area to buy yams, okra, melon, and local baskets, all of which I sold at Afia eze and at Eke market. These markets were in Utagba-ogbe. It was my habit then to sell whatever was in season. Most times I attended the market at Ashaka and sold my goods there. Until the 1950s the Ashaka market was famous and attracted traders from far and near. Its importance declined when other traders became offended with the attitude of their colleagues from Ashaka. The exorbitant prices they fixed for their goods made other traders shift their attention elsewhere. Afia eze, located close to the creek, was accessible to traders from distant places including those from the non-Igbo areas. It replaced Ashaka market as the main trading center in Ukwuani. It enjoyed a wide patronage from communities in Ukwuani and in the non-Igbo areas. Afia eze remained popular until the time federal soldiers arrived in Ukwuani.

The coming of the Biafran soldiers was a big boost to trade for those who traded in Afia eze. I secured a pass from Biafran soldiers, which I used to trade with them. I supplied them with bags of food items, cartons of tomatoes, tins of cigarettes, and medicines, procured through the Ukwuani Central Hospital. I moved the goods from the purchasing centers to the selling sites with the help of my husband and children. We trekked long distances, from Utagba-ogbe in Ndokwa West to Okpai in Ndokwa East, which was close to the river Niger. At Okpai Biafran traders who came in canoes from Oguta and Ossomari across the Niger bought our goods. I later lost my pass to a man from Umutu who stole it from me.

I was forced to abandon the trade with people from Biafra when the federal soldiers arrived. They came on a day I went to the farm with my son. We ran away to Ogume but we did not spend many days outside Utagba-ogbe. We returned to our homes after the announcement by the town crier that the soldiers promised not to harm us.

Some Biafran soldiers were caught off by the sudden arrival of the federal soldiers. They remained with us instead of returning to Biafra. The federal soldiers warned women against trading with people from Biafra. They moved Afia eze to the center of the town, and from that time the market ceased to be the big market it used to be. Traders could no longer move about freely or trade as we were used to. We were stopped from going to distant places. I had to think up something else to do and decided on processing garri. I would buy cassava, prepare the tubers, fry them into garri and sell to people. With time the military unit in Ukwuani began to buy garri from me. Their cook was a tenant in my father's house. When there was an increase in the demand for my garri I started buying cassava farms and harvesting the yield in stages.

Many people also started paying in advance for the quantity of garri they needed because the demand was very high. About the same period I was nicknamed mama garri. I bought cassava farms at £30 (US$ 56.45) each but I was able to recover that amount from the proceed from a little less than half the entire farm. My children helped with peeling and grating the cassava tubers. Then we were using hand graters made by perforating metal tins. On many occasions I worked from one evening to the next. Most times I would be so thoroughly exhausted from grating that I would have pains all over my chest.

Another thing I did was to sell locally brewed liquor. There were days I was able to sell 20 liters of it. Even with the war, women in Ukwuani were able to do a lot of things unlike men. Emu women were very good in making the local gin. They prepared it from palm wine, sugar cane, and other ingredients. I would buy 20 liters of it with £20 (US$ 37.63) but I made sure that I concealed it amidst a whole lot of other goods to avoid detection at the checkpoints. The police used to conduct raids for it before the war but no such raid was carried out to the best of my knowledge in Utagba-ogbe during the war. We were able to sell the gin during the war much more than we did when there was no war.

I used the profit I made from my business in feeding my children and training two of them in primary school. I had nobody to assist me. My husband, a fisherman, was an alcoholic and could not take proper care of his children...

MARIA ONOJARUMA

Utagba-ogbe, January 2000

The war sent us away from the market. As a trader I bought and sold fish, yams, and garri at Afia eze. Before the war I could buy a bag of garri for less than two pennies and I packed them in UAC bags with the same amount of money. These were very big bags made by the United African Company for packing goods. Traders used them a lot those days for storing foodstuffs and in moving large quantities of foodstuffs and other goods from place to place.

Ijaw traders who came through the waterways in their canoes to trade with us were prevented by the war from visiting our town. Because of the war I could not go to Okpai to purchase yams and fish for sale or to Aboh for okra and potato. The war drove the people of Aboh into the bush. People in Utagba-ogbe spent only a day at Isumkpe but those in Aboh stayed a long time, more than a year, in the bush.

In Utagba-ogbe, we were unable to visit our distant farms to harvest yams or to fish in the water. The soldiers monitored us very closely. It was even difficult getting passes from them. Fortunately food was not very scarce here unlike in Aboh. Fear and thoughts of being killed kept me from moving outside my town. The soldiers were very brutal, and we found it hard accommodating them. They behaved like animals. On our way to market one day they took our bicycles from us. We had to cover the distance on foot and still if they think an individual was not walking very fast, they beat up the person. Those of us whose bicycles were taken never received them back.

I stopped trading in the market and started selling goods from my house. Eventually, I obtained a pass with which I went to Obiaruku from where I bought a few food items that I sold at Utagba-ogbe. There were many roadblocks on the way and sometimes the soldiers would seize our goods when we got to these checkpoints. Without bicycles we often walked the long distance to Obiaruku. We might be lucky to hitch a ride in a private vehicle but sometimes we might run into soldiers who would order all the passengers to disembark and drive off with the vehicle. It was the proceeds from my trade that I used to look after myself. My husband was working in another town when the war broke out. It was difficult for him to visit us regularly...

MRS. B. OMODON

Alisimie, June 2000

The war got to Agbor a few weeks after the delivery of my fifth child. I never anticipated that Nigerian soldiers would overrun Agbor. If I had known this would happen, I would not have allowed my husband, who was the chief clerk in the Eastern Regional Government, to remain in Biafra. His absence affected me immensely during the war. I had to look after five children and myself alone.

We are happy to be alive. None of us died or sustained an injury during the war. Some of our relatives that were in Biafra returned safely. For those of us who remained here, when we remember what we saw in this town we pray that there should be no war again. We suffered then. I had never before seen something like what I witnessed here during the war. People were careful of their behavior to avoid being victims of the soldiers' meanness. There was serious looting of people's property by the soldiers. We lost a lot of things ourselves to looters.

I was in my home with my children when the federal soldiers came. The shelling of the town preceded their arrival. Many people ran away at the sight of them. The shelling caused people to leave the town. The soldiers disturbed women a lot. I was intensely scared during the period but my greatest problem was my inability to communicate with my husband. I was so unsure of his safety. It was difficult convincing myself that he was alive, yet I could not prove that he was dead. The torture alone from that uncertainty was unbearable. I had to take solace in my job at the General Hospital, Agbor, where wounded soldiers were brought for treatment. A good number of the federal soldiers were brought from Onitsha and other parts of Biafra.

I always dressed in my professional outfit when going to work to prevent any molestation. When off work, I made sure I carried my baby with me whenever I leave house. It was just God that helped us to survive that period. All classes of the society were affected by the war and suffered throughout the crisis. Even though women traded, there was still a shortage of food and other provisions. Ordinary food items were exiguous and very dear. I could not provide all the necessary things we needed in my family. It was also difficult supplementing my baby's feeding with baby fomular. I had to depend on *akamu* [local pudding]. Corn was available and *akamu* was easy to prepare. Sometimes the hospital would receive a consignment of milk and cereals. I always made sure that I bought as much as I could from them because we did not receive these consignments often.

I did not have any savings but I was able to pay the school fees of my children. I still remember the day I got a letter from my husband through a Red Cross official in 1969. It was a memorable day for me...

GLADYS OKWUASHI

Onicha-ugbo, February 2000

I was about thirty-two years old when the war broke out. This October I will be sixty-five years. My education beyond the primary level was difficult. I started training as a nurse after primary school but did not complete it. It was not a very popular thing educating female children then. Moreover, my family was large, and at a point it was difficult for my parents to finance my schooling. I had to give up the training and started working as an attendant in a petrol station. In 1963 I was married and three years later had my first child.

We were living in Benin City when the news of the disturbances in northern Nigeria reached us. Many people ran home to their respective towns and many small businesses folded up, including the place where I worked. I had to return to my town. I thought of what to do. I felt that I should not be idle. I have never liked idleness, not even as a girl. I needed to have a means of taking care of my immediate family and myself. From my village I moved to Onitsha. It was part of the Igbo area. We speak the same Igbo and it is our place too. I was convinced that there was nothing I could not do there. I took my child with me to Onitsha but later returned him to my mother at Onicha-ugbo. At Onitsha, I picked a job as a telephone operator with the police force. One morning, on my way to work, I saw some young women running. I made inquiries and learnt that they were members of the civil defense. I was so attracted by the sight that I decided to join them.

Before this time, we were at work one day when our group [the Biafran army] crossed into the Midwest to Ore in Nigeria. Another morning we were trying to contact other units on the phone and we were told that there was trouble. The Nigerians were after our group. They were pushing them back from Ore. We prayed and begged God that He should support our cause. My friends and I followed the news of their retreat from town to town until they got to Agbor. It was at that point that we lost touch with them. We did not need to be told that the situation had become serious...

Although I had joined the militia by this time, I was still working as a telephone operator. I belonged to the ROB, that is, militia members from Anioma. We were part of the Biafran army but actually we were giving Biafra a helping hand. Every morning we had some training. We were taught a lot of things including how to take cover, how to defend ourselves from assaults or attacks, and how to leave a besieged area. We were also taught other life-saving devices. Our instructors started our training with Mac 2 rifle. They would dismantle it and ask us to re-assemble the parts. We became familiar with its various parts and their functions.

When the Nigerian army took Onitsha was when I was fully commissioned as a militia member. I had completed my training and was issued with a set of uniforms. With the fall of Anioma to federal control, my mother and nineteen others – her children, my son, other grandchildren, and some relatives – joined me in Biafra. I had to take care of them.

From Onitsha we moved to Ogidi. Many girls had joined the militia and our number increased considerably. We stayed in a camp at Ogidi. I was chosen with another girl, Joy, to head the girls. Before the commencement of any major movement, retreats, or evacuation, we would request for a car for the evacuation of the girls. I never left a camp until I had settled my mother and other relations somewhere near me. We still continued with our routine exercises. These helped us to keep in shape, to be alert, and ever prepared.

At Ogidi in 1968 we were split into companies and attached to some army units. We did a number of minor jobs for these units. From the time we were split up we ceased to be together but moved with our different army units. The militia was an interesting group to belong to. My experiences with them were enjoyable ones. We felt we were fighting our personal battles. We were not forced to belong but volunteered to be militia members. I was happy and I fed very well. The physical training made me very strong. I was proud of being a Biafran. I never thought I would answer a Nigerian again in my life. We knew our sufferings but we prayed that they would not be in vain. In the militia I dressed like any other soldier. I did not put on earrings. The day Ojukwu, Biafran military leader, came to inspect the soldiers in our unit, he shook hands with me not knowing that I was a woman. I was the only female in their midst.

Much later in the war we taught civilians some of what we learnt in the militia. Some of them occasionally visited our camps. Most of the women came from nearby refugee camps to see us. The sight of women in military uniforms seemed to surprise them. Some would bring us gifts and spend a little time with us before leaving. It was during such visits that we taught them some of what we were taught. We taught them not to run in a confused manner at the noise of an approaching plane. If standing, they either remain motionless or they lie flat on the ground without moving their bodies to avoid attracting the attention of a hovering craft. By so doing they might forestall an intended bombing.

At a point during the war I was selected as one of the intelligence officers to work with prisoners of war. I was often sent for to interview prisoners of war from such places as Idoma. I speak Idoma, Hausa, Yoruba, Edo, Urhobo and Igbo. I am conversant with both the Anioma dialect and that of the Igbo heartland. We extracted information from federal soldiers captured by Biafran soldiers. We quizzed them concerning federal operations and used the information to plan our troops' movement. Such intelligence often helped us to avoid the federal onslaught and to work out where and how to station our troops before a military confrontation. I was able to work as an intelligence officer because of my ability to speak these languages. I was born in Oturkpo where Idoma is spoken. Hausa was the *lingua franca* of the Benue area. It was impossible to live in that section of the country and not become familiar with the Hausa language. Besides growing up in Idoma, I spent some years in Jos. I equally had the privilege of living and later working in Warri and Benin, where the Urhobo and Edo languages are spoken.

I never visited any of the war fronts. Most of the women were ignorant of the war fronts, but we did watch as soldiers left the camp for military engagements. Women were not asked to take up arms or to go to war fronts. The war never got to the stage that women were expected to fight. There were girls who would sneak out and accompany their soldier friends to battle. Some of them also took part in spying. Spying, though, was not a hectic job. Female spies merely disguised themselves as common people in order to move freely in and out of Biafra. In the same manner there were girls from areas under the control of the Nigerian government who visited Biafra. We had some rough girls in our group. If we get a report that one or two were proving difficult we changed their duties.

I joined the militia as an ordinary recruit. There was no regimented or formal system of promotion for the women. We also did not enjoy rapid promotion. The condition for our promotion was based on our attitudes and display of responsible behavior.

I worked very hard for every promotion I earned. I was first a cadet officer, then a second lieutenant, full lieutenant, and lastly a captain. It rarely bothered me during the war that the group was not properly organized, and that the members were not regularly promoted. We were engrossed with the mission of fighting for survival. I am sure that if we had won the war we would have been properly recompensed. They gave some of us ranks as a mark of distinction and to distinguish us from those under us. Joy and I were given further military training where we learnt more military tactics. I was assigned a gun for our protection and that of some forty girls under us. It would look absurd if we were left without any means of protecting ourselves. If the enemy had come against us and I, as a woman, gunned down at least one of them I would have tried, even if they eventually overpowered us in the encounter.

When the war became more serious, the men in the militia joined the army and only the women remained as militia members. We worked in refugee camps where we assisted with the distribution of food items and drugs. We also gave a helping hand to the Red Cross and other humanitarian organizations that operated in Biafra. The Biafran government made sure that we were well taken care of, were healthy and received medical attention when the need arose. We lacked nothing. Our daily rations were sent along with that of the army.

The war put everybody on the same level. For instance, those who previously could afford to eat twice a day had to stop. Life was so uncertain that people did not think too highly of themselves. My only regrets after Biafra's loss were for those few wasted years of the war. We could have made something out of our lives within that period. I lost so much in the war. All my property left behind in Onisha-ugbo was looted. If we had won the war I am sure that I would have gained back all those things and more...

Midway through 1969, the burden of shouldering the responsibility for my family members with me in Biafra became more than I could handle. I was shaken by the death of my infant nephew. My sister had a number of female children before him. The little boy died after an illness in spite of the medical attention he received. By that time, too, life had become very difficult in Biafra. I was afraid of any other member of my family dying under my care when God may have wanted to save them. I decided to take them away from Biafra. I left my uniforms and told those that were curious of my movements that I was taking my mother and siblings to Atani. We took a car to Atani where we took a canoe and crossed into Anioma.

Shortly after my arrival at Onicha-ugbo I was arrested by armed soldiers along with all the members of my family who returned with me. Nigerian soldiers came with a lorry load of soldiers to arrest us. We were taken to Agbor and later transferred to Uromi. One of my sisters gave birth in detention while we were at Uromi and the rest of them were released, but I was moved to Benin City, where I remained until the end of the war.

Nigerian soldiers got hints of my activities in Biafra. When they heard that I had returned they made haste and picked me up. They must have considered me a security risk. It was because of me that they arrested other members of my family. I was thoroughly interrogated on the role I played in Biafra. I told them bluntly that I joined Biafra with reasons. We did not beg for war but when it came I played my own part.

I was not badly treated in detention. I was well fed but they denied me some necessary things that would have made me comfortable. I needed at least a razor for my facial hairs. I shave every two days or my face would be dotted with beards. Throughout the period I was in detention I did not shave. I looked just like a man. Was that not punishment? People who came to visit me were thoroughly interrogated and properly searched before they were allowed to see me. I was not allowed to leave my room except for the bathroom. And when I did, I had an escort of two armed soldiers. Anytime I was in the bathroom I made sure I stayed as long as I could. Somehow I was proud of the hassles of being escorted to the bathroom by armed soldiers because it also gave me the opportunity to inflict my own punishment on them. I would simply sit in one corner of the room and leave the tap on. Every effort to hurry me up was a waste. Occasionally I would remind my escorts that it was their duty to wait on me.

I was in detention for about nine months. The circumstances of my arrest and incarceration after the war motivated my changing my name... I felt that my first name, which had become popular then, would expose me to further mistreatment. Fortunately, the new name stuck and gave me a good coverage after my detention and throughout the period of readjusting to peacetime.

Notes

INTRODUCTION

1. J. A. Sluka, "The Anthropology of Conflict," in *The Paths to Domination, Resistance, and Terror,* ed. C. Nordstrom and J. Martin (Berkeley: University of California Press, 1992), 19.
2. E. Ukasonwa, "Aspects of the Pre-colonial History of Obinofia (in Ezeagu Local Government Area, Anambra State) to 1900" (B. A. project, University of Nigeria, 1989), 18.
3. Sayre P. Sheldon, ed., *Her War Story, Twentieth Century Women Write about War* (Carbondale: Southern Illinois University Press, 1999), x.
4. S. L. A. Marshall, *Men against Fire: The Problem of Battle Command in Future War* (New York: William Morrow, 1947), 27; David Perlmutter, *Visions of War: Picturing Warfare from The Stone Age to the Cyber Age* (New York: St. Martin Griffin, 1999), 9.
5. Sheldon, ed., *Her War Story,* x.
6. Ignomar Hauchler and Paul Kennedy, *Global Trends* (New York: Continuum Publishers, 1994).
7. "Women and War," a publication of the International Committee of the Red Cross (August 1995), 4.
8. Patricia Smyke, "Refugee Women," *The Courier*, no. 150 (1995), 54.
9. Uta Klein, "War and Gender: What Do We Learn from Israel?" in *The Women and War Reader,* ed. L. A. Lorentzen and J. Turpin (New York: New York Press, 1998), 151.

10. The people of Aniocha, meaning people of the white land, also called *ndi enuani*, are found in Oshimili North and South and in Aniocha North and South Local Government Areas. The Ika are in Ika Northeast and Ika South, while the Ndokwa or Ukwuani are in Ukwuani, Ndokwa West, and Ndokwa East Local Government Areas. The word *enuani*, implying people of the highland, when used in reference to the Aniocha area, is restrictive and misleading since it cannot be applied to territories along the Niger, namely, Asaba, Illah, and Akwukwu-Igbo, all of which are in a lowland.
11. Midwest Government, *Investigation into the Role of Chiefs in the Midwestern State: Divisional Report in Respect of the Aboh Division* (1972), 13.
12. The major political parties in the country before the civil war were the Northern People's Congress (NPC) for Northern Region; the Action Group (AG) for Western Region; and the National Council of Nigerian Citizens (NCNC) for the Eastern Region, formerly the National Congress for Nigeria and the Camerouns.
13. O. Oyediran, ed., *Nigerian Government and Politics under Military Rule,* 1966–1979 (London: Macmillan Press, 1979), 19.
14. Remi Anifowose, *Violence and Politics in Nigeria: The Tiv and Yoruba Experience* (New York: Nok Publishers, 1982), 55 – 66.
15. Ibid., 251 – 53. See also J. S. Olawoyin, "My Recollections of the Strengths and Weaknesses of the First Republic, 1960–1966," in *Inside Nigerian History* 1950 - 1970*: Events, Issues and Sources,* ed. Y. B. Usman and G. A. Kwanashie (Zaria: Ahmadu Bello University Press, 1995), 206; John de St. Jorre, *The Nigerian Civil War* (London: Hodder and Stoughton, 1972), 42 – 43.
16. St. Jorre, *The Nigerian Civil War,* 43–44.
17. R. B. Alade, *The Broken Bridge* (Ibadan: Caxton Press, 1975), 1; St. Jorre, *The Nigerian Civil War,* 59.
18. As noted, the Midwest, where the Anioma lived, was constituted from minority groups of the old Western Region by the referendum of 1963. Other groups that shared the region with the Anioma were the Urhobo/Isoko, Itshekiri, and some Ijaw. Their excision from Western Region was informed by their complaints

of neglect and domination by the Yoruba, the dominant ethnic group in the Old Western Region.

19. M. M. Green, *Igbo Village Affairs* (London: Sidgwick and Jackson, 1947), xiii; Phoebe V. Ottenberg, "The Changing Economic Position of Women among the Afikpo Ibo", in *Continuity and Change in African Cultures,* ed. W. R. Bascom and M. J. Herskovits (Chicago: The University of Chicago Press, 1959), 205.
20. Ottenberg, "Changing Economic Position of Women" in *Continuity and Change.* "The Afikpo Igbo of Eastern Nigeria," in *Peoples of Africa,* ed. James C. Gibbs (New York: Holt, Rinehart and Winston, 1965); with Simon Ottenberg, "Afikpo Markets: 1900-1960," in *Markets in Africa,* eds. Bohannan and G. Dalton (Northwestern University Press, 1962); as Phoebe Miller, "Sex Polarity Among the Afikpo Igbo," in *African Religious Groups and Beliefs,* ed. S. Ottenberg (Meerut, India: Archana Publications, 1982).
21. G. T. Basden, *Niger Ibos* (London: Frank Cass, 1937); Elizabeth Isichei, *The Ibo People and the Europeans* (London: Faber and Faber, 1970); and Don Ohadike, *Anioma, A Social History of the Western Igbo People* (Athens: Ohio University Press, 1994). Don Ohadike's book is the first concise work on Anioma besides Elizabeth Isichei's discussion of some Anioma communities in *The Ibo People and the Europeans* (1970) and her collection of oral history in Anioma published in 1977 as *Igbo Worlds.* Ohadike traced the historical origin of Anioma, giving various aspects of it from the precolonial period up to 1960.
22. Claude Phillips, *The African Political Dictionary* (Oxford: Clio Information Services, 1984), 123.
23. Carolyn Nordstrom, "Girls behind the Front Lines," in *The Women and War Reader,* 83.
24. S. Oyeweso, ed., *Perspectives on the Nigerian Civil War* (Lagos: O. A. P., 1992), v.
25. Part of the discussion in Appendix A deals with the lopsidedness of the studies on the Nigerian civil war. The review of the civil war literature shows clearly that the activities of men dominate the contents of the majority of works on the subject.

26. Silence about women's roles in warfare is also discussed in Meredith Turshen and Clotilde Twagiramariya, eds., *What Women Do in Wartime: Gender and Conflict in Africa* (London: Zed Books, 1998), in which several authors discussed the conflicts in Mozambique, Sudan, South Africa, Liberia, and Rwanda, and noting among many other issues some of the roles played by women during civil strife.
27. Jenny Hammond and Nell Druce, *Sweeter than Honey, Ethiopian Women and Revolution: Testimonies of Tigrayan Women* (Trenton, N.J.: The Red Sea Press, 1990); and Tanya Lyons, *Guns and Guerilla Girls: Women in the Zimbabwean Liberation Struggle* (Trenton, N.J.: Africa World Press, 2004).
28. Hammond and Druce, *Sweeter than Honey*, 8.

CHAPTER ONE

29. Annual rainfall in Delta State, heaviest in July, averages some 260 centimeters in the coastal areas and 190 centimeters in the extreme north of the state. Natural resources include kaolin, crude oil, granite, rubber, and natural gas. See Delta State Government, *Understanding Delta State: Delta State at Seven* (Asaba: 1998), 36.
30. Elizabeth Isichei, *The Ibo People and the Europeans* (London: Faber and Faber, 1970), 17.
31. Asaba Development Association, *Asaba History and Development* (Benin: Manla Enterprises, 1978), 11.
32. The nine local government areas that make up Anioma are Oshimili North, Oshimili South, Aniocha North, Aniocha South, Ika Northeast, Ika South, Ukwuani, Ndokwa West, and Ndokwa East. Their corresponding headquarters are Akwukwu-Igbo, Asaba, Issele-ukwu, Ogwashi-ukwu, Owa-oyibu, Agbor, Obiaruku, Utagba-ogbe (kwale), and Aboh. Anioma is divided into three subsections – Aniocha, Ika, and Ukwuani.
33. Ohadike, *Anioma, A Social History of the Western Igbo People* (Athens: Ohio University Press, 1994), xvi.
34. Delta State was recorded as having a population of 2,570,181 in 1991. Source: Federal Republic of Nigeria, 1991 *National Population Census* (Lagos).

35. Ohadike, *Anioma*, 15.
36. Isichei, *The Ibo People and the Europeans*, 19.
37. E. O. Oko, "The Aniocha People at the Crossroads, 1866–1911" (M.A. diss., University of Benin, 1982).
38. Ohadike, *Anioma*, 69-74.
39. The kinship structure among towns that claim Igala and Yoruba origin is presented in those languages. For instance, in Ebu, which claims Igala origin, the *unor* is called *Ibe efiniomi*; the *umunna – ibe atamuka*; the *idumu – ibe adaka*, and the *ebo* or *ogbe – alubu*. For Ukwunzu who claim Yoruba origin the kinship units are *imaba, imabawa, ozule*, and *ibo*.
40. John Enemoh, "Grandwork History of Asaba" (unpublished, 1999), 73–74.
41. Chief J. Enemoh, age 75, Asaba, interviewed in January 2000.
42. Isichei, *The Ibo People and the Europeans*, 161; and Obaro Ikime, "Native Administration in Kwale-Aboh 1928-50: A Case Study," *Journal of the Historical Society of Nigeria* 3, no. 4 (June 1967), 663–682.
43. Source: D.C. Ohadike, *Anioma, A Social History of the Westrern Igbo*. Used with the permission of the author.
44. E. Uchendu, "Rating of Slaves in the West Niger Igbo Area in the 19th Century," *Nsukka Journal of the Humanities* 12 (2002), 190–191.
45. Among the Igbo the freeborn are the legitimate members of the society. They are not ritual outcasts or slaves. They enjoy the right of full citizenship in the society.
46. Mr. B. C. Oforgu, age 82, Asaba, interviewed in June 2000.
47. Uchendu, "Rating of Slaves in the West Niger Igbo Area," 192–193.
48. Ohadike, *Anioma*, 196.
49. Chief J. Enemoh, age 80, Asaba, interviewed in April 2004.
50. Chief S. O. Akumwata, age 90, Asaba, interviewed in November 2002; and Chief J. Enemoh, age 80, Asaba, interviewed in April 2004.

51. E. Uchendu, "Culture: The Obstacle to Active Female Participation among the Igbo of Nigeria," *Asian Women* 15 (Winter 2002), 77.
52. Kenneth Little, *African Women in Towns* (London: Cambridge, 1973), 6.
53. It was forbidden for the wife of an Eze title holder to wear a blouse, beginning from the day the husband completed rites associated with his title.
54. Enemoh, "Grandwork History of Asaba," 75.
55. Enemoh, see note 49.
56. The following expressed this opinion: Chukuka Gbenoba, age 48, Agbor-obi, interviewed in January 2000; Chief S. O. Ubah, age 67, Utagba-ogbe, interviewed in January 2000; Obi Okada Okorie and Obi Nweze, Okpanam, interviewed in January 2000; Chief D. Aniogwu, age 65, Aboh, interviewed in January 2000, and Peter Okobi, age 60, Asaba, interviewed in November 1999.
57. Enemoh, see note 49.
58. The major responsibility of the *umuada* was the maintenance of peace in the lineage. They also played important roles during local festivals and ceremonies. For instance, the leader of the *umuada*, called the *ada isi,* offered the mourning stick to a widow (or widower) before her/his confinement prior to the burial process of her/his deceased spouse. The *inyemedi* teamed up among themselves for their mutual welfare in their husbands' town. While *umuada* could sometimes react to unacceptable legislation by the men folk, the *inyemedi* were not supposed to interfere with the administration of their husbands' village. In the Ika section of Anioma, women played no recognized administrative roles.
59. Richard Henderson, *The King in Everyman: Evolutionary Trends in Onitsha Ibo Society* (New Haven: Yale University Press, 1972); and Zulu Sofola, "Feminism and African Womanhood," *Sisterhood, Feminism and Power: From Africa to the Diaspora*, ed. O. Nnaemeka (Trenton, N.J.: Africa World Press, 1998).
60. The omu institution has been treated in detail in Egodi Uchendu, "Mordernizing Female Chieftaincy Institution in Anioma in the 21st century."(Paper presented at the Seventh Annual Confer-

ence of the Mid-America Alliance for African Studies (MAAAS) held at St. Louis, Missouri, September 28-29, 2001.)

61. Information on the ada institution came from interviews with Mr. S. Nwabam (Ossissa), Chief Aniogwu (Aboh), Felicia Ekeke (Obiaruku), Chief S. O. Ubah (Utagba-ogbe), Chief Enemoh (Asaba), and Regina Ije (Akwukwu-Igbo).
62. Enemoh, "Grandwork History of Asaba," 112.
63. Ubah and Aniogwu, see note 56.
64. Madam Mary Ihedi, age 65, Ubulu-ukwu, interviewed in January 2000.
65. Obi Okada Okorie, see note 56. Mr. Gabriel Ogbue, age 67, Onicha-ugbo; and Madam Veronica Ikem, age 65, Onicha-ugbo, interviewed in January 2000.
66. At present, pressure is being mounted on the Nigerian federal government by various feminist and humanitarian groups to eradicate this rite all over Nigeria. Official efforts to end the rite are noted in UNICEF/Federal Government of Nigeria, *National Baseline Survey of Positive and Harmful Traditional Practices Affecting Women and Girls in Nigeria*. 1998.
67. Madam Lucy Emili, age 54, Utagba-ogbe; and Mr. James Oyita, age 58, Utagba-uno, interviewed in January 2000. National Archives Ibadan, BP 203/151, 1935.
68. Mr. N. N. Eboigbe, age 73, Igbanke, interviewed in June 2000; see also, A. E. Idure, "History of the People of Ika L. G. A. of Bendel State" (unpublished, 1989), 41–42.
69. Gbenoba, see note 56; Madam Lucy Mordi, age 60, Asaba, interviewed in November 1999.
70. Eboigbe, see note 68.
71. Okobi, see note 56; Mrs. A. Omo, age 62, Asaba, interviewed in June 2001.
72. D. Davies, "Introduction," in *Rites of Passage,* ed. Jean Holm (London: Pinter Publishers, 1994), 6.
73. G. T. Basden, *Niger Ibos* (London: Frank Cass, 1966), 290–291.
74. Ibid.
75. Ubah, see note 56; Mr. C. C. Omodon, age 73, Alisimie, interviewed in June 2000.

76. Constantina Bailly, "Asian Religions," in *Encyclopedia of Women and World Religion*, ed. Serenity Young, vol. 2, 623.
77. R. F. Fortune, *Sorcerers of Dobu: The Social Anthropology of the Dobu Islanders of the Western Pacific* (London: Routlege, 1932), 52, 153.
78. Basden, *Niger Ibos,* 294.
79. Bonny Ibhawoh, *Between Culture and Constitution: The Cultural legitimacy of Human Rights in Nigeria* (Copenhagen, Denmark: The Danish Centre for Human Rights, 1999), 48.
80. Madam Okodike, the omu of Akwukwu-Igbo, age 77, and Ejime Chizea, the omu of Asaba, age 72, interviewed in January 2000.
81. S. A. Agboola, *An Agricultural Atlas of Nigeria* (London: Oxford University Press, 1979), 13.
82. S. Ogbobine, *Bendel Law Series, Oshimili and Aniocha, Their People and Land Tenure* (Benin City: Government Press, 1981), 63.
83. Aderanti Adepoju and Christine Oppong, eds., *Gender, Work and Population in Sub-Saharan Africa* (London: James Currey Ltd., 1994).
84. Mid-West Government, *Investigation into the Role of Chiefs in the Midwestern State, Divisional Report in respect of Aboh Division*, 42.
85. Ikem, see note 65; Madam Lydia Akazue, age 70, Isheagu, interviewed in January 2000, and Omodon, see note 75.
86. Nwabam, see note 61.
87. Agboola, *Agricultural Atlas of Nigeria*, 115.
88. Ikem and Ogbue, see note 65; Rose Ikem, age 38, Onicha-ugbo, interviewed in January 2000.
89. Madam M. Onojaruma, age 65, Utagba-ogbe, interviewed in January 2000.
90. Ohadike, *Anioma*, 179.
91. National Archives, Ibadan. File no. 48/19, Asa Div. 2/1.
92. Information on trade came from the following: Madam Lydia Akazue (Isheagu), Madam Maria Onojaruma (Utagba-ogbe), Chief D. Aniogwu (Aboh), and Mr. S. O. Nwabam (Ossissa). Mr. Ebu, age 47, Ozanogogo, interviewed in January 2000.

93. Mordi, see note 69.
94. Okada Okorie, see note 56.
95. Federal Republic of Nigeria, *The National Atlas of the Federal Republic of Nigeria* (Lagos: Government Press, 1978), 86.
96. Madam Gladys Obi, age 65, Obamkpa, interviewed in January 2000; Chief S. O. Okocha, age 88, Asaba, interviewed in June 2000, and Omodon, see note 75.
97. Cotton is a shrubby plant growing some 4–6 meters high when under cultivation. It produces soft spongelike creamy flowers that soon turn deep pink and fall off, leaving the cotton bolls containing the seeds and the fibers or seed hairs. The cotton bolls burst open upon maturity, revealing soft white to yellowish-white masses.
98. Mrs. Nwaka, age 48, Issele-ukwu, interviewed in November 1999. See also, E. O. Egboh, "Northern Nigeria Cotton for Lancashire, 1902 – 1913," *Nsukka Journal of History,* vol. 1 (December 1989), 134–150.
99. Ebu, see note 92.
100. Dr. D. Gbenoba, age 58, Agbor-obi, interviewed in January 2000.
101. Justice Maido, age 70, Onicha-ugbo, interviewed in January 2000; and Tina Okwuashi, age 65, Onicha-ugbo, interviewed in February 2000.
102. Eboigbe, see note 68.
103. Eboigbe and Maido, see notes 68 and 101; Mrs. B Omodon, age 71 years, Alisimea, interviewed in June 2000.
104. Some of these authors include Sylvia Leith-Ross, *African Women* (London: Faber and Faber, 1939); M. M. Green, *Igbo Village Affairs* (London: Frank Cass and Co. Ltd., 1964), 169–176; Judith Van Allen, " 'Aba Riots' or 'Igbo Women's War'? Ideology, Stratification, and the Invincibility of Women," and Kamene Okonjo, "The Dual Sex Political System in operation: Igbo Women and Community Politics in Mid-Western Nigeria," in *Women in Africa: Studies in Social and Economic Change,* eds. N. J. Hafkin and E. G. Bay (Stanford, Calif.: Stanford University Press, 1976); Ifi Amadiume, *Male Daughters, Female Husbands* (London: Zed Press, 1987); Z. Sofola, "Feminism and African Womanhood,"

in *Sisterhood, Feminism and Power: From Africa to the Diaspora*, ed. O. Nnaemeka (Trenton, N. J.: Africa World Press, 1998); and, Misty Bastian, " "Vultures of the Market Place": Southeastern Nigerian Women and Discourses of the Ogu Umunwaanyi (Women's War) of 1929," in *Women in African Colonial Histories*, eds. Jean Allman, Susan Geiger, and Nakanyike Musisi (Bloomington, Indiana: Indiana University Press, 2002).

105. Green, *Igbo Village Affairs*, 169–171.
106. Allen, " 'Aba Riots' or 'Igbo Women's War'?...," 80.
107. Sofola, "Feminism."
108. Towns that claim Benin ancestry are Issele-ukwu, Issele-azagba, Issele-mkpitime, Onicha-olona, Onicha-ukwu, Obior, and Ezi.
109. Ubah, Aniogwu, and Gbenoba, see note 56.
110. Enemoh, "Grandwork History of Asaba."

CHAPTER TWO

111. C. Okonjo, "The Western Ibo," in *The City of Ibadan,* eds. P. C. Lloyd, A. L. Mabogunje, and B. Awe (Cambridge: Cambridge University Press, 1967), 99.
112. O. Nnoli, *Ethnic Politics in Nigeria* (Enugu: Fourth Dimension, 1978), 97.
113. Remi Anifowose, *Violence and Politics in Nigeria: The Tiv and Yoruba Experience* (New York: Nok Publishers, 1982), 251–253; J. S. Olawoyin, "My Recollections of the Strength and Weaknesses of the First Republic, 1960–1966," in *Inside Nigerian History* 1950 – 1970*: Events Issues and Sources*, eds. Y. B. Usman and G. A. Kwanashie (Zaria: Ahmadu Bello University Press, 1995), 206.
114. J. J. Oluleye, *Military Leadership in Nigeria,* 1966 – 1979 (Ibadan: University Press, 1985), 45.
115. Okobi, see note 56.
116. Chizea, see note 80.
117. Ogbue, see note 65.
118. Nigeria's four regions were split into twelve states in May 1967 in one of the federal government's attempts at finding a lasting solution to the national crisis. It was also intended to deny the Eastern

Regional Government the support of the minority groups in the region, thereby discouraging the plan for secession. Under the twelve states structure, Eastern Region was split into three states, namely East Central State, populated by the Igbo; Southeastern State, populated by the Ekois, Efik, and Ibibio; and Rivers State, populated by the Ijaw and marginal Igbo. The division of the country into twelve states was ignored by the Eastern regional government, which went ahead and seceded from the Nigerian federation.

119. Midwest Government, *Rehabilitation in the Midwest State,* 1963-1970 (Benin City, 1970), 2.
120. Prof. J. O. Ijoma, an eyewitness of the disturbances in the Midwest.
121. *Daily Times,* 9 December 1966, 1.
122. Enemoh, see note 41.
123. *Daily Times,* 22 September 1966, 3.
124. Mrs. B. Nwandu, age 55, Asaba, interviewed in January 2000; and Mr. J. I. O. Badifu, age 54, Ogwashi-ukwu, interviewed in June 2000.
125. Members of the Ika Ibo Association (IIA) who attended the Consultative Assembly include Obi Rufus Osemena of Issele-ukwu; Eugene Oba, president of the IIA; Mark Uzoma, a minister in the Midwest government, and J. O. G. Achuzia.
126. J. O. G. Achuzia, *Requiem Biafra* (Enugu: Fourth Dimension, 1986), 3.
127. Letters to the *Biafran Sun* include "What Happens to Ika Ibos " (18 June 1967, p. 2); "Ika Ibos, What Do You Say?" (28 July 1967); "Ika Ibos Cross Over to Protest" (19 June 1967. p. 8); and "Midwest offers Men" (29 August 1967, p. 3).
128. "Ika Ibos Cross over to Protest," *Biafran Sun*, 19 June 1967, 8.
129. *Daily Times*, 10 May 1967, 3; *Daily Times,* June 1967, 5.
130. O. Ojukwu, *Selected Speeches with Journal of Events* (London: Harper and Row, 1969), 198.
131. B. Odogwu, *No Place to Hide: Crises and Conflicts inside Biafra* (Enugu: Fourth Dimension, 1985), 54.
132. Ibid.

133. *Daily Times*, 1 June 1967, 1.
134. Mr. W. Mokogwu, age 58, Issele-ukwu, interviewed in November 1999.
135. S. O. Ogbemudia, *Years of Challenge* (Ibadan: Heinemann, 1991), 93.
136. Ibid.
137. The economic blockade was the federal government's response to Biafra's (then Eastern Region) "survival edicts" by which its military governor, Lt. Col. Chukwuemeka O. Ojukwu, appropriated from April 1967 federal revenue in his region.
138. Ogbemudia, *Years of Challenge*, 101.
139. Ibid., 102.
140. St. Jorre, *The Nigerian Civil War*, 163.
141. Fola Oyewole, *The Reluctant Rebel* (Akure: Olaiya Fegbamigbe Ltd., 1977).
142. Okobi, see note 56.
143. Mr. B. Oforgu, age 82, Asaba, interviewed in June 2000.
144. See chapter 1, page 32.
145. "The Meeting of the Nigerian Military Leaders Held at Aburi, Accra, Ghana," Official Document no.5 of 1967 (Enugu: 1979). See also St. Jorre, *Nigerian Civil War*, 97.
146. *Daily Times*, 17 May 1967, 1.
147. O. Obasanjo, *My Command* (Ibadan: Heinemann, 1980), 35.
148. Ibid., 166–167.
149. J. I. Elaigwu, *Gowon* (Ibadan: West Books, 1986), 113.
150. Ogbemudia, *Years of Challenge*, 105.
151. Oluleye, *Military Leadership in Nigeria*, 108.
152. Emma Okocha, *Blood on the Niger: The Untold Story of the Nigerian Civil War* (Port Harcourt: Sunray, 1994), 24.
153. Omodon, see note 75.
154. Mrs. Esther Nwanze, age 48, Ibusa, interviewed in November 1999.
155. Obasanjo, *My Command*, 46.
156. Ibid., 39.

157. Mr. Nwabudike Adigwe, age 95, Isheagu, interviewed in January 2000.
158. St. Jorre, *Nigerian Civil War*, 164.
159. Mordi and Omodon, see notes 69 and 75. Prof. S. Okobiah, age 60, Abraka, February 2000.
160. Ibid.

CHAPTER THREE

161. *Daily Times*, 27 September 1967, 1.
162. Federal soldiers moved into Akwukwu-Igbo before dawn and strategically positioned themselves at the entrance and exit doors of unsuspecting indigenes. Each building was assigned four soldiers. This approach caused quite some stir among the residents, who upon waking found themselves under arrest in their homes. They were marched to a field and ordered to produce Biafrans hiding in their midst, which of course they could not do.
163. Mr. E. Aminu, age 43, Boji-boji Agbor, interviewed in November 1999.
164. Madam Catherine Agbon, age 65, Otolokpo, interviewed in June 2002.
165. N. P. Biose, "The Impact of the Nigerian Civil War on Umunede" (B.A. project, Delta State University, Abraka, 1997), 33.
166. Badifu, see note 124.
167. Mr. I. M. Onyemushani, age 58, Isheagu, interviewed in January 2000.
168. Ikem, see note 65.
169. Nicole Dombrowski, ed., *Women and War in the Twentieth Century* (New York: Garland Publishing House, 1999), 26.
170. Madam Mary Ihedi, age 65 years, Ubulu-ukwu, interviewed in January 2000.
171. Ubah, Emili, and Badifu; see notes 56, 67, and 124; Mrs.Gboliwe Nwoji, age 65, Asaba, interviewed in June 2000.
172. Mr. S. Megwai, age 49, Onicha-olona, interviewed in November 1999.
173. What connected Asaba with Benin City was the old trunk A road that cut through Agbor, demarcating Agbor from Owa.

Accessing Asaba from Benin City were twin towns that faced each other, Boji-boji Agbor on the north and Boji-boji Owa on the south. Boji-boji Agbor had been a farm settlement belonging to the Agbor royal family and in the early twentieth century it grew, along with Boji-boji Owa, into a thriving commercial area. During the war, residents of Boji-boji were drawn from the surrounding Ika towns and from other parts of Anioma. Agbor-obi, the heart of Agbor, and Owa-oyibu, the heart of Owa, were a little removed from the Boji-boji settlements.

174. Achuzia, *Requiem Biafra*, 42.
175. Okada Okorie, see note 56; Mr. M. Amolo, age 47, Okpanam, interviewed in November 1999.
176. Elizabeth Isichei, *A History of Nigeria* (London: Longman, 1983), 364.
177. It was alleged that Obi Izedimo, the reigning obi of Ogwashi-ukwu, had previously been informed by a diviner that there would be war in the course of his reign and warned not to flee the town if he wanted to save it. This prior information, it was alleged, gave him the boldness to organize his chiefs to welcome the soldiers.
178. Agbor and Owa are the two major clans in the Ika area.
179. Gbenoba, see note 56.
180. Omodon, see note 75. "Na my pickin" is corrupt English for "That is my child."
181. Gbenoba, see note 56.
182. Atina Grossman, "A Question of Silence: The Rape of German Women by Soviet Occupation Soldiers," in *Women and War in the Twentieth Century ...*, ed. Nicole Dombrowski , 165, 169.
183. Geneva Conventions Relative to the Protection of Civilian Persons in Time of War, common art. 3, 1(a) and (c); arts. 27 and 76, 97 (hereafter, Geneva Convention IV); Protocol Additional to the Geneva Conventions of 1949, and Relating to the Protection of Victims of Non-International Armed Conflicts (Protocol II), art. 4 and 76 in Human Rights: A Compilation of International Instruments, vol. 1, part 2 (1993), 799–939.
184. J. Turpin, "Many Faces: Women Confronting War," in *The Women and War Reader,* ed. L. A. Lorentzen and J. Turpin, 5.
185. Mrs. B. Omodon, age 71, Alisimie, interviewed in June 2000.

186. Grossman, "A Question of Silence," 171.
187. Omodon, see note 75.
188. *Daily Times*, 9 November 1966, 1.
189. Of the nine Anioma senior military officers four were from Ibusa. These were S. Nwajei, H. Igboba, M. Okwechime, and Major (M.D.) Albert N. Okonkwo, the administrator of the short-lived Republic of Benin.
190. *Sunday Times* (Nigeria), 15 October 1967, 7–8.
191. Okobi, see note 56.
192. Ebu, see note 92.
193. Mr. G. Okafor, age 57, Ogwashi-ukwu, interviewed in October 1999.
194. Nwabam, see note 61.
195. Emili and Onojaruma; see notes 67 and 89. Madam Agnes Odagwe, age 69, Utagba-unor, interviewed in June 2000.
196. Ubah, Emili, Oyita, Onojaruma, and Odagwe; see notes 56, 67, 89, and 195 respectively.
197. The people were expected to maintain complete silence. It was an offense to be caught listening to a radio transmission during the curfew hours. Soldiers could enjoy that privilege but not the local people. The ban did not deter everybody from the satisfaction of secretly listening to Biafran broadcasts, but it turned out that more men than women enjoyed this luxury. Many women found themselves depending on men for information and were satisfied with secondary transmissions that have been sifted or restructured by the original recipients to suit their emotional state and imagination. In such cases, the disseminated information was often inaccurate.
198. Nwabam, see note 61.
199. Okada Okorie, see note 56.
200. The excision of Rivers State from Eastern Region made Mrs. Nwajei ethnically a non-Biafran except for her marriage to an Ibusa man. Women who felt that her presence in Ibusa threatened their safety blamed her for the federal attack on the town. (Mrs. Nwajei, age 60, Ibusa, interviewed in February 2000.)
201. Nwabam, see note 61.

202. Reverend Martins' church was believed to be affiliated to the Southern Baptist Convention of the United States.
203. Nwaka and Mokogwu; see notes 98 and 134.
204. Ubah, Emili, Oyita, Onojaruma, and Odagwe; see notes 56, 67, 89, and 195 respectively.
205. The 12th battalion of the Biafran army, called the Liberation Army, was responsible for harassing federal units in Anioma all through the war.
206. Achuzia, *Requiem Biafra*, 52.
207. Ibid.
208. Ms. P. Ejere, age 50, and Mr. M. Egbuniwe, age 48. Both were from Asaba and interviewed in November 1999.
209. Mr. and Mrs. Azuka Iwebi, Asaba, interviewed in June 2000.
210. E. C. K. Uwafili, "The Effects of the Nigerian Civil War on Asaba" (B.A. project, University of Nigeria, Nsukka, 1992), 58.
211. Enemoh, see note 41. See also Uwafili, "The Effects of the Nigerian Civil War on Asaba," p. 49.
212. Ibid.
213. Obasanjo, *My Command*, 39–41.
214. Ejere, see note 208.
215. Human Rights Watch, *Proxy Targets: Civilians in the War in Burundi* (March 1988), 32–33.
216. *The New Encyclopaedia Britannica*, vol. 12 (Chicago: Encyclopaedia Britannica Inc. 1995), 1491.
217. St. Jorre, *The Nigerian Civil War*, 165.
218. John Osu, age 60, Idumuje-unor, interviewed in January 2000.
219. Madam Eunice Oganwu, age 85, Illah, interviewed in January 2000; and Mr. F. O. Egwuatu, age 48, Illah, interviewed in November 1999.
220. What the people of Ibusa, Asaba, Isheagu, and Ogwashi-ukwu were subjected to was considerably more traumatic than in any other part of Anioma.
221. Anasthesia Okommah, age 55, Ibusa, interviewed in November 1999.
222. Dr. W. O. Nwegbe, age 60, Ibusa, interviewed in October 2000.
223. Maido, see note 101.

224. Mr. G. Okafor, age 57, Ogwashi-ukwu, interviewed in October 1999.
225. Onyemushani, see note 167. Mrs. A. Okogo, age 52, Isheagu, interviewed in January 2000; and Mr. V. Chenimuya, age 73, Isheagu, interviewed in November 1999.
226. Ibid.
227. *The Nigerian Observer*, 20 June 1968, 2.
228. The estimated number of casualties in Isheagu cannot be verified because of improperly kept records.
229. Okocha, *Blood on the Niger*, 33.
230. These were my observations in Isheagu. Most people in the community were unwilling to receive me. Those who accepted to be interviewed were cautioned by their neighbors and were specifically told to remember what happened during the civil war. Women, more than men, expressed fear for strangers.
231. *The Nigerian Observer*, 9 July 1968, 3.
232. Biose, "The Nigerian Civil War on Umunede," 44.
233. Ejere, see note 208.
234. Biose, "The Nigerian Civil War on Umunede," 54.
235. Mr. M. Ofuani, age 55, Ogwashi-ukwu, January 2000.
236. Comfort Obianeze never remarried after losing her husband and son in the Asaba massacre in 1967. (Madam Obianeze, age 65, Asaba, interviewed in January 2000.)
237. Turpin, "Many Faces: Women Confronting War," 5.
238. See chapter 1 page 28 for the link between male children and women's social and economic status.
239. Okonmah and Okogo; see notes 221 and 225 respectively.
240. Antonella Fabri, "Silence, Invisibility, and Isolation: Mayan Women's Strategies for Defense and Survival in Guatemala," in *Women and War in the Twentieth Century,* ed. Nicole Dombrowski, 291–296.
241. Gerard Prunier, *The Rwandan Crisis: History of a Genocide* (London: Hurst and Company, 1998), 255.
242. See chapter 3, pages 88–94.
243. Okobi and Chizea; see notes 56 and 80 respectively.
244. Osu, see note 218.

245. Stacy Young, *Women and language* (Urbana: Fall 1988). Available from wysiwyg://60/http://proquest.umi.co...3&Deli=1&mtd=1&idx=20&sid=3&RQT=309.
246. Prashant Bordia, Ralph Rosnow, *Human Communication Research*, (1998, December). Available from wsyiwyg://48/http://proquest.umi.co...=4&Deli=1&mtd=1&idx=2&sid=3&RQT=309.
247. Ibid.
248. Nwoji, see note 171.
249. T. Shibutani, *Improvised News: A Sociological Study of Rumor* (New York: Bobbs- Merrill Coy., 1966), v.
250. L. A. Samovar and J. Mills, *Oral Communication: Message and Response* (Iowa: W. C. Brown, 1977), x

CHAPTER FOUR

251. Achuzia, *Requiem Biafra*, 4.
252. The Biafran segment of the militia was made up largely of junior civil servants. The officers were mostly university lecturers, members of different professions, and other highly educated persons in Biafra. This was thought the easiest way of involving highly placed individuals in the fighting who were unwilling to join the regular army and be controlled by those less educated than themselves. Some famous Biafran army commanders, including Achuzia from Anioma, started as members of the militia. See N. U. Akpan, *The Struggle for Secession* 1966 – 1970 (London: Frank Cass, 1972), 97.
253. J. O. G. Achuzia, age 69, Asaba, interviewed in January 2000.
254. Nwandu, see note 124.
255. Mrs. B. Omodon, see note 185.
256. Okwuashi, see note 101.
257. Nwandu, see note 124.
258. Mrs. Edith Dibie, age 48, Onicha-ugbo, interviewed in January 2000.
259. Arlene Eisen, *Women and Revolution in Vietnam* (London: Zed Books, 1984), 94.

260. Helen Praeger Younger, "Why We joined the Revolution: Voice of Chinese Women," in *Women and War in the Twentieth Century*, ed. Nicole Dombrowski (New York: Garland Publishing, 1999), 92.
261. Hammond and Druce, *Sweeter than Honey*, 11.
262. Nwandu, see note 124.
263. Nwandu and Achuzia; see notes 124 and 253 respectively.
264. Dibie, see note 258.
265. Mr. M. Amolo, age 47, Okpanam, interviewed in November 1999; and Mr. Obuzoma, age 57, Ebu, interviewed in November 1999.
266. Akpan, *The Struggle for Secession*, 77.
267. Hammond and Druce, *Sweeter than Honey,* 11; W. W. Selassie, "The Changing Position of Eritrean Women: An Overview of Women's Participation in the EPLF," in *Beyond Conflict in the Horn: Prospects for Peace, Recovery, and Development in Ethiopia, Somalia, and the Sudan*, ed. Martin Doornbos et al. (Trenton, N. J.: The Red Sea Press, 1992), 67–9. Tanya Lyons, "Guerilla Girls and Women in the Zimbabwean National Liberation Struggle," in *Women in African Colonial Histories*, eds. J. Allman, S. Geiger, and N. Musisi (Bloomington: Indiana University Press, 2002), 305–312.
268. Okwuashi and Nwandu; see notes 101 and 124 respectively.
269. Dibie, see note 258.
270. Okwuashi, Nwandu, and Dibie; see notes 101, 124, and 258 respectively.
271. Achuzia, see note 253.
272. M. McFadden, ed., *Women's Issues* vol. 1. (California: Salem Press, 1997), 160.
273. Hammond and Druce, *Sweeter than Honey*, 50–52.
274. Nwandu and Dibie; see notes 124 and 258 respectively.
275. Mr. Ezendo, age 52, Ibusa, interviewed in November 1999.
276. Okwuashi, see note 101.
277. Mrs. D. Gbenoba, age 48, Agbor-obi, interviewed in January 2000.
278. Okobi and Gbenoba; see note 56.

279. Okwuashi and Achuzia; see notes 101 and 253 respectively. Also Colonel C. Nwawo, age 75, Onicha-olona, interviewed in January 2000.
280. Achuzia, *Requiem Biafra*, 178–179.
281. Ibid.
282. Achuzia, see note 253.
283. Okwuashi and Dibie; see notes 101 and 258 respectively.
284. Ibid.
285. Mrs. D. Gbenoba, see note 277.
286. Dan Jacobs, *The Brutality of Nations* (New York: Alfred A. Knopf, 1987), 189, 309.
287. Information came from interviews in Anioma. See also Sofala, "Feminism".
288. Ogbemudia, *Years of Challenge*, 113–114.
289. Maido, see note 101.
290. Federal Government of Nigeria, "The Dawn of Lasting Peace," Broadcast to the Nation by Major-General Yakubu Gowon, Head of the Federal Military Government and Commander-in-Chief of the Armed Forces (Lagos: March 1968), 6.
291. Okocha, *Blood on the Niger*, 234–235.
292. Okodike, see note 80.
293. Uwafili, "The Effects of the Nigerian Civil War on Asaba," 45.
294. Mr. Nwokolo, age 68, Asaba, interviewed in June 2000; and Enemoh, see note 41.
295. In Illah one of such women was Eunice Oganwu, whose husband ran the local post office and was for some time in detention for going into hiding on the arrival of federal troops.
296. Enemoh (2004), see note 49.
297. These were the General Hospital, Agbor; the Central Hospital, Ukwuani; the General Hospital, Asaba (from 1968); the Dispensary at Ozanogogo; Mission Hospital, Ogwashi-ukwu; the Maternity at Onicha-olona; Anglican Maternity, Ubulu-ukwu; and, Pilgrims Maternity, Issele-ukwu. The last four belonged to different Church groups.
298. Mr. Frank Ijeh, age 62, Asaba, interviewed in January 2001.
299. *The Observer*, 8 June 1968, 12.

300. Odagwe, see note 195.
301. *The Nigerian Observer,* 29 May 1968, 2.
302. Doornbos et al., (eds.), *Beyond Conflict in the Horn,* 9.
303. Sheldon, ed., *Her War Story*, x.
304. See chapter 3, 103–105.
305. See chapters 4 and 5 of Ohadike, *Anioma, A Social History of the Western Igbo People* (Athens: Ohio University Press, 1994).
306. Enemoh (2004), see note 49.
307. Ibid.
308. Ibid.

CHAPTER FIVE

309. Richard Nixon, *Six Crises* (New York: Doubleday, 1962), xvi.
310. Mrs. Azuka Iwebi, Okommah, Okogo, and Akazue; see notes 209, 221, 225, and 85 respectively.
311. Nwoji, see note 171.
312. Aniogwu and Ubah, see note 56.
313. Nwaka and Iwebi, see notes 98 and 209.
314. Agboola, *Agricultural Atlas*, 13.
315. Nwabam, Onojaruma, and Ofuani, see notes 61, 89, and 235 respectively.
316. See Chapter 3, page 118. Mrs. Igwe Obu died from a stray bullet on her way from the farm.
317. Nwabam, see note 61.
318. Ohadike, *Anioma*, 202 – 203.
319. *Daily Times* (Nigeria), 20 May 1967, 4 - 5.
320. *Daily Times* (Nigeria), 20 June 1967, 4.
321. Enemoh, "Grandwork History of Asaba," 277.
322. *The Nigerian Observer*, 20 June 1968, 2.
323. John Oyinbo, *Nigeria: Crisis and Beyond* (London: Charles Knight & Co., 1971), 98.
324. Mrs. I. Onyemushani, age 50, Isheagu, interviewed in January 2000.
325. Enemoh, see note 49.

326. Oyinbo, *Nigeria: Crisis and Beyond,* 98. Also, Central Bank of Nigeria, *History of Nigerian Currency.* Available from http://www.centbank.org/currency/historycur.asp.
327. Ibid.
328. Gloria Chuku, The Changing Role of Women in Igbo Economy, 1929–1985 (Ph.D. thesis, University of Nigeria, 1995), 292.
329. Information on the trans-border trade came from the following: Eboigbe (Igbanke), Nwanze (Ibusa), Amolo (Okpanam), Mr. and Mrs. Onyemushani, and Okogo (Isheagu); Odagwe (Utagba-unor), Ofuani and Okafor (Ogwashi-ukwu); see notes 68, 154, 175, 167, 225, and 324; 195, 235 and 224. Mrs. E. Menewe, age 50, Onicha-ukwuani, interviewed in January 2000.
330. Uwafili, "The Effects of the Nigerian Civil War on Asaba," 62.
331. *The Nigerian Observer*, 8 June 1968, 3, and July 9, 1968, 3.
332. Nwoji, see note 171.
333. Biose, "The Nigerian Civil War on Umunede," 56.
334. *The Nigerian Observer,* 8 June 1968, 1.
335. Federal Government of Nigeria, "Broadcast to the Nation by Major-General Yakubu Gowon, Head of the Federal Government of Nigeria and Commander-in-Chief of the Armed Forces" (Lagos: March 1968), 6.
336. Okocha, *Blood on the Niger*, 236.
337. *The Nigerian Observer,* 21 January 1969, 3.
338. St. Jorre, *The Nigerian Civil War*, 388.
339. Okafor, see note 224.
340. Onojaruma, see note 89.
341. Onojaruma and Ijeh, see notes 324 and 61.
342. Eboigbe, see note 68. See also Biose, "The Nigerian Civil War on Umunede," 44.
343. Okobi and Nwoji, see notes 56 and 171.
344. Nwoji, see note 171.
345. Ijeh, see note 61.
346. Ibid.
347. Odagwe, see note 195.
348. Obi, see note 96.
349. Iyase-omu is the spokesperson of the Omu group.

350. Madam Ifesonye, Iyase-omu, age 70, Issele-ukwu, interviewed in January 2000.
351. Badifu, see note 124.
352. Eboigbe, see note 68. Also *Atlas of the Federal Republic of Nigeria*, 82–83.
353. Mrs. Ngozi Ochei, age 62, Onicha-olona, interviewed in January 2000.
354. Dr. E. Mordi, age 45, Ubulu-ukwu, interviewed in January 2000.
355. Jodi York, "The Truth about Women and Peace," in *The Women and War Reader,* eds. L. A. Lorentzen and J. Turpin (New York: New York University Press, 1998), 23.
356. *Magajiya* was originally the title for the queen mothers in Hausa land in the last two centuries.
357. Nwoji and Iwebi, see notes 171 and 209.
358. Nwegbe, see note 222.
359. St. Jorre, *The Nigerian Civil War,* 382.
360. *Daily Times* (Nigeria), 23 June, 1967, 1.
361. Ibid.
362. Mokogwu, see note 134. Mrs. A. Omo, age 62, Asaba, interviewed in February 2000.
363. Nwegbe, see note 222.
364. St. Jorre, *The Nigerian Civil War*, 383.

CHAPTER SIX

365. Elaigwu, *Gowon*, 135.
366. Julian Critchley and A. J. Parrington, *The World and the School: Crisis Paper* No. 7 (n.p. 1970), 1.
367. Elaigwu, *Gowon*, 136.
368. Towns in Oshimili North Local Government Area are Asaba, Ibusa, Illah, Ebu, Okpanam, Oko, Okwe, and Akwukwu-Igbo.
369. Nwanze, see note 154.
370. Akazue and Okogo, see notes 85 and 225.
371. Mrs. Stella Benyeogo, age 48, Asaba, interviewed in December 2000.
372. *Daily Times* (Nigeria), 28 October 1970, 1.

373. Mrs. M. M. Ojogwu, age 48, Okpanam, interviewed in January 2001.
374. Oluleye, *Military Leadership in Nigeria*, 154.
375. Omodon, see note 75. St. Jorre, *The Nigerian Civil War*, 402.
376. See pages 171–73.
377. Ojogwu, see note 373.
378. Okwuashi, see note 101.
379. Mokogwu, see note 134.
380. Nwoji, see note 171.
381. Achuzia, *Requiem Biafra*, 329.
382. Midwest Government, *Rehabilitation in Midwestern State*, 10.
383. Akazue, Nwanze, Okogo, and Ojogwu, see notes 85, 154, 225, and 373.
384. Midwest Government, *Rehabilitation in Midwestern State*, 8.
385. Mrs. Eziuno Eboka, age 65, Asaba, interviewed in January 2001.
386. Sayre Sheldon, ed., *Her War Story*, x.
387. St. Jorre, *The Nigerian Civil War*, 238.
388. *Daily Times* (Nigeria), 25 September 1970, 28.
389. East Central State is populated by the Igbo; Rivers by the Ijaw and some Igbo; and the Southeastern State by the Ekoi, Efik, and Ibibio.
390. Elaigwu, *Gowon*, 141.
391. Federal Ministry of Information, *Blue Print for Post-War Reconstruction* (Lagos: Government Press, 1968), 4–5.
392. Midwest Government, *Rehabilitation in Midwestern State*, 5.
393. Lt. Col. S. O. Ogbemudia, "Winning the Peace." An Address by the Military Governor of Midwest State to the Traditional Rulers and People of the Midwest State at Benin City on 7 February 1970. Page 9.
394. Midwest Government, *Rehabilitation in Midwestern State*, 3–6.
395. Nwanze, see note 154.
396. Federal Military Government, "Ending the War: The Last Lap." Broadcast to the Nation by His Excellency Major-General Yakubu Gowon, Head of the Federal Military Government and Commander-in-Chief of the Armed Forces, July 1968. Page 9.

397. Mrs. Rhoda Chenimuya, age 64, Isheagu, interviewed in January 2001.
398. *The Nigerian Observer*, 22 January 1970, 12.
399. Paul Obi-ani, *Post Civil-War Social and Economic Reconstruction of Igboland* 1970–83 (Enugu: Mikon Press, 1998), 16.
400. St. Jorre, *The Nigerian Civil War*, 251.
401. Enemoh, see note 49.
402. *Daily Times* (Nigeria), 14 August 1970, 5.
403. *Udeaku* is an ointment made from frying palm nuts.
404. Nwanze, see note 154.
405. The towns in question include Isheagu, Achalla, Oko-ogbele, Oko-anala, Okpanam, Okwe, Asaba, Ibusa, Ukala, Amakom, and others.
406. Ijeh, see note 298.
407. *Daily Times* (Nigeria), September 17, 1970, 14.
408. Enemoh, see note 49.
409. Enemoh, see note 41.
410. Mrs. N. M. Awachie, age 41, Awka – Anambra State, interviewed in October 2002.
411. Nwanze, see note 154.
412. Ojogwu, see note 373.
413. Midwest Government, *Rehabilitation in Midwestern State*, 10.
414. *The National Atlas of Nigeria*, 82–83.
415. *Daily Times* (Nigeria), 25 September 1970, 28.
416. *The Nigerian Observer*, 31 October 1970, 1.
417. *The Nigerian Observer*, 28 October 1970, 1.
418. Enemoh, see note 49.
419. *The Nigerian Observer*, 25 October 1970, 7–9.
420. *Daily Times* (Nigeria), 30 July 1970, 24; and *The Nigerian Observer*, 9 October 1970, 5.
421. Okocha, *Blood on the Niger*, 159.
422. Ibid., 205.
423. Ibid.
424. Enemoh, see note 49.
425. Ibid.

426. Oluleye, *Military Leadership in Nigeria,* 156.
427. "The Public Officers (Special Provisions) Decree 1970, No. 46" in *Annual Volume of Laws of the Federal Republic of Nigeria Containing Decrees and Subsidiary Legislation made in the Year* 1970 (Lagos: Federal Ministry of Information, Printing Division, 1971), A 205.
428. Ibid., A 206–7.
429. Okocha, *Blood on the Niger*, 236.
430. Ibid.
431. Achuzia, *Requiem Biafra*, 345.
432. Obi-ani, *Post Civil-War Reconstruction of Igboland*, 69, 72.
433. Nwajei, see note 200.
434. Oluleye, *Military Leadership in Nigeria,* 156.
435. "Clearing the Air," in *Daily Times* (Nigeria), 19 August 1970, p. 3. Obiani, *Post Civil-War Reconstruction of Igboland*, 66.
436. *The Guardian* (Nigeria), 12 November 1995, B4.
437. St. Jorre, *The Nigerian Civil War*, 403.
438. Oyinbo, *Nigeria: Crisis and Beyond,* 119.
439. Ibid.
440. *Daily Times* (Nigeria), 18 May 1970, 1.
441. *Daily Times* (Nigeria), 29 May 1970, 1, 8.
442. Mrs. S. Igbeka, age 66, Asaba, interviewed in November 1999.
443. Obi-ani, *Post Civil-War Reconstruction of Igboland*, 88.
444. Shehu Shagari, *Shehu Shagari: Beckoned to Serve, An Autobiography* (Ibadan: Heinemann, 2001), 170–171.
445. Enemoh, see note 49.
446. *The Nigerian Observer*, 2 October 1970, 1–3.
447. *Daily Times* (Nigeria), 6 August, 1970, 6.
448. *Daily Times* (Nigeria), 5 March 1971, 1.
449. Uwafili, "The Effects of the Nigerian Civil War on Asaba," 28.
450. Mr. V. Ebuwa, age 48, Illah, interviewed in January 2000.
451. Ogbemudia, "Winning the Peace," 9.
452. Federal Military Government, "Ending the War: The Last Lap," 4.
453. *Daily Times* (Nigeria), 25 September 1970, 28.
454. Enemoh, see note 49.

455. C. Okonjo, "The Western Ibo," in *The City of Ibadan*, eds., P. Lloyd, A. L. Mabogunje, and B. Awe (Cambridge: Cambridge University Press, 1967), 109–113.
456. Mr. Gabriel Ogbukor, age 56, Ubulu-ukwu, interviewed in January 2001. Interviews with the following also support this information: Ijeh, Enemoh, Nwanze, and Ojogwu; see notes 298, 49, 154, and 373.
457. Benyeogo and Igbeka, see notes 371 and 442.
458. Federal Military Government, "Ending the War: The Last Lap," 9.
459. Amolo, see note 265.
460. Enemoh, Chenimuya, and Nwanze; see notes 49, 397, and 154.
461. Okwuashi and Nwandu, see notes 101 and 124.
462. Chenimuya, see note 397.
463. *The Nigerian Observer*, 16 January 1970, 3.
464. Eboka, see note 385.
465. Ojogwu, see note 373.
466. Elaigwu, *Gowon*, 144. Also, Midwest Government, *Rehabilitation in the Midwestern State*, 101.
467. Oluleye, *Military Leadership in Nigeria*, 157, 169–173.
468. Elaigwu, *Gowon*, 145.
469. Shagari, *Beckoned to Serve*, 164.

CONCLUSION

470. Editorial comment in *The Times* (London), reproduced in Julian Critchley and A. J. Parrington, *The World and the School: Crisis Paper* No. 7 (1970), 14.
471. Pope Pius XII in *The Mind Opener* vol. 9, 2000-2001, 4.
472. Raph Uwechue, *Reflections on the Nigerian Civil War* (New York: Africana Publishing Corporation, 1971), 50–52.
473. Federal Government of Nigeria, "Ending the War: The Last Lap," 10.
474. See Chapter 2.
475. Betty Reardon, "Women or Weapons?" in *The Women and War Reader*, 292.
476. St. Jorre, *The Nigerian Civil War*, 165.

477. Information from interviews with the following: Okobi, Omodon, Nwaka, and Ejere, see notes 56, 75, 98, and 208.
478. Nicole Dombrowski, "Soldiers, Saints or Sacrificial Lambs? Women's Relationship to Combat and Fortification of the Home Front in the 20th Century," in *Women and War in the Twentieth Century,* ed. Nicole Dombrowski (New York: Garland Publishing, 1999), 2.
479. Akpan, *The Struggle for Secession*, 159.
480. Chizea, Badifu, Nwoji, Nwajei, and Ochei; see notes 80, 124, 171, 200, and 353.
481. Okocha, *Blood on the Niger*, 26, 33–34.
482. Enemoh, see note 49.
483. Sydney Emezue, "Women and the War," in *A Social History of the Nigerian Civil War*, A. Harneit Sievers (et al.) (Enugu: Jemezie Associates, 1997).
484. Turpin, "Many Faces: Women Confronting War," 4–6.
485. St. Jorre, *The Nigerian Civil War*, 405.
486. Turpin, "Many Faces: Women Confronting War," 9.
487. *Daily Times* (Nigeria), 31 October 1970, 1.
488. Okwuashi, Ejere, Okonmah, and Ojogwu; see notes 101, 208, 221, and 373 respectively.
489. The following expressed this opinion: Gbenoba (Agbor-obi), Okobi (Asaba), and Ubah (Utagba-ogbe); see note 56.
490. *The Guardian* (Nigeria), 23 March 2001, 4.
491. *The Guardian on Sunday* (Nigeria), 29 October 2000, 1.

APPENDIX

492. Other works in this category include: H. G. Hanbury, *Biafra: A Challenge to the Conscience of Britain* (London: Routledge and Kegan Paul, 1968); John de St. Jorre, *The Nigerian Civil War* (London: Hodder and Stoughton, 1971); J. Hatch, *Nigeria: Seeds of Disaster* (Chicago: Henry Regenry, 1971); Z. Cervenka, *A History of the Nigerian Civil War,* 1967 – 1970 (Ibadan: Onibonoje Publishers, 1972); S. Cronje and A. Waugh, *Biafra: Britain's Shame* (London: Michael Joseph, 1969); F. Forsyth, *The*

Biafran Story (London: Penguin, 1969), and *Emeka* (London: Hodder and Stoughton, 1982).

493. See the following: Eric Opia, *Why Biafra?: Aburi, Prelude to the African Tragedy* (San Rafael, California: Leswing Press, 1972); O. Nnoli, *Ethnic Politics in Nigeria* (Enugu: Fourth Dimension Publishers, 1978); J. Irukwu, *Nigeria at the Crossroads* (London: Witherby and Co., 1983); R. Olaniyan, ed. *Nigerian History and Culture* (Ibadan: Longman, 1985); T. N. Tamuno and S. U. Ukpabi, eds. *Nigeria since Independence: The First Twenty-five Years* (Ibadan: Heinemann, 1989); S. O. Oyeweso, ed. *Perspectives on the Nigerian Civil War* (Lagos: Obafemi Awolowo University Press, 1992); and Y. B. Usman and G. A. Kwanashie, eds. *Inside Nigerian History,* 1950 – 1970*: Events, Issues and Sources* (Zaria: Ahmadu Bello University Press, 1995).

494. Other books are Odumegwu Ojukwu, *Biafra: Random Thoughts* (London: Harper and Row, 1969) and *Biafra: Selected Speeches with Journal of Events* (London: Harper and Row, 1969); R. Uwechue, *Reflections on the Nigerian Civil War* (New York: Africana Publishing Co., 1971); A. Nwankwo, *Nigeria: The Challenge of Biafra* (London: Rex Collings, 1972); Wole Soyinka, *The Man Died* (London: Rex Collings, 1972); Elechi Amadi, *Sunset in Biafra* (London: Heinemann, 1973); R. B. Alade, *The Broken Bridge* (Ibadan: The Caxton Press, 1975); and D. S. Obikeze and A. A. Mere, *Children and Civil War, A Study of the Rehabilitation Programme for Displaced Children* (Enugu: Star Printing and Publishing Co.,1985).

495. Another book in this category is J. J. Oluleye's, *Military Leadership in Nigeria,* 1966 – 1979 (Ibadan: University Press, 1985).

496. Other relevant fictional works are: J. P. Clark, *Casualties* (London: Longman, 1970); Chinua Achebe, *Girls at War* (Ibadan: Heinemann, 1972); Chukwuemeka Ike, *Sunset at Dawn* (London: Collins of Harvill Press, 1976); and T. A. C. Ezeigbo, *Facts and Fiction in the Literature of the Nigerian Civil War* (Lagos: Unity Publishers, 1991).

497. Gloria Chuku, "The Changing Role of Women in Igbo Economy" (Ph. D. thesis, University of Nigeria, 1995); Ngozi Ezeigwe, "Women in Combat" (B. A. project, University of Nigeria, 1996).

Bibliography

ORAL SOURCES *(INFORMATION ON INTERVIEWEES)*

Mr. C. Abagbodi, age 65, Rtd. Civil Servant, Akwukwu-Igbo, January 2000.

Col. J. O. G. Achuzia, age 69, Former Biafran Officer, Asaba, January 2000.

Mr. Nwabudike Adigwe, age 95, Ritual Specialist, Isheagu, January 2000.

Madam C. Agbon, age 65, Trader, Otolokpo, June 2000.

Madam Lydia Akazue, age 70, Potter, Isheagu, January 2000.

Mr. P. Aminu, age 46, Civil Servant, Agbor, November 1999.

Mr. M. Amolo, age 47, Headmaster, Okpanam, November 1999.

Chief D. O. Aniogwu, age 64, Rtd. Civil Servant, Aboh, January 2000.

Mrs. Victoria Ashedu, age 60, Professional farmer, Issele-ukwu, January 2000.

Mrs. N. M. Awachie, age 41, Lecturer, Awka, October 2002.

Mr. J. I. O. Badifu, age 52, Lecturer, Ogwashi-ukwu, June 2000.

Mrs. Stella Benyeogo, age 48, Civil Servant, Asaba, January 2000.

Mr. Gideon Biachi, age 54, Former Biafran Soldier, Illah, January 2000.

Madam Rhoda Chenimuya, age 67, Isheagu, January 2001.

Mr. Victor Chenimuya, age 73, Civil Servant, Isheagu, November 1999.

Madam Ejime Chizea, age 72, Omu of Asaba, January 2000.

Mrs. Edith Dibie, age 48, Civil Servant, Onicha-ugbo, January 2000.

Ms. Martha Dunkwu, age 47, Oza-Omu of Okpanam, January 2000.
Mr. E. Ebu, age 47, Plumber, Ozanogogo, January 2000.
Mr. N. N. Eboigbe, age 73, Rtd. Civil Servant, Igbanke, June 2000.
Mrs. Eziuno Eboka, age 65, Asaba, January 2001.
Mr. Val Ebuwa, age 48, Public Relations Consultant, Illah, January 2000.
Mr. C. Echeruo, age 45, Civil Servant, Uli, January 2000.
Madam O. Edebatu, age 75, Omu (Ukwumega) of Illah, January 2000.
Mr. M. Egbuniwe, age 49, Civil Servant, Asaba, November 1999.
Mr. F. O. Egwuatu, age 48, Civil Servant, Illah, November 1999.
Mrs. P. Ejere, age 52, Civil Servant, Asaba, November 1999.
Mrs. Felicia Ekeke, age 44, Civil Servant, Obiaruku, January 2000.
Mrs. Lucy Emili, age 54, Butcher, Utagba-ogbe, January 2000.
Chief John Enemoh, age 75, Rtd. Civil Servant, Asaba, January 2000.
Mr. S. Ezendo, age 52, Civil Servant, Ibusa, November 1999.
Mrs. D. Gbenoba, age 49, Civil Servant, Agbor-obi, January 2000.
Prince C. Gbenoba, age 47, Civil Servant, Agbor-Obi, January 2000.
Prince D. Gbenoba, age 56, Lecturer, Agbor-Obi, January 2000.
Madam S. Ifesonye, age 70, Iyase-Omu, Ritual Specialist, Issele-ukwu, January 2000.
Mr.and Mrs. C. Igbeka, ages 74 and 66, Rtd. Civil Servants, Asaba, November 1999.
Mrs. Mary Ihedi, age 65, Ubulu-ukwu, January 2000.
Mr. E. U. D. Ijeh, age 54, Civil Servant, Asaba, November 1999.
Mr. Frank Ijeh, age 62, Red Cross Official, Asaba, January 2001.
Mrs. Patience Ijeh, age 48, Trader, Akwukwu-Igbo, January 2000.
Mrs. Regina Ijeh, age 66, Trader, Akwukwu-Igbo, January 2000.
Madam J. Ikebude, age 68, Trader, Illah, January 2000.
Mrs. Rose Ikem, age 38, Civil Servant, Onicha-ugbo, January 2000.
Madam Veronica Ikem, age 65, Trader, Onicha-ugbo, January 2000.
Mr. and Mrs. Azuka Iwebi, ages 75 and 60, Asaba, June 2000.
Madam Onwunwenkewaso Iyama, age 70, Omu of Onicha-ugbo, January 2000.

Justice L. Maido, age 70, Rtd. Chief Judge, Onicha-ugbo, January 2000.

Mr. S. Megwai, age 50, Civil Servant, Onicha-olona, November 1999.

Mrs. C. Mekwunye, age 48, Weaving, Ubulu-ukwu, January 2000.

Mrs. Esther Menewe, age 50, Civil Servant, Onicha-ukwuani, January 2000.

Mr. W. O. Mokogwu, age 58, Civil Servant, Issele-ukwu, November 1999.

Dr. E. Mordi, age 45, Lecturer, Ubulu-ukwu, January 2000.

Mrs. L. Mordi, age 60, Civil Servant, Asaba, November 1999.

Mr. S. O. Nwabam, age 52, Headmaster, Ossissa, January 2000.

Madam Angelina Nwadiagu, age 68, Trader, Issele-azagba, November 1999.

Mrs. L. A. Nwajei, age 58, Ibusa, February 2000.

Mrs. N. Nwaka, age 48, Civil Servant, Issele-ukwu, November 1999.

Rev. Mike Nwaka, age 52, Clergy, Ogwashi-ukwu, January 2000.

Mrs. B. Nwandu, age 51, Civil Servant, Asaba, January 2000.

Mr. Anthony, and Mrs. Esther, Nwanze, ages 55 and 48, Ibusa, November 1999.

Mrs. Mary Nwaso, age 38, Civil Servant, Obamkpa, January 2000.

Col. Conrad Nwawo, age 70, Biafran Officer, Onicha-olona, January 2000.

Dr. W. O. Nwegbe, age 58, Lecturer, Ibusa, November 2000.

Obi Mordi Nweze, age 85, Ritual Specialist, Okpanam, January 2000.

Mrs. Gboliwe Nwoji, age 65, Trader, Asaba, June 2000.

Mr. L. Nwokolo, age 68, Rtd. Civil Servant, Asaba, June 2000.

Mrs. Chizoba Nzelibe, age 48, Lecturer, Issele-ukwu, November 1999.

Mrs. A. Nzelibe, age 38, Seamstress, Issele-ukwu, November 1999.

Mr. S. Nzelibe, age 48, Civil Servant, Issele-ukwu, November 1999.

Mrs. Gladys Obi, age 50, Trader, Opu, Akwukwu-Igbo, January 2000.

Madam Gladys Obi, age 65, Ritual Specialist, Obamkpa, January 2000.

Mrs. Comfort Obianeze, age 65, Nurse, Asaba, January 2000.

Mrs. Martha Oburo, age 58, Rtd. Civil Servant, Asaba, January 2001.

Mr. Obuzorma, age 57, Civil Servant, Ebu, November 1999.

Rev. Canon C. Ochei, age 70, Clergy, Onicha-olona, January 2000.

Madam Mgbolie Ochei, age 72, Weaving, Onicha-ugbo, January 2000.

Mrs. Ngozi Ochei, age 62, Rtd. Civil Servant, Onicha-olona, January 2000.

Col. P. O. Ochei, age 64, Biafran Officer, Asaba, January 2000.

Mrs. Agnes Odagwe, age 65, Trader, Utagba-uno, June 2000.

Dr. (Mrs.) Odiase, Director, UNDP Programs (Delta State), January 2000.

Mr. G. C. Oforgu, age 75, Rtd. Military Officer, Asaba, June 2000.

Mr. Matthew Ofuani, age 55, Police Inspector, Ogwashi-ukwu, January 2000.

Madam Eunice Oganwu, age 78, Illah, January 2000.

Mr. Gabriel Ogbue, age 67, Cobbler, Onicha-ugbo, January 2000.

Mr. Gideon Ogbukor, age 56, Civil Servant, Ubulu-ukwu, January 2001.

Madam Regina Ogbolu, age 65, Trader, Akwukwu-Igbo, January 2000.

Mrs. M. M. Ojogwu, age 48, Civil Servant, Okpanam, January 2001.

Mr. G. Okafor, age 57, Civil Servant, Ogwashi-ukwu, October 1999.

Dr. (Mrs.) R. Okoh, Commissioner, Federal Refugee Commission, January 2001.

Mr. P. Okobi, age 61, Civil Servant, Asaba, November 1999.

Madam Dorothy Okodike, age 77, Omu of Akwukwu-Igbo, January 2000.

Mrs. Theresa Okojie, age 62, Ewulu, January 2000.

Mrs. Augustina Okogo, age 52, Isheagu, January 2000.

Mrs. Anasthesia Okonmah, age 57, Civil Servant, Ibusa, January 2000.

Obi Okada Okorie, age 75, Cobbler, Okpanam, January 2000.

Ms. Njoabuzia Okwuashi, age 63, Hotelier, Onicha-ugbo, January 2000.

Ms. Tina Okwuashi, age 65, Onicha-ugbo, February 2000.

Mrs. Augustina Omo, age 62, Asaba, February 2000.

Mrs. B. Omodon, age 71, Rtd. Nursing Officer, Alisimie, June 2000.

Mr. C. C. Omodon, age 73, Rtd. Civil Servant, Alisimie, June 2000.
Mrs. Maria Onojaruma, age 68, Trader, Utagba-ogbe, January 2000.
Mr. Felix Onwugbenu, age 45, Politician, Abavo, January 2000.
Mr. J. and Mrs. I. Onyemushani, ages 58 and 50, January 2000.
Opuyemeze, age 86, Opu, Akwukwu-Igbo, January 2000.
Mrs. Anuli Osakwe, age 55, Civil Servant, Ubulu-ukwu, November 1999.
Major John Osu, age 60, Rtd. Military Officer, Idumuje-uno, January 2000.
Mr. James Oyita, age 58, Tailor, Utagba-uno, January 2000.
Chief S. O. Ubah, age 64, Rtd. Civil Servant, Utagba-ogbe, January 2000.
Mr. Gabriel Udoma, age 42, Engineer, Agbor-obi, January 2000.
Mr. G. Ugbo, age 58, Civil Servant, Agbor-nta, April 2000.
Mrs. F. K. Uyaelemor, age 54, Civil Servant, Ebu, January 2000.

ARCHIVAL MATERIALS

National Archives, Enugu

FRP/X19	Commentaries and Write-ups on the Nigerian Civil War by Foreign Journalist, 1968.
FRP/X21	Extracts from Foreign Newspapers on the Civil War in Nigeria, 1967.
G. P/ X. 2	The Nigerian Crisis, 1966.
G. P/ X. 4	The Problem of Nigerian Unity, 1961.
G. P/ X. 7	Introducing the Republic of Biafra, 1967.
G. P/ X. 8	The Case for Biafra, 1968.
G. P/ X. 13	Gowon, Soldier of Honour (nd).
G. P/ X. 14	Guide to the National Military Government, 1967.
G. P/ X. 15	Ibos in a United Nigeria, 1968.
G. P/ X. 43	The Struggle for Survival, 1967.
MM/ X. 5	Meeting of the Nigerian Military Leaders at Aburi, 1967.
PD/ X. 6	Professor Aluko on the War, 1968.
SD/ A. 6	What Biafrans Know about the War 1968.

SD/ G3	The Dawn of Lasting Peace, 1968.
SD/ G4	Ending the Fighting: The Last Lap 1968.
SD/ 1. 3	B. J. Ikpeama on the Non-Igbo Minorities, 1968.
SD/ 0. 28	Major A. Okonkwo's Broadcast to the People of the Mid-West, 1967.
____	No Victor, No Vanquished, Opinions 1967 – 1968.
____	Nigeria—Biafra Conflict, Report of a One day Conference, Washington, 1969.
MINLOC 17/2	Southern Provinces, Tribal Customs and Superstitions, 1922.

National Archives, Ibadan

Intelligence Reports

Benin Prof. 1	B. P. 203/83, Vol. 11, 1934.
Benin Prof. 1	B. P. 203/87, Vol. 11, 1934.
Benin Prof. 1	B. P. 203/94, Vol. 11, 1934.
Benin Prof. 1	B. P. 203/111, 1933 – 34.
Benin Prof. 1	B. P. 203/151, 1935.
Benin Prof. 1	B. P. 203/329, 1938.
Benin Prof. 1	B. P. 203/336, 1938 – 39.

Civil War Documents

CWC 1/1/5	Ending the Fighting, 1968.
CWC 1/2/9	The Collapse of a Rebellion and Prospects of Lasting Peace (nd).
CWC 1/2/12	Blue Print for Post-war Reconstruction, 1968.
CWC 1/5/5	I Believe in One Nigeria, 1968.

GOVERNMENT PUBLICATIONS

Federal Government of Nigeria

Government Gazettes, July – December 1968.

Annual Volume of Laws of the Federal Republic of Nigeria Containing Decrees and Subsidiary Legislation made in the Year 1970, 1971.

The National Atlas of the Federal Republic of Nigeria, 1978.

Midwest Government

Understanding the Nigerian Crisis, 1968.

The Nigerian Crisis and the Mid-West Decision, 1968.

Rehabilitation in the Mid-West State, 1963 – 1970.

"Winning the Peace," An Address by the Military Governor of the Midwest State on the Occasion of the Launching of the Midwest Rehabilitation Fund, February 1970.

Investigation into the Role of Chiefs in the Midwestern State, Divisional Report in Respect of Aboh Division, 1972.

Investigation into the Role of Chiefs in the Midwestern State, Divisional Report in Respect of Asaba Division, 1972.

Delta State Government

Delta State Handbook, Vol. 1. 1991 –1995, 1996.

Understanding Delta State, Delta State at Seven, 1998.

BOOKS

Achebe, C. *Girls at War*. Ibadan: Heinemann, 1972.

______. *The Trouble with Nigeria*. Ibadan: Heinemann, 1983.

Achuzia, J. O. G. *Requiem Biafra*. Enugu: Fourth Dimension, 1986.

Adepoju, A., and C. Oppong, eds. *Gender, Work and Population in Sub-Sahara Africa*. London: James Currey Ltd., 1994.

Agboola, S. A. *An Agricultural Atlas of Nigeria*. London: Oxford University Press, 1979.

Akeosu, P. C. A. *The History of Great Isi-ile-uku (Issele-uku) Kingdom*. Onitsha: Etukokwu Press, 1992.

Akinjogbin, I. A. *Topics on Nigerian Economic and Social History*. Ife: Obafemi Awolowo University Press, 1980.

Akpan, N. U. *The Struggle for Secession*. London: Frank Cass, 1972.

Alade, R. B. *The Broken Bridge*. Ibadan: The Caxton Press, 1975.

Allman, J. Geiger, S. and Musisi, N. eds. *Women in African Colonial Histories* (Bloomington, Indiana: Indiana University Press, 2002).

Amadi, E. *Sunset in Biafra*. London: Heinemann, 1973.

Amadiume, I. *Male Husbands and Female Daughters: Gender and Sex in an African Society*. London: Zed Press, 1987.

Anifowose, R. *Violence and Politics in Nigeria: The Tiv And Yoruba Experiences.* New York: Nok Publishers, 1982.

Anyanwu, U. D., and J. C. Aguwa, eds. *The Igbo and the Tradition of Politics*. Enugu: Fourth Dimension, 1993.

Bascom, W. R., and M. J. Herscovits, eds. *Continuity and Change in African Cultures.* Chicago: The University of Chicago Press, 1959.

Basden, G. T. *Among the Ibos of Nigeria.* London: Frank Cass, 1966.

______. *Niger Ibos*. London: Frank Cass, 1966.

Benneth, O., et al., eds. *Arms to Fight, Arms to Protect: Women Speak Out About Conflict.* London: Panos,1995.

Bohannan, P., and G. Dalton, eds. *Markets in Africa*. Chicago: Northwestern University Press, 1962.

Caroll, B. A., ed. *Liberating Women's History: Theoretical and Critical Essays.* Chicago: University of Illinois Press, 1976.

Cervenka, Z. *A History of the Nigerian Civil War, 1967–1970.* Ibadan: Onibonoje Press, 1972.

Clark, J. P. *Casualties.* London: Longman, 1970.

Claude, P. *The African Political Dictionary*. Oxford: Clio Information Services, 1984.

Cronje, S., and A. Waugh. *Biafra: Britain's Shame*. London: Michael Joseph, 1969.

De Groot, J., and M. Maynard, eds. *Women Studies in the 1990's: Doing Things Differently*. London: Macmillan Press, 1993.

Dornbos, M., et al., eds. *Beyond Conflict in the Horn: Prospects of Peace, Recovery, and Development in Ethiopia, Somalia, and the Sudan.* Trenton, N. J.: The Red Sea Press, 1992.

Elaigwu, J. I. *Gowon*. Ibadan: West Books Publishers, 1983.

Ezeigbo, T. A. *Facts and Fiction in the Literature of the Nigerian Civil War*. Lagos: Unity Publishers, 1991.

Emecheta, B. *Destination Biafra.* London: Allison and Busby, 1982.

Forsyth, F. *The Biafran Story*. London: Hodder and Stoughton, 1969.

Fortune, R. F. *Sorcerers of Dobu: The Social Anthropology of the Dobu Islanders of the Western Pacific*. London: Routlege, 1932.

Gardiner, J., ed. *What Is History Today...?* London: Macmillan Press, 1988.

Green, M. M. *Igbo Village Affairs*. London: Sidgwick & Jackson (1947), Frank Cass (1964).

Goldstein, A. T. *Recognizing Forced Impregnation as a War Crime under International Law*. New York: Center for Reproductive Law and Policy, 1993.

Gbulie, B. *Nigeria's Five Majors*. Awka: Africana Publishers, 1981.

Gibbs, J. C., ed. *Peoples of Africa*. New York, Holt, Rinehart and Winston, 1965.

Hafkin, N. J., and E. G. Bay, eds. *Women in Africa: Studies in Social and Economic Change*. Stanford, Calif.: Stanford University Press, 1976.

Hallet, R. ed. *The Niger Journal of Richard and John Lander*. London: Routledge and Paul, 1965.

Hammond, J., and B. Neil. *Sweeter than Honey, Ethiopian Women and Revolution: Testimonies of Tigrayan Women*. Trenton, N. J.: The Red Sea Press, 1990.

Hanbury, H. G. *Biafra*: *A Challenge to the Conscience of Britain*. London: 1968.

Harneit-Sievers, A., et al. *A Social History of the Nigerian Civil War: Perspectives from Below*. Enugu: Jemezie Associates, 1997.

Hatch, J. *Nigeria: Seeds of Disaster.* Chicago: Henry Regenry, 1971.

Hauchler I., and P. Kennedy, *Global Trends*. New York: Continuum Publishers, 1994.

Henderson, R. *The King in Everyman: Evolutionary Trends in Onitsha Ibo Society* (New Haven, Conn.: Yale University Press, 1972).

Holm, J., and J. Bowler, eds. *Rites of Passage*. London: Pinter Publishers, 1994.

House-Midamba, B., and F. Ekechi, eds. *African Women and Economic Power*. Westport, Conn.: Greenwood Press, 1995.

Human Rights Watch, *Proxy Targets: Civilians in the War in Burundi.* March 1988.

Ibhawoh, B. *Between Culture and Constitution: The Cultural legitimacy of Human Rights in Nigeria*. Copenhagen, Denmark: The Danish Centre for Human Rights, 1999.

Ifemesia, C. *South eastern Nigeria in the 19th Century*. London: Nok Publishers, 1971.

______. *Traditional Humane Living among the Igbo: An Historical Perspective*. Enugu: Fourth Dimension, 1979.

Ike, C. *Sunset at Dawn*. London: Collins of Harvill Press, 1976.

Ikime, O., ed. *Groundwork of Nigerian History*. Ibadan: Heinemann, 1984.

International Committee of the Red Cross, *Women and War*. 1995.

Irukwu, J. O. *Nigeria at the Crossroads*. London: Witherby and Co., 1983.

Isichei, E. *The Ibo People and the Europeans*. London: Faber and Faber, 1970.

_____. *A History of the Igbo People*. London: Macmillan, 1976.

_____, ed. *Igbo Worlds*. London: Macmillan, 1977.

_____. *A History of Nigeria*. London: Longman, 1983.

Jacobs, D. *The Brutality of Nations*. New York: Alfred A. Knopf, 1987.

Jorre, J. *The Nigerian Civil War*. London: Hodder and Stoughton, 1972.

Kirk-Greene, A. H. M. *Crisis and Conflict in Nigeria: A Documentary Source Book, 1966 – 1970. London: Oxford University Press, 1971.*

Leith-Ross, S. *African Women*. London: Faber and Faber, 1939.

Lloyd, P. C., Mabogunje, A. L., and B. Awe, eds. *The City of Ibadan*. Cambridge: Cambridge University Press, 1967.

Lorentzen, L. A., and J. Turpin, eds. *The Women and War Reader*. New York: New York Press, 1988.

Lyons, T. *Guns and Guerilla Girls: Women in the Zimbabwean Liberation Struggle*. Trenton, N. J.: Africa World Press, 2004.

Madiebo, A. *The Nigerian Revolution and the Biafran War*. Enugu: Fourth Dimension, 1980.

Marshall, S. L. A. *Men against Fire: The Problem of Battle Command in Future War*. New York: William Morrow, 1947.

Mcfadden, M., ed. *Womens Issues*, Vols. 1–3. Pasadena, Calif.: Salem Press, 1997.

Nnoli, O. *Ethnic Politics in Nigeria*. Enugu: Fourth Dimension, 1978.

Nordstrom, C., and J. Martin, eds. *The Paths to Domination, Resistance, and Terror*. Berkeley: University of California Press, 1992.

Norton, P. *The New Encyclopaedia Britannica*. Vols. 3 and 12. Chicago: Encyclopaedia Britannica Inc. 1995.

Nwankwo, A. A., and S. U. Ifejika, *BIAFRA: The Making of a Nation*. London: Hurst and Co., 1969.

Nwankwo, A. A. *Nigeria: The Challenge of Biafra*. London: Rex Collins, 1972.

Nwapa, F. *Never Again*. Enugu: Nwanife Publishers, 1975.

Obasanjo, O. *My Command*. Ibadan: Heinemann, 1980.

Obiani, P. O. *Post-Civil War Social and Economic Reconstruction of Igboland, 1970–1983*. Enugu: Milkon Press, 1998.

Obikeze, D. S., and A. A. Mere, *Children and the Nigerian Civil War: A Study of the Rehabilitation Programme for War Displaced Children*. Enugu: Star Printing and Publishing Co., 1985.

Odogwu, B. *No Place to Hide: Crises and Conflicts inside Biafra*. Enugu: Fourth Dimension, 1985.

Ofonagoro, W. I. *Trade and Imperialism in Southern Nigeria, 1881 – 1929*. London: Nok Publishers, 1979.

Ogbemudia, S. O. *Years of Challenge*. Ibadan: Heinemann, 1991.

Ogbobine, R. A. *Bendel Law Series-Oshimili and Aniocha: Their People and Land Tenure*. Benin City: (np), 1981.

Ohadike, D. *Anioma: A Social History of the Western Igbo People*. Athens: Ohio University Press, 1994.

Ojukwu, O. *Biafra: Selected Speeches with Journal of Events*. London: Harper and Row, 1969.

_____. *Random Thoughts*. London: Harper and Row, 1969.

Okocha, E. *Blood on the Niger: An Untold Story of the Nigerian Civil War*. Port Harcourt: Sunray, 1994.

Okpaku, J., ed. *Nigeria, Dilemma of Nationhood: An African Analysis of the Biafran Conflict*. New York: The Third Press, 1972.

Okwechime, C. *Onicha-ugbo through the Centuries*. Lagos: Max-Hernie, 1994.

Olaniyan, R., ed. *Nigerian History and Culture*. Ibadan: Longman, 1985.

Oluleye, J. J. *Military Leadership in Nigeria, 1966 – 1979.* Ibadan: University Press, 1985.

Opia, E. *Why Biafra? Aburi: Prelude to the African Tragedy.* St. Rafael, Calif.: Leswing Press, 1972.

Ottenberg, S., ed. *African Religious Groups and Beliefs.* Meerut, India: Archana Publications, 1982.

Oyeweso, S., ed. *Perspectives on the Nigerian Civil War.* Lagos: Obafemi Awolowo Press, 1992.

Oyinbo, J. *Nigeria: Crisis and Beyond.* London: Charles Knight & Co., 1971.

Parkin, D., and D. Nyamwaya, eds. *Transformations of African Marriage.* Manchester: Manchester University Press, 1987.

Prunier, G. *The Rwandan Crisis: History of a Genocide.* London: Hurst & Company, 1998.

Samovar, L. A., and J. Mills, J. *Oral Communication: Message and Response.* Dubuque, Iowa: W. C. Brown Company Publishers, 1989.

Sheldon, S. P. ed. *Her War Story: Twentieth Century Women Write about War.* Carbondale: Southern Illinois University Press, 1999.

Nnaemeka, O. ed. *Sisterhood, Feminism and Power: From Africa to the Diaspora.* Trenton, N. J.: Africa World Press, 1999.

Soyinka, W. *The Man Died.* London: Rex Collings, 1972.

Talbot, P. A. *Tribes of the Niger-Delta.* London: Frank Cass, 1967.

______. *The Peoples of Southern Nigeria.* Vol. 1. London: Frank Cass, 1969.

Tamuno, T. N., and S. Ukpabi, eds. *Nigeria since Independence: The First Twenty-five Years, The Civil War Years.* Ibadan: Heinemann, 1989.

The Encyclopedia Americana. International Edition. Vol. 9. Connecticut: Grolier Inc., 1996.

Turshen, M., and C. Twagiramariya, eds. *What Women Do in Wartime: Gender and Conflict in Africa.* London: Zed Books, 1998.

Uchendu, V. C. *The Igbo of South Eastern Nigeria.* Winston, New York: Holt, Rinehart and Winston, 1965.

UNCHR. *The State of the World's Refugees: A Humanitarian Agenda.* New York: Oxford University Press, 1977.

UNICEF/Federal Government of Nigeria. *National Baseline Survey of Positive and Harmful Traditional Practices Affecting Women and Girls in Nigeria.* 1998.

Usman, Y. B., and G. Kwanashie, eds. *Inside Nigerian History, 1950–1970: Events, Issues and Sources.* Zaria: Ahmadu Bello University Press, 1995.

Uwechue, R. *Reflections on the Nigerian Civil War.* New York: Africana Publishing Corporation, 1971.

Waugh, A., and S. Cronje. *Biafra: Britain's Shame.* London: Michael Joseph, 1969.

Young, S., ed. *Encyclopedia of Women and World Religion.* Vols. 1–2. New York: Macmillan U.S.A., 1999.

ARTICLES

Central Bank of Nigeria, *History of Nigerian Currency.* Available from http://www.centbank.org/currency/historycur.asp

Egbo, E. O. "Northern Nigeria Cotton for Lancashire, 1902–1913." *Nsukka Journal of History* 1, no. 1 (1989): 134–150.

Ekejiuba, F. "Omu Okwei, The Merchant Queen of Ossomari: A Biographical Sketch." *Journal of the Historical Society of Nigeria* 3, no. 4 (1967): 633–646.

Isichei, E. "Historical Change in an Ibo Polity: Asaba to 1885." *Journal of African History X*, 3 (1969): 421–438.

Ikime, O. "Native Administration in Kwale-Aboh, 1928–1950: A Case Study." *Journal of the Historical Society of Nigeria* 3, no. 4 (1967): 663–682.

Rosnow, R., and P. Bordia. *Human Communication Research* December, 1998. Available from wsyiwyg://48/http://proquest.umi.co...=4&Deli=1&mtd=1&idx=2&sid=3&RQT=309.

Symke, P. "Refugee Women." *The Courier,* no. 150 (1995): 54–55.

Young, Stacy. *Women and language* (Urbana: Fall 1988). Available from wysiwyg://60/http://proquest.umi.co...3&Deli=1&mtd=1&idx=20&sid=3&RQT=309.

Uchendu, E. "Rating of Slaves in the West Niger Igbo Area in the 19th Century." *Nsukka Journal of the Humanities* 12 (2002): 180–191.

______. "Culture: The Obstacle to Active Female participation in Governance among the Igbo of Nigeria." *Asian Women* 15 (2002): 73–94.

NEWSPAPERS AND MAGAZINES

***Daily Times* (Lagos).**
November 9, 22, 1966.
December 9, 1966.
May 1, 4, 10, 17, 20, 31, 1967.
June 1, 19, 20, 23, 1967.
July 3, 31, 1967.
September 22, 27, 1967.
May 18, 29, 1970.
July 7, 30, 1970.
August 4, 6, 14, 24, 1970.
September 17, 25, 1970.
October 25, 28, 31 1970.
March 5, 1971.

***Sunday Times* (Lagos)**, October 8, 15, 1967.

***Sunday Vanguard* (Lagos)**, October 15, 1997.

***The Biafran Sun* (Enugu).**
June 8, 11, 19, 1967.
July 28, 1967.
August 29, 1967.
September 12, 1967.

***The Guardian* (Lagos).**
November 26, 1988.
November 3, 2000.
March 23, 2001.

***The Guardian on Sunday* (Lagos).**
January 14, 1966.
May 29, 1968.

October 3, 1999.
October 29, 2000.

***The Nigerian Observer* (Benin City).**
June 1, 2, 5, 8, 20, 22, 1968.
July 9, 1968.
January 3, 14, 21, 30, 1969.
March 6, 1969.
June 2, 1970.
October 2, 1970.

***The Times* (London).**
August 10, 1967.
August 21, 1968.
January 15, 1970.

***Sunday Telegraph* (London)**, January 18, 1970.

***Svenska Dagbladet* (Stockholm, Sweden)**, January 13, 1970.

***Los Angeles Times* (Los Angeles, California)**, April 23, 1967.

***Spectator* (United Kingdom)**, January 17, 1970.

***U. S. News and World Report* (New York)**, May 1967.

UNPUBLISHED WORKS

Ademola, K. "The Impact of Colonialism on Women's Education." Paper presented at a symposium in the Institute of African Studies, University of Ibadan, 1989.

Awe, B. "Notes on the Institution of Iyalode within the Traditional Yoruba Political System." Paper presented at the 20th Annual Congress of the Historical Society of Nigeria, 1974.

Biose, N. P. "The Impact of the Nigerian Civil War on Umunede." B.A. project, Delta State University, Abraka, 1997.

Chuku, G. "The Changing Role of Women in Igbo Economy, 1929–1985." Ph.D. thesis, University of Nigeria, 1995.

Edozien, J. C. "Lecture on the Occasion of the N.Y.S.C. Orientation Course at Issele-ukwu, February 9, 1998.

Enemoh, J. "Grandwork History of Asaba" (Asaba, Nigeria: 1999).

Ezeigwe, N. "Women in Combat." B.A. project, University of Nigeria, 1995.

Idure, A. E. "A History of Ika Local Government Area of Bendel State" (Agbor, Nigeria: 1989).

Ohadike, D. "Western Igbo Communities Claiming Origin from Nri." B.A. project, University of Nigeria, 1975.

Oko, E. O. "The Aniocha People at the Crossroads, 1866–1911." M.A. project, University of Benin, 1982.

Onyenuwe, P. N. "Pre-Colonial Economic Activities in Umutu." B.A. project, Delta State University, Abraka, 1988.

Ukasonwa, E. "Aspects of the Pre-Colonial History of Obinofia in Ezeagu L.G.A. of Anambra State to 1900." B.A. project, University of Nigeria, 1989.

Uwafili, E. C. K. "The Effects of the Nigerian Civil War on Asaba." B.A. project, University of Nigeria, 1992.

Index